TIMPSON'S

Adaptables

Timpson's Adaptables
Travels Through England's Hidden Heritage

Designed and produced by
Jarrold Publishing, Whitefriars, Norwich NR3 1TR

Written by John Timpson

Editorial:	Paula Granados, Donald Greig
Design and mapping:	Visual Image
Photography:	John Brooks, Neil Jinkerson
Text research:	Jan Tavinor
Picture research:	Paula Granados

Cover pictures
Above, from left: Sherborne House grandstand, Gloucestershire; the maltings, Saffron Walden, Essex, now a youth hostel; the 'summerhouse', Eyton-on-Severn, Shropshire, now a cottage; the game larder, Gunton Hall, Norfolk, now a cottage. *Below, clockwise from left*: water tower, Steyning, West Sussex, now occupied; the old police station, Helmsley, North Yorkshire, now a café; bus-shelter at Snape in Suffolk, formerly a hump-back bridge; telephone-box aquarium, Fyfield Hall, Essex; 'Little Church', near Gosport, Hampshire, now a health centre; Paull Lighthouse, East Yorkshire, now occupied.

ISBN 0-7117-0900-9

Printed by Jarrold Book Printing, Thetford, Norfolk 1/97

TIMPSON'S

Adaptables

TRAVELS THROUGH ENGLAND'S HIDDEN HERITAGE

JOHN TIMPSON

JARROLD
PUBLISHING

Contents

• • • • • • • • • • •

Bryant and May's old match factory at Bow, London – now apartments

Top left: Thornbury Castle near Bristol – now a hotel
Top right: The Smith's Arms at Godmanstone in Dorset – formerly a smithy
Above: Bishopsdale Oast in Kent, now a guest-house

Foreword

• • • • • • • • • • •

'Adapt or perish!' thundered H.G. Wells in one of his more apocalyptic moods. He was writing under the title *Mind at the End of Its Tether*, and it turned out to be the year in which he died, so he probably wasn't feeling at his best.

But he had a point. He was actually referring to the world of Nature – 'Adapt or perish, now as ever, is Nature's inexorable imperative'. However, he could also have said it about the man-made features of the landscape (from great castles to tiny telephone boxes, from stately homes to public lavatories) which are featured in this book. For one reason or another, they have outlived their original purpose. If they had failed to adapt, they would not have survived.

I think of them as Adaptables. They have found a new role to play. They have not just been turned into museums, relying on trusts or charities or the public purse. They have adapted to a new, active role in the community, and they still pay their own way.

There are the obvious examples: the barns converted into genteel residences, the 'Old Rectories' and 'Old Schoolhouses' no longer occupied by rectors or schoolteachers, the redundant churches which are used as (rather chilly) community centres. But I prefer the more unlikely Adaptables, with a strange history behind them or a bizarre future ahead.

Sometimes there have been curious exchanges of roles. I found a church which became an Indian restaurant, and a windmill which became a church; a town hall which is now a filling station, and a Mechanics' Institute which is now a town hall. I am still looking for the reverse of the corset factory which became council offices, and the stocking factory which is now a supermarket...

But once you start looking for Adaptables, you come across them in every field of activity. As each new form of transport was introduced, for instance, the existing facilities were made obsolete. So, a ticket office for stage-coaches became, in due course, the branch office of a building society, a canal warehouse became a pub, and a sailing barge is used for adventure holidays. Any number of railway carriages have been converted into country cottages (I found

Holme Lacy House, Hereford and Worcester – once a stately home, now a hotel

one which is even thatched), and redundant railway stations now serve as almost anything, from a sale-room for classic motorcycles to a Greek Orthodox Church.

Unwanted military installations have become Adaptables, too. Barracks and military hospitals built during the Napoleonic wars have been converted into luxury apartments, Martello towers into holiday cottages and coastal pillboxes (the Martello's modern equivalent) into beach cafés. An RAF control tower is being used as a nursery school, and the building where targets were tethered on a Royal Naval air station for low-flying machine-gun practice is now an amusement arcade. They are even trying to find a new use for perhaps the most prestigious military Adaptable of them all, Admiralty Arch.

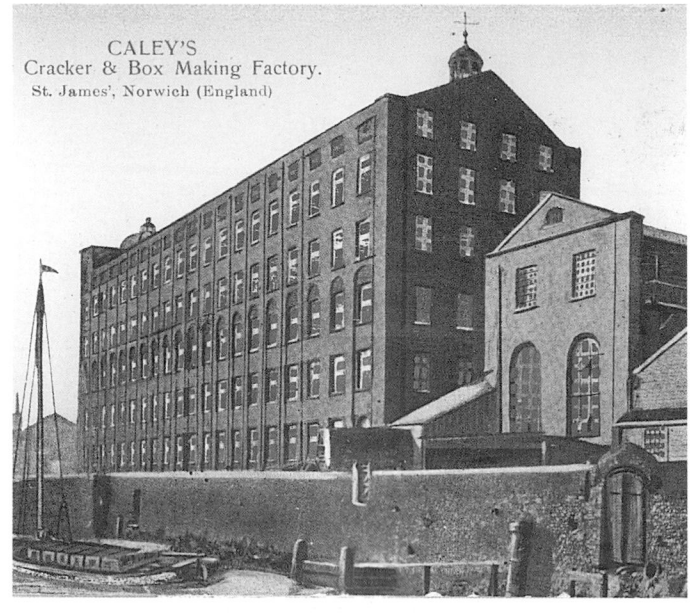

CALEY'S
Cracker & Box Making Factory.
St. James', Norwich (England)

In education, schools have become inns, stately homes have become schools. In medicine, a leper hospital is now a public library, a block of stables (admittedly a very large one) has become a hospital. Jehovah's Witnesses meet in a former ambulance station, a restaurant has taken over a morgue...

On a grander scale, a bank has become a hotel, a Guildhall has become a bank. Corn exchanges and assembly rooms are adapted for films, or concerts, or bingo. Dockside warehouses have been turned into arts centres, a matchstick factory into apartments, a maltings into a world-famous concert hall. Not least, an historic yarn mill is now the headquarters of the publishers of this book...

And among the smaller Adaptables, a village lock-up is doing duty as a lamp-post, smithies are being used as bus shelters, and telephone kiosks have been converted into mini-bars, shower cubicles, and king-sized fish-tanks. Most bizarre of all, perhaps, a Victorian bathing hut (itself adapted, so they say, from an ammunition wagon used in the Crimean War) has become a terminal building at one of England's tiniest international airports.

There is no limit, it seems, to the potential uses of redundant buildings, nor to the ingenuity of those who adapt them. Some of our greatest historic houses have been kept alive in new roles, and just as importantly, in my view, so have many ordinary, everyday features of our heritage; England's countryside and cities would not be the same without them.

So the Adaptables survive, as do some of their stranger stories in this book. H.G. Wells should be glad to know that his warning has not gone unheeded.

St James' Mill in Norwich has been a yarn mill and a factory and is now used as offices

A note on the maps

• • • • • • • • • •

This book includes two sets of maps to help locate the Adaptables.

The first page of each chapter features a countrywide map showing the location of each Adaptable in that chapter. A table alongside gives the location of each Adaptable, its old use and its new use.

On pages 168 to 185 are the regional maps, numbered 1 to 11. These show the positions of the Adaptables in each particular region in greater detail.

In addition, there is a full alphabetical index at the end of the book. Where appropriate, entries include a map number as well as a page number. This refers to the number of the regional map where the entry is shown.

A number of the Adaptables referred to in this book are privately owned and occupied. Please respect that privacy if you do travel to see them.

Waterside Adaptables

● ● ● ● ● ● ● ● ●

*Lighthouses, coastguard
stations, quayside warehouses
and a bathing hut*

	Location	Old use	New use(s)
1	Blyth, Northumberland: the *Calshot Spit*	Lightship	Yacht Club HQ
2	Boscastle, Cornwall	Stables	Youth hostel
3	Bristol: Arnolfini Arts Centre	Tea warehouse	Arts centre
	The Old Library, King Street	Library	Restaurant
4	Cadgwith, Cornwall	Fish storage cellar	Restaurant
5	Colchester, Essex: The *Colne Light*	Lightship	Sea Cadet Corps HQ
6	Droskyn Point, Cornwall	Research station	Youth hostel
7	East Portlemouth, South Devon: Gara Rock Hotel	Coastguard station	Hotel
8	Hoylake, Wirral	Lighthouse	Private residence
9	Little Petherick, Cornwall	Grain store	Holiday flats
10	Liverpool: The Tate Gallery	Dockland buildings	Art gallery
11	Northrepps, Norfolk: International Airport	Bathing hut	'Terminal building'
12	Paull, East Yorkshire	Lighthouse	Private residence
13	Portloe, Cornwall: United Church	Lifeboat station	Church
14	Rock, Cornwall	Coal store	Sailing Club HQ
15	Sutton Bridge, Lincolnshire	Lighthouses	Private residences
16	Tollesbury, Essex	Lightship	Floating hostel
17	Wells-next-the-Sea, Norfolk	Grain mill	Luxury apartments
18	Whitehaven, Cumbria	Mine buildings	Coastguard station

'...For buildings in peril by the sea'

The Pharos of Alexandria, the first recorded lighthouse and one of the Seven Wonders of the Ancient World, would have made a splendid Adaptable. It was commissioned in 300 BC by King Ptolemy II of Egypt, who liked to do things on a grand scale – not surprisingly, for someone who had the Pyramids on his doorstep. I have not

It may look like a monster anti-aircraft gun, but this is how an eighteenth-century artist visualised the world's first lighthouse, the Pharos of Alexandria

actually seen the Pharos, of course, but according to artists' impressions it looked rather more like the Empire State Building than a lighthouse.

It stood on a narrow islet known by the Greek name Pharos, linked to the mainland by a three-hundred-yard causeway. The base section was a tower, over two hundred feet high, with a viewing gallery around the roof. From the centre of that rose a second section, making it a hundred feet higher, and finally an eighty-foot cylindrical section, nearly thirty feet across, which looked like an enormous gun barrel pointing vertically at the heavens. The gun-

barrel effect was strengthened by the smoke rising from it; a fire burned permanently on the roof, nearly four hundred feet above sea level. At night, it was said, the flames could be seen thirty-five miles away.

The whole structure was made of stone faced with white marble, with a handsome arched entrance and windows on all sides, at several different levels. It could have accommodated not just a couple of lighthouse keepers, but the entire staff of Trinity House. Transfer it to New York and it could have blended in nicely with all the other skyscrapers. In London, it would be on a par with Centre Point. Almost anywhere, it could have adapted into the most prestigious office block in town.

As well as building big, they built to last; the Pharos stood there for sixteen hundred years. Some say it took an earthquake to demolish it, but more likely it was superceded by later navigational aids and allowed to simply crumble away.

Only its name survives; the science of lighthouses is still known as pharology.

These days, when coastal lighthouses become redundant, they fare rather better. Sometimes they are preserved, for old times' sake, as an attractive feature of the landscape, sometimes they are adapted, with neighbouring buildings, to form novel living quarters, though finding furniture to fit a lighthouse is even trickier than furnishing a windmill – the diameters of the rooms are that much smaller.

One early example is at **Paull**, on Humberside in East Yorkshire. Trinity House built a lighthouse there in 1836, and it has been a familiar landmark for mariners using the Humber ever since. However, it was only in service until 1870, when it was replaced by other lights further along the river and, with the adjoining cottage, it was converted into living accommodation. As one ecstatic local reporter wrote: 'If you want an ivory tower with all modern conveniences, salty air, a view of the Humber and two counties, a balcony overlooking the river and a studio or study which is both light and silent – take a look at Paull lighthouse.'

The view from the railed balcony that encircles it is certainly spectacular. On one side is the river with Lincolnshire beyond, on the other the lush Holderness Plain, and the village of Paull is clustered below.

The location of **Hoylake** lighthouse, beside the Mersey in Wirral, is not quite so rural. As the estate agent who had it on his books helpfully pointed out: 'The property is conveniently situated a quarter of a mile from Market Street Shopping Centre and public transport services, including Merseyrail commuter link to Liverpool and the M53 mid-Wirral motorway...'

But it does have just as spectacular a view, plus mahogany panelling, moulded skirtings and Gothic-style windows; the

Two examples of lighthouses adapted as private residences – at Hoylake on Merseyside...

...and at Paull on Humberside. It is probably difficult to fit the furniture, but the views are splendid

oil-fired central heating and Aga cooker came a little later. It all looks very typically – and rather boringly – Victorian, but it is a Grade II listed building, so in case you fancy living in an up-market lighthouse and it is still on the market, the asking price is £195,000.

The two lighthouses at the entrance to the River Nene at **Sutton Bridge** in Lincolnshire are a lot smaller than those at Paull and Hoylake, a mere sixty-two feet high – just a couple of candlesticks compared with the Pharos. And there is a more basic difference: these 'lighthouses' never had a light. They were built in the 1820s by the company which widened and straightened the river, partly to guide ships into its mouth (though only in daylight), and partly as ornamental follies, to celebrate the successful completion of the project. On top of each tower, instead of a lantern, there is just an empty room with two round windows.

The lighthouse that never was: one of the two decorative landmarks at the entrance to the River Nene in Lincolnshire, now privately occupied

The East Light is set in a wildfowl reserve, and in the 1930s it was the home of a young naturalist called Peter Scott. Lincolnshire folk will tell you that this is where he learned all he knew about wild birds, and it formed the basis for the wildfowl reserve he founded at Slimbridge ten years later. In what is now the dining-room, which he used as a study, he etched a frieze of wild ducks over the fireplace, with his name and the date, November 1937. It is also thought he constructed one of the doorways, but he may not have been as good at carpentry as he was at painting and etching, because later occupants have found it rather too low for comfort.

The East Light is well off the beaten track, but the one on the opposite side of the river, more grandly named Guy's Head Lighthouse, is just beside the coastal road, and its easier access may make it a more desirable residence (how easy to slip into estate agents' jargon with this kind of Adaptable). Certainly, it was looking a lot smarter than its twin on the far bank when I saw it, freshly painted and displaying the proud inscription: 'Built 1829, Restored 1986–89.' It also boasts an elegant conservatory and other additions. Perhaps one day Guy's Head Lighthouse may even boast a light...

Redundant lightships have been found various uses. The one at Hythe Quay in Colchester is the headquarters of the local Sea Cadet Corps...

Not every navigational light is attached to a lighthouse, of course. Lightships are out there too and, like lighthouses, they can become redundant and qualify as Adaptables. They are not quite so simple to convert into residences, perhaps, but they can acquire different nautical roles. The one moored at Hythe Quay on the River Colne in **Colchester** for instance, the *Colne Light*, is now the headquarters of the local Sea Cadet Corps, and the former Light

...another, now without its light, is the House Yacht of the Royal Northumberland Yacht Club at Blyth...

Vessel 50, named *Calshot Spit*, is now H.Y. *Tyne III*, House Yacht of the Royal Northumberland Yacht Club at **Blyth**.

By coincidence, the *Tyne III* also originated in East Anglian waters, just up the coast from *Colne Light*. When the yacht club bought her in 1952 she was lying in Harwich Roads at the mouth of the River Orwell. The club's previous headquarters yacht had capsized at her moorings in the early hours during a violent northerly gale – the steward and his wife just managed to escape in their nightclothes.

After two years in temporary headquarters, the club discovered that Trinity House was advertising the *Calshot Spit* for sale. A viewing party travelled down from Northumberland to inspect the vessel, which was sturdily constructed of

...and this one at Tollesbury in Essex is a floating hostel for Fellowship Afloat, a trust which provides sailing holidays for youngsters. Its shore headquarters are in a converted sail loft

teak on oak – sturdy enough, they decided, to withstand Blyth's devastating northerly gales. They eventually agreed terms, and the lightship was towed up the coast by a tug which was itself a conversion – from steam to diesel.

The newly named *Tyne III* was put into commission as the club's House Yacht in 1954, though it was another three years before the wreck of her predecessor was finally cleared away. She was towed to her present berth and has remained there ever since, apart from a period in dry dock in 1976 to have a leak repaired. Unfortunately, the shell of the light on the mast, and the topmast above it, have had to be removed for safety, so she is now a lightship without any vestige of a light, but as a House Yacht she provides a warm and dry headquarters for the club.

Perhaps the most imaginative and appropriate new use for a lightship has been found at **Tollesbury**, back in Essex. It has been acquired by a Christian charitable trust called Fellowship Afloat, and converted into a floating hostel, moored in the harbour and accessible by boardwalks across the salt-marsh. It has been fitted out with thirty-six beds, and the existing saloon and galley are now the lounge-dining-room. It has been connected up

The entrance lodge to Wellington Pit, overlooking the sea at Whitehaven in Cumbria, is now a coastguard station – but the plaque close by is a reminder of those who were in peril underground instead of on the sea

Indeed, Portloe United Church now has toilets and other amenities which some, much larger, churches could envy – but one feature of it has remained unchanged. In the little Cornish copper belfry there is a bell which was retrieved from a ship that ran ashore over a century ago. Although no lifeboat was needed for the rescue, it is a reminder of the building's original role.

Linked with the lifeboat service are the coastguards, and their stations and lookouts around the coast have also qualified as Adaptables. In some rare cases the stations have actually been adapted from something else, and perhaps the most unusual example is at **Whitehaven** in Cumbria, where it occupied what used to be the entrance lodge to Wellington Pit, on a cliff overlooking the sea.

with electricity, water, a sewage disposal system and a telephone.

Youngsters live on board ship while they enjoy sailing and wind-surfing holidays, subsidised if necessary by the trust, which has also adapted a sail loft by the harbour, within sight of the lightship, as its shore headquarters.

It is also appropriate that Adaptables which were originally designed to help those in peril on the sea should now be used as places to pray for them. This has happened at **Portloe** on the south Cornish coast, where the old lifeboat station is now in regular use as Portloe United Church. As it happened, the lifeboat was only stationed there for a few years, and in that period it was never called out to a shipwreck (which presumably is why it closed), so the building serves a rather more valuable purpose today.

It was originally Church of England, but the congregation dwindled, even for such a modest building as this, and in an admirable demonstration of ecumenical harmony, the local Methodists, who were having a similar problem, sold their own church, spent the money on modernising the former lifeboat station, and now take part in combined services which regularly attract twenty or more worshippers.

Portloe United Church in Cornwall started life as a coastguard station; its bell was retrieved from a ship that ran aground in the last century

The biggest mine owner in the area during the eighteenth century was the first Earl of Lonsdale, who had a taste for turrets. He built Whitehaven Castle (which itself became an Adaptable and was converted into a hospital) and he put battlements on most of his mine buildings, too. After nearly two hundred years, Wellington Pit was closed in 1932. In the

early 1980s it was a café; then the coastguards moved in.

More commonly, however, the coastguards have moved out, and as they always have splendid sea views, their stations are often snapped up as some form of holiday accommodation – youth hostels, holiday homes, hotels. At **East Portlemouth** in South Devon, for example, the old Rickham Coastguard Station has been developed into the Gara Rock Hotel.

It was built in 1847, at the request of the Admiralty to Parliament, to protect the shipping which used Salcombe Harbour from the smugglers and wreckers who frequented that stretch of coast. The 1851 census showed a complement of one Royal Navy lieutenant, the coastguard chief, and seven assistants living there with their families, a community of over forty.

Despite their numbers, the coastguards were kept extremely busy. So much contraband came ashore in that area that it is said two public ale houses in East Portlemouth were actually closed down

and demolished because of the part they played in the smuggling trade.

The other important role of the coastguards, of course, was saving shipwrecked crews that ran aground on the rocks just below their station. In 1872 an entire crew of sixteen was saved – though most of the two thousand tons of cargo was lost, one way or another; and in 1880 two coastguards died while trying to save a sailor from another wrecked vessel.

But by 1909, the Board of Trade decided that the

The former coastguard cottages at Rickham Coastguard Station in South Devon, now part of the Gara Rock Hotel

smuggling problem was over and, presumably, shipwrecked mariners could get help from elsewhere. The station was sold to the Jordan family, who converted four of the cottages into accommodation and the other two into a dining-room and lounge, and reopened the place as a boarding-house.

Conditions, I gather, were rather primitive in the early days. One of the first guests recorded an unnerving visit to the outside lavatory, in complete darkness. 'I found the right place, but when I sat down the seat sank down and down, apparently some primitive "flush". I leapt up in case I went for good...'

Droskyn Point youth hostel in Cornwall is officially described as a former coastguard station, but the locals say the Admiralty used it to test secret tracking devices during the war

can even be mistaken for them. For instance, a youth hostel on **Droskyn Point** at Perranporth is described in the YHA handbook as 'a former coastguard station', but the locals will tell you it was never occupied by coastguards. It was actually an Admiralty research station, which had a number of curious devices on the cliff during the war for detecting enemy maritime activity. But the rest of the description is accurate enough: 'It offers wonderful views over an exciting coastline, with untamed seas and isolated bays, and three miles of excellent surf beach.' With all that to enjoy, I doubt the youth hostellers care whether their predecessors saved ships or helped to sink them.

In the last ninety years conditions have somewhat improved – though it was requisitioned as a headquarters for the nearby radar station during the last war, which set things back a bit. But since then the hotel has been greatly modernised and expanded. The circular lookout on the cliff was given a thatched roof and used for a time as a bar. It still provides the same panoramic sea view that the coastguards enjoyed – but without the smugglers.

Other types of buildings can be found on lonely Cornish cliff tops with just as commanding views as coastguard stations; indeed, they

Quayside warehouses and granaries generally have good sea views too, but they are often too big and bleak to adapt comfortably as hotels or homes. One exception is the quayside grain mill which has stood since 1902 at **Wells-next-the-Sea** in Norfolk. The town was originally called Wells-on-Sea, but over the centuries the tide went out and never came back.

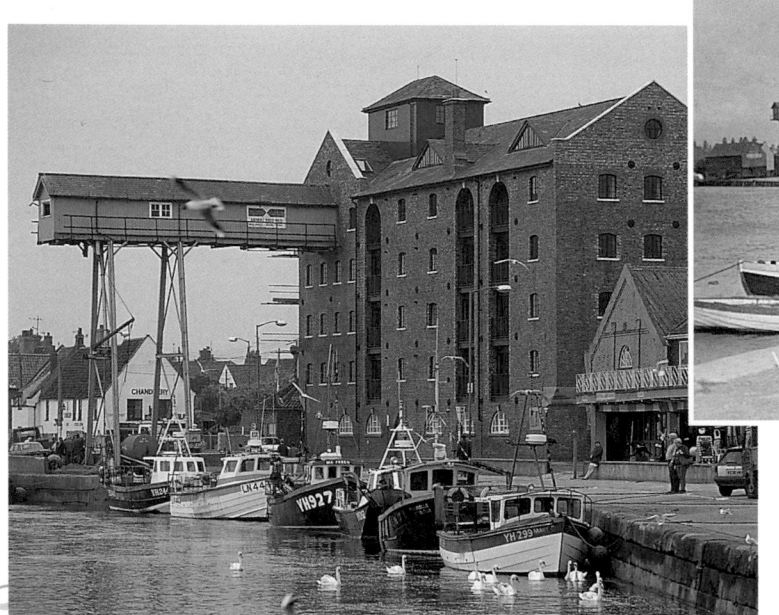

The grain mill at Wells-next-the-Sea in Norfolk has been adapted as apartments, without altering the distinctive skyline. Only the boats – and the dress fashions – have changed

A grain store at Little Petherick in Cornwall has been converted into holiday flats...

From the quayside at ground level, therefore, all you can see is the channel that winds its way through the salt-marshes to the sea, but from the upper floors of the mill the view extends beyond the marshes to the sand dunes and the shoreline. This has turned out to be one of the most useful selling points for the mill's new role as luxury apartments. New windows and balconies have been installed to make the most of the view, but the old wooden gantry at one end of the building, soaring over the quayside, has been left in place. It still looks like a mill – but a very up-market one.

The same thing has happened, although on a smaller scale, to the grain store at **Little Petherick** in Cornwall. It stands beside the creek where schooners used to sail up from Padstow Harbour to load or unload corn and flour. The store has been converted into holiday flats, perhaps not quite so tastefully as its Norfolk counterpart, and the mill itself, a

few yards upstream, is a similar Adaptable; it has been turned into a guest-house.

Just along the coast at **Boscastle** a stable block stands at the high-water line where the River Valency meets the sea. It was built to accommodate the horses which hauled up the boats, but today it accommodates youth hostellers. There are beds beneath the beams in the hayloft, and a welcoming open fire in the stable-cum-lounge below.

...and along the coast at Boscastle, a stable block for the horses which used to haul up the boats is now a youth hostel

Harbours in the great ports and industrial cities cannot offer such attractive views, but there have been some spectacular Adaptables among the vast assortment of redundant warehouses in places like Liverpool and Bristol. The 'Tate of the North' at

The Tate Gallery, part of the major adaptation of Liverpool Docks

Liverpool is perhaps the best known, part of the comprehensive conversion of the city's Victorian docks, but the arts and media centres on the dockside at **Bristol** are rapidly catching up.

The Bristol development began in the 1970s, when a massive tea warehouse on the Narrow Quay, built nearly one hundred and fifty years ago in the heyday of the Port of Bristol, became an ideal Adaptable for the Arnolfini organisation. Arnolfini, itself, was founded in 1961, taking its name from a fifteenth-century painting in the National Gallery by Jan van Eyck, *The Arnolfini Marriage*. The Arnolfini family were important patrons of the arts, and the organisation follows this theme by providing facilities for the development and understanding of contemporary arts.

The former tea warehouse has become a centre for visual arts, exhibitions, films and live events, which between them now attract nearly half a million visitors a year. It set a precedent which has been followed up by similar conversions of other warehouse Adaptables on Bristol's Broad and Narrow Quays.

It is perhaps ironic that just behind these quayside conversions, which have changed redundant buildings into active

centres for the intellectual and the artistic, there is an Adaptable which went the other way. The Old Library in King Street was much frequented by the poets Coleridge and Southey at the end of the eighteenth century. It may well have been here that they dreamed up a political creed which was given the rather unfortunate name of 'pantisocracy'. It had nothing to do with underwear, but described a Utopian form of democracy involving equal rule by all, and was the philosophy on which they planned to found a community in America. But somehow they never got around to it. They married a pair of sisters instead, and went to live in the Lake District. The Old

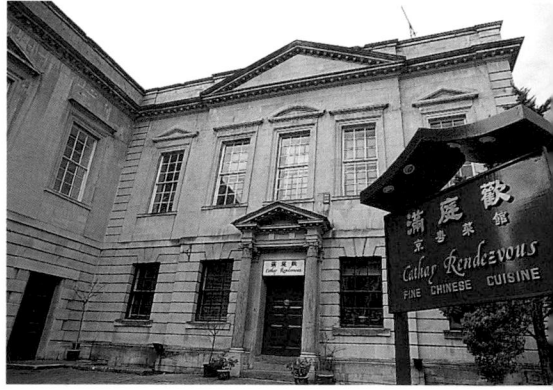

The old library in Bristol, much frequented by Coleridge and Southey, now a restaurant

This former tea warehouse on Bristol's quayside now serves refreshment for the eyes in its new role as an arts centre

Library possibly never recovered – and became a restaurant.

While I greatly admire the large-scale adaptations at Bristol and elsewhere, I am rather more taken with the smaller and more picturesque waterside Adaptables, with unusual histories behind them. For instance, there is a former coal store on the quay at **Rock** in Cornwall which is now, rather more grandly, the headquarters of the Rock Sailing and Water Ski Club.

'Coal store' conjures up the wrong kind of picture. It is not a waterside version of a grimy backyard coal shed, but a warehouse of considerable character, which stored grain as well as coal in its earlier days, and became such a familiar feature that when its owners, the Duchy of Cornwall, threatened to demolish it, there was a public outcry. As a result, the building was listed, and thus reprieved.

The sailing club first became involved with it fifty-odd years ago. The building was rented out as a boat store and workshop, and the club was offered the upper floor as a clubroom during the summer season. But in 1969 it was found to be in danger of imminent collapse. For more than a century, twice daily, the tide had washed through the foundations,

causing the wooden supports to rot away. The floor joists had rotted too, so they were only held up by the floors they were supposed to support.

It became clear that, instead of repairing it, the Duchy wanted to knock it down and allow the club to build a new headquarters on the site. It reached the stage in the 1970s when tenders were invited to demolish it; at the eleventh hour, the protesters persuaded the local MP to get it listed. The Duchy, now landed with the expensive responsibility of maintaining a building they did not want, agreed to lease it to the club for a peppercorn rent of ten pounds a year – on condition the club took on the restoration work, too.

With the help of the Sports Council and the English Tourist Board, the club raised the necessary £65,000, the work was completed in two years, and the former 'coal shed' was formally reopened as a modernised, well-equipped clubhouse in 1977. It has stood there, Rock-steady, ever since.

A pilchard cellar sounds just about as modest as a coal shed, but there was nothing modest about the pilchard catches that used to be brought ashore at **Cadgwith**, another picturesque Cornish harbour. The record for a single day was one million three hundred thousand pilchards, and a great many of them passed through this cellar. Then the pilchards swam away, never to return, and the cellar first became Sharkey's Cafe, then the Old

The headquarters of Rock Sailing and Water Ski Club in Cornwall once served as a storehouse for grain and coal. It came perilously close to demolition but is now a listed building

Cellars Restaurant. It sees rather fewer pilchards today, but there are still the grooves in the floor where the natural oil from the fish was channelled away, to be drained into tanks and used to fuel the lamps. The grooves could still come in handy, if a diner spilt his soup...

Finally, a waterside Adaptable which is no longer by the water. Tucked away in the North Norfolk countryside is a flat stretch of grass between fields of corn and sugar beet, which serves as the runway for the magnificently named **Northrepps** International Airport. The story goes locally that it acquired the title after a Dutch helicopter took the wrong turning over the North Sea and landed there by mistake but, in fact, it does receive quite a few international flights by private planes from the Continent.

The airstrip was originally for the use of the men building the nearby Bacton gas terminal. When the job was completed the strip was taken over by a local land-owning family, the Gurneys, and it now has two 'terminal buildings' at the end of the runway. The more sophisticated of the two is a caravan, but the earlier one, which still stands beside it, is actually a former bathing hut which used to be on Overstrand beach.

Its history, though, is said to go back much further than that. The Gurneys believe it was used as an ammunition limber in the Crimean War; an alternative and rather more romantic theory is that it was one of Florence Nightingale's ambulances. Whatever its role then, after the war it was brought home and installed at Overstrand, where it provided discreet changing accommodation for genteel Victorian bathers.

In the Second World War it saw active service again, this time as a sentry box for the Home Guard. Then it was acquired by

a local smallholder, who hauled it off to house his chickens. In due course, the smallholding was taken over as a caravan site, and the much-travelled wooden hut was in grave danger of being smashed up and used as firewood. It had already lost its original big wheels and shafts, dating back to its horse-drawn days, when it was rescued by the Gurneys, who re-equipped it with small metal wheels and trundled it off to Northrepps Airport.

Some of that early history is difficult to verify, and it seems remarkable that such a primitive wooden structure could survive so many astonishing adventures, over a period of a century and a half. But I do not wish to push the bounds of credibility – nor that much-travelled hut – too far. Let's not delve too deeply into its activities in the Crimea: seaside bathing hut into airport terminal building is a good enough Adaptable for me.

Cadgwith in Cornwall had a thriving pilchard fleet until the pilchards swam elsewhere. A former pilchard cellar by the beach is now a restaurant

The two distinctive airport terminals at Northrepps in Norfolk. A converted caravan is not too unusual – but a bathing hut?

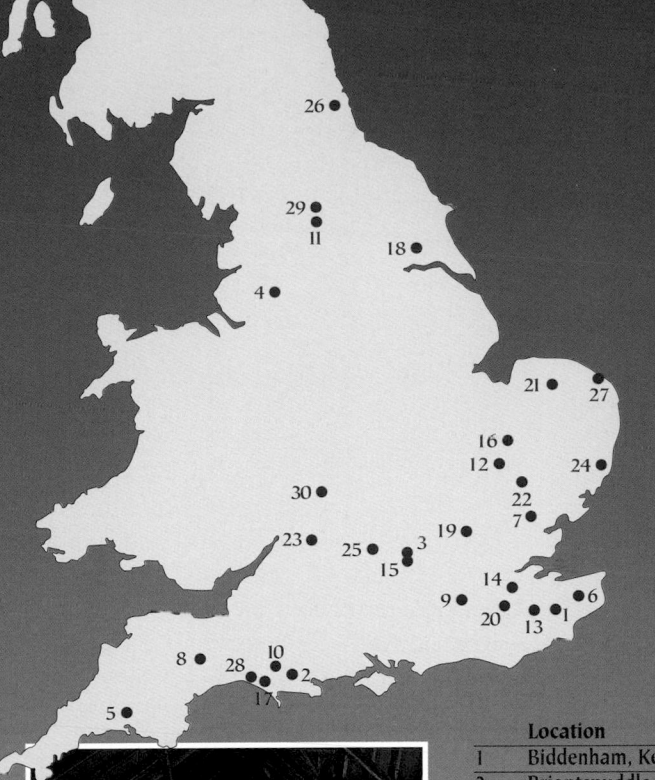

Countryside Adaptables

• • • • • • • • • •

Barns and granaries, dovecotes and smithies, maltings and oast-houses, hammer ponds and gravel pits

	Location	Old use	New use(s)
1	Biddenham, Kent: Bishopsdale Oast	Oast-house	Guest-house
2	Briantspuddle, Dorset	Cowsheds	Cottages
3	Brightwell-cum-Sotwell, Oxfordshire	Granary	Private residence
4	Bromley Cross, Bolton: Last Drop Village	Farm buildings	Leisure centre
5	Calstock, Cornwall: Cotehele mine	Engine room	Holiday accommodation
6	Chartham, Kent: Thruxted Oast	Oast-house	Guest-house and picture-framer's
7	Dunmow, Essex	Farm buildings	Workshops
8	Escot, Devon	Farm buildings	Exotic fish breeder's
9	Farley Green, Surrey: St. Michael's Church	Barn	Parish church
10	Godmanstone, Dorset: The Smith's Arms	Smithy	Pub
11	Grassington, North Yorkshire:	Barn	Theatre; private residence
	Pletts Barn	Barn	Mountaineering shop
	Tom Lee's Smiddy	Smithy	Florist; art gallery
12	Great Shelford, Cambridgeshire	Pigeon-house	Private residence
13	Horsmonden, Kent	Furnace pond	Fishing pond
14	Ightham, Kent: The Old Forge	Smithy	Private residence
15	Ipsden, Oxfordshire	Granary	Chemical store
16	Little Thetford, Cambridgeshire: The Round House	Dovecote	Private residence
17	Litton Cheney, Dorset	Barn	Youth hostel
18	Lund, East Yorkshire	Smithy	Bus shelter
19	Node Court, Hertfordshire	Dairy farm	Luxury residence
20	Penshurst, Kent	Smithy	Garage
21	Pensthorpe, Norfolk	Gravel pits	Nature reserve
22	Saffron Walden, Essex	Maltings	Evacuation centre; youth hostel
23	Sherborne Park, Gloucestershire	Dovecote	Army base; school; flats
24	Snape, Suffolk	Maltings	Concert hall
25	Wantage, Oxfordshire	Barns	Youth hostel
26	Washington, Sunderland: Biddick Farm	Farm buildings	Arts centre
27	Waxham, Norfolk: Waxham Barn	Barn	Restored but unused
28	West Allington, Dorset	Flax mill	Youth hostel; training centre
29	West Burton, North Yorkshire	Smithy	Bus shelter
30	Winson, Gloucestershire	Farm buildings	Fish-processing works

Koi carp in the cowshed, dormers in the dovecote

Ever since the invention of the threshing machine, there have been redundancies among farm workers, but some farm buildings were becoming redundant long before that, from the time when the church stopped collecting tithes and its vast tithe barns were no longer required. Many other rural buildings have also outlived their original uses, from granaries and dovecotes to stables and smithies, but the barn is still by far the most familiar Adaptable in the English countryside.

There was a period when even the most handsome redundant barn

Farm complexes which have taken on new roles: this one at Washington in Sunderland is now an arts centre with theatre and art gallery...

... and at Bromley Cross near Bolton, a lonely moorland farm is now a luxury hotel and leisure centre

might not have survived. In 1987 there were more applications to demolish listed barns than any other single type of building, and nobody will ever know just how many unlisted ones disappeared. But, during the last ten years, with the increasing popularity of country living and the growing influence of conservationists, the trend seems to have been halted. 'Barn conversion' is one of the most overworked phrases in the estate agent's vocabulary.

No need to quote examples. You can see them all over the country, sometimes lovingly preserved in almost their original form, more often embellished with dormer windows, fanlights in the roof, fancy porches, front gardens copied from suburbia – anything to disguise what they used to be.

It is hardly surprising because, let's face it, there are few buildings that look more boring than your average barn. But, now and again, someone shows a little imagination, and a barn can become a

really interesting Adaptable, while still looking like a barn.

It can happen in the most unexpected places. **Washington**, in Sunderland, is not the leafiest of New Towns, even though the cramped streets of miners' houses have been demolished and the pit heap which dominated the landscape has been moved away. But, amidst all the modern houses and shops in this almost entirely industrial area, a cluster of farm buildings has survived, in what is now the Washington Arts Centre.

In the 1970s the Washington Development Corporation found itself with this Victorian farm inside the boundaries of the New Town. Instead of flattening it, which must have been a temptation, they adapted it to the cultural needs of a population of eighty thousand incomers. The biggest barn was converted into a theatre seating one hundred and thirty people. Others became craft workshops, an art gallery, a community meeting room. Just a couple became what the Corporation called 'residential units' and estate agents call 'barn conversions'.

In all, the work took ten years to complete, and the last section was opened in 1983. Five years later the arts centre was taken over by the City of Sunderland Community Services as one of their more unusual properties.

There was another ingenious adaptation of large barns and sheds at **Bromley Cross**, near Bolton. A collection of eighteenth-century moorland farm buildings became almost a self-contained leisure complex, known as the Last Drop Village – I suppose the last drop of use was squeezed out of them. One has been converted into a pub, another into a bakery and tea-shop, and what used to be a cattle-shed became the restaurant of the Last Drop Village Hotel. It kept its original

cow stalls, and the tables were made out of cartwheels.

'Model' dairy farms created by idealistic millionaires between the wars for happy cows were obvious Adaptables, because they looked a little unreal anyway. **Node Court** in Hertfordshire, with its thatched cow barns and a thatched silo looking like the turret of a fairy castle, is now a luxury home – the old manure store, known as the Dungery, functions as a swimming-pool. And at **Briantspuddle** in Dorset, where Sir Ernest Debenham of the London department store created a similar 'model farm' (but with two thatched turrets instead of one), the cowsheds have been turned into cottages.

Smaller groups of farm buildings have proved more versatile. Stock sheds are particularly popular, because they generally face inwards on to a paved courtyard, which creates a cosy atmosphere for holiday cottages, or craft centres, or small workshops. In former farm buildings just outside **Dunmow** in Essex, for example, the products now range from boats to hospital equipment; in a group of Cotswold barns at **Winson** in Gloucestershire they smoke and process fish; and on the **Escot estate** in Devon they breed ornamental varieties, with fish tanks in the pigsties, aquaria in the tractor sheds, and Koi carp in the cow stalls.

The model farm at Briantspuddle in Dorset already had thatched cowsheds and turrets before they were turned into cottages

Pletts Barn at Grassington in North Yorkshire still looks like a barn, but inside is a mountaineering shop

Isolated barns in the middle of nowhere are rather more tricky, particularly if they are the massive medieval kind, which delight the conservationists, but are singularly impractical for most modern uses. This was certainly true of **Waxham Barn** in Norfolk, one of the finest medieval barns in the country, which was restored at a cost of half a million pounds, but stood empty for years after the work was completed, and the last I heard was empty still.

Pletts Barn at **Grassington** in North Yorkshire has fared rather better, because it is in the heart of a thriving village, in popular tourist country. It is a massive Wharfedale barn dating back to the sixteenth or seventeenth century, with the traditional high-porched entrance for carts, and ventilation slits instead of windows. It now serves as a mountaineering shop, but there has been a minimum of alteration to the original structure. Thomas Plett, if he revisited his barn today, would easily recognise it.

Another barn in the village has had a rather more varied career since it became redundant in the early 1800s. An enterprising local postmaster called Tom Airey adapted it as a theatre, and Edmund Kean was among the famous actors of the day who performed there, fresh from his

triumph as Richard III at Drury Lane. But Kean died young, in 1833, and so did Tom Airey's theatre. He turned his attention to mail coaches, a business which his family continued until the end of the century, and the theatre was closed. It became just another 'barn conversion', but its brief foray into the world of entertainment is not forgotten; it is called Theatre Cottage.

A rather different use for a big old barn, albeit a wooden one, has been found at **Farley Green** in Surrey. At the end of a track, leading into what looks like a farmyard, there is, indeed, a yard surrounded by weather-boarded barns, about a hundred and fifty years old, but one of them has a tiny cross on the end gable and a simple wooden belfry above the porch. Its original doorway, large enough to take a horse and cart, has been reduced in size, though the original outline and hinges are still there. The conversion –

Theatre Cottage at Grassington was originally a barn, but as its name suggests, it had an interim role as a theatre in the early 1800s. Edmund Kean was one of the famous actors who appeared there

A weatherboarded barn at Farley Green in Surrey is now the parish church, but from the outside the only clues are the little cross on the gable and the bell-cote over the door

Grain stores were built on stone 'mushrooms' to discourage the rats, and they discouraged adaptors too. But at Sotwell in Oxfordshire one is now part of a private residence

an appropriate word – took place in the 1920s, and the barn was consecrated in 1930. It has been the parish church of St. Michael's ever since.

The bell rope still hangs from the belfry, but the bell itself, alas, has gone; it was stolen a few years ago. But one particular memory of it still lives on in the village, the occasion during the last war when it was heard being tolled, even though that was normally not allowed. In wartime it could only mean that the Germans had invaded, and the villagers rushed to the Barn Church, as it is always known, to find who had raised the alarm. Instead, they found a very irritated cow, with its horns entangled in the bell rope...

The little field barns which are dotted all over the Peak District and the Yorkshire Dales might have been abandoned to the elements once they had outlived their original use, but someone had the bright idea of converting them into 'stone tents' for use by long-distance walkers. They provide just the basic essentials – a sleeping area, a cooking area and a toilet – plus, more importantly, shelter from the cold and wet. The idea got the backing of both the Countryside Commission and the Youth Hostels Association, and under the title of 'camping barns' they have been included in the itineraries of countless energetic holiday-makers with a taste for spartan living.

There are more elaborate versions, of course. In a chalk-pit, outside **Wantage** in Oxfordshire, five redundant barns from local farms were re-erected to form a youth hostel and community centre, with accommodation for seventy people. The attraction was not living in a chalk pit but in its location; it lies midway along the Ridgeway Long-Distance Path.

More specialised farm buildings have become Adaptables, too, though they required a little more ingenuity. Granaries, for instance, can be a problem, because they are usually perched on straddle stones, those little stone mushrooms, to prevent rats getting at the floorboards and gnawing their way through. Not everybody wants to live in mid-air but, at **Brightwell-cum-Sotwell** in Oxfordshire, for instance, one of these mushroom-mounted buildings is used as part of a converted residence, and nobody has fallen out of it yet.

25

This former grain store at Ipsden in Oxfordshire no longer houses the harvested crop – instead it stores the chemicals which help to produce it

England, plus the cotes built into the walls of buildings – Plett's Barn at Grassington for one. Then somebody thought of using root crops for winter fodder, so they could eat fresh beef and pork all the year round, and the popularity of pigeon pie plummeted. The massive dovecotes built by sixteenth-century landowners, some of them big enough to accommodate three thousand birds, became redundant, and have mostly disappeared. Only the more familiar circular ones survive in any number, too small to be worth the cost of demolishing, but too small also for most practical uses.

More commonly, these granaries are still used for storage, but instead of grain, they are particularly useful for pesticides and the like. There is one at **Ipsden**, also in Oxfordshire, which looks just as it did centuries ago, but now contains chemicals instead of corn.

Another specialised rural building is the dovecote, once an essential source of fresh meat during the winter months. There were twenty-six thousand of them in

One exception is at **Little Thetford** in Cambridgeshire, where a former dovecote is now The Round House, a delightful circular cottage with dormer windows in its thatched roof. Elsewhere in Cambridgeshire, **Great Shelford** has a converted timber-and-plaster pigeon house built around 1700. It is easy to spot among the modern dwellings around it, but it is just called, unromantically, 42 Granhams Road.

Perhaps the most remarkable dovecote conversion is at **Sherborne Park** in Gloucestershire, where the hall itself was converted into a wartime army base, then a private school, an assortment of study centres and, finally, luxury flats. The little octagonal dovecote in the grounds – which some say was a meat larder, but dovecote experts disagree – has come in very handy as an electricity substation.

Another feature of the countryside used to be the smithy. A few still survive in their original role, for the benefit of the comparatively few horses which have survived the motor age, but most have been adapted for other uses. Logically, a smithy should evolve into a garage, and this has happened at **Penshurst** in Kent, for instance, where the garage has happily retained the large horseshoe-shaped door

A former dovecote at Little Thetford in Cambridgeshire is now occupied by people instead of birds

Not for the birds – this imposing cottage was once a dovecote

Adapted smithies which are still easy to identify: the garage at Penshurst in Kent has retained its horseshoe-shaped door...

Charles II dropped in to have his horse reshod, and was so disappointed at not getting a drink that he promptly gave it a licence. The Smith's Arms still occupies the six-hundred-year-old smithy, and claims to be the smallest pub in the world, but it may equally claim to be the first smithy-pub Adaptable.

and the symbolic hammer and spikes on the gable. Other smithies have also adjusted to meet the needs of mechanised transport, but in another way; at **Lund** in East Yorkshire and **West Burton** in North Yorkshire, for instance, they now serve as bus shelters.

A good many of them became pubs, as all those Blacksmith's Arms and Horseshoe Inns bear witness. Sometimes the building fulfilled both functions, with the blacksmith as landlord, too. Perhaps the earliest example is the Smith's Arms at **Godmanstone** in Dorset, where the blacksmith was just a blacksmith until

...and the tiny Smith's Arms at Godmanstone in Dorset has a sign you cannot mistake

The Old Forge at Ightham in Kent only has its old anvil as a reminder of its former role...

Other smithies became private residences rather than public houses, but they like to display reminders of their origin, like the timbered Old Forge at **Ightham** in Kent, which still has the old anvil on show. In contrast, the smithy at

...and Tom Lee's Smiddy at Grassington in North Yorkshire, now an art gallery, just has its long sloping roof to identify it

Grassington (a happy hunting-ground for Adaptables) in North Yorkshire forsook any memories of the smoke and heat of the forge when it became a florist's shop. It was subsequently turned into an art gallery, and its links with the past became even more blurred, but it is still known locally as Tom Lee's

Smiddy and, indeed, Tom Lee himself is unlikely to be forgotten – not as a blacksmith, but as a murderer.

It is said that, in 1766, he was boasting in the Anglers' Arms at nearby **Kilnsey** – another Adaptable, now a private house – about his exploits as a robber, when he was overheard by a local physician, Dr Petty, who threatened to expose him. The doctor's body was found later in the River Wharfe, and Lee was arrested, charged with his murder, and executed at York. His body was hung in chains in Grass Wood, just outside Grassington. After his death, the smithy passed through several hands, and several adaptations, before it became the Shenstone Gallery a couple of years ago.

The oast-house, like the smithy, relies on heat to fulfil its function and, like the smithy, it has suffered widespread redundancy. But, unlike the smithy, it is difficult to disguise in a different role. The tapering roof surmounted by a swivelling cowl, reminiscent of the paper hats that chefs put on lamb cutlets, is quite unmistakable, and the kiln inside, where the hops are laid on a slatted floor with a heated draught passing through them, does not seem immediately appropriate for conversion to living accommodation.

Bishopsdale Oast in Kent, which was derelict for thirty years, is now a guest-house – there is even a bedroom in the kiln

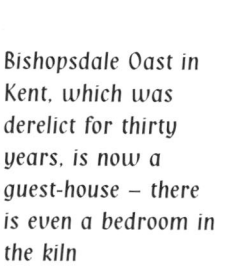

However, some have been successfully adapted as private houses or modest hotels. Bishopsdale Oast at **Biddenham** in Kent was built about 1750, ceased to operate as an oast-house some fifty years ago, and stood empty for thirty, until it was adapted as a guest-house, with one bedroom in the kiln; the heated draught has presumably been excluded. The hop press and sulphur pans are still around. Not far away near **Chartham**, the upper areas of three oast-houses at Thruxted Oast are now guest-rooms, with the original tie-beams and trapdoors still featured, and the other part is now a picture framing business.

Along with oast-houses, maltings are probably the most familiar rural buildings associated with the drinks industry – apart from pubs, of course – and the best-known of the maltings Adaptables must surely be at **Snape** in Suffolk, home of the Aldeburgh Festival. During the first half of the last century a corn and coal business operated on the site, until it was bought by a maltster called Newson Garrett. He decided the buildings needed expanding, and he is said to have marked out the front of the maltings with his walking-stick. He may have been sampling some of his own products, because he failed to draw a straight line – which accounts for the slight bend in the front wall. In the end it made little odds, because most of the walls became hidden beneath Virginia creeper.

The maltings were conveniently placed for barges bringing in the barley from American grain ships lying offshore, but when English farmers started growing barley in quantity the malting industry became more centralised, and Snape found itself, almost literally, out on a limb. The maltings closed in 1965, and a year

later they were taken on by the Aldeburgh Festival Committee, headed by Benjamin Britten and Peter Pears, who converted them into an opera house and concert hall.

They were opened by the Queen in 1967, but two years later, on the opening night of the season, a fire broke out which gutted the interior. The restoration work took twelve months – then the Queen came back and opened them all over again. Today, the maltings complex includes shops, coffee and wine bars, an art gallery and a piano workshop – with river trips available as a bonus in the summer.

The maltings at **Saffron Walden** in Essex is even more picturesque than the

Hop into bed – Thruxted Oast near Chartham in Kent has guest bedrooms in the upper floors

The Snape maltings in Suffolk is now the home of the famous Aldeburgh Festival

 *(second photograph, top right)*

At **Litton Cheney**, not far from the Chesil Beach, a Dutch barn where cheese used to be manufactured is now equipped to provide simple self-catering accommodation – in other words, bring your own cheese – and at **West Allington**, on the outskirts of Bridport, the accommodation is in a converted flax mill, one of the main industries on which Bridport was founded.

In 1996, however, the old building was taken over by a housing association and the district council, who are making use of this accommodation in quite a different way. The flax mill is now a 'Foyer', which provides affordable accommodation, vocational training, social facilities, and help with finding a job, for young local people between sixteen and twenty-five.

After nineteen years as a youth hostel it was ideal for the purpose. Very few

The maltings at Saffron Walden in Essex, the family business and home of the Gibsons throughout the last century, is now a youth hostel

one at Snape; it is probably the finest medieval building in the town. More accurately, it was originally a house, probably owned by a wealthy cloth merchant, to which the maltings were added during the eighteenth century. The occupier in 1790, George Gibson, is listed as owning 'a house etc., maltings and offices'. The property remained in the Gibson family until the 1930s, when it was sold to the Society for the Preservation of Ancient Buildings.

It had its first experience of youthful occupation during the last war, when Middlesex Education Committee rented it to house evacuees. Then, in 1947, it was acquired by the Youth Hostels Association, and it has been a youth hostel ever since.

Within seven miles of each other in Dorset are examples of two less familiar rural industries, housed in rather less picturesque buildings, which became Adaptables and were also taken over by the YHA.

A former cheese factory at Litton Cheney in Dorset now offers holiday accommodation but no cheese – it is self-catering

A former flax mill at Bridport in Dorset is now a 'Foyer', providing accommodation, training and other help to young people seeking jobs

property, in a very different setting.

Only the old engine house survives intact among the derelict buildings. The mine has not been worked since 1900, like the other abandoned mines in the woods around it. But the engine house, surprisingly, became an Adaptable when the Landmark Trust leased it, along with the other buildings, and made it habitable. Groups of four can now take their holidays there, in the building where the massive rotary beam engine, with its forty-inch cylinder, used to provide the power for what the Trust describes as 'a dreadful but romantic trade'.

There are two rural industries, one now extinct, the other at its peak, which

alterations were needed, and seventeen young people can be accommodated there with all the necessary facilities, from training rooms to a laundry. There is a network of 'Foyers' in the United Kingdom and across Europe, but this was the first of its kind in the south-west. It means that the flax mill, which used to provide employment for hundreds of local people, is now once again playing its part in getting young people jobs, in a very different world.

A rural industry which was unique to one part of the country has left behind very few Adaptables – its buildings are almost as unattractive as the industry itself. Cornwall and Devon used to have their copper and arsenic mines; the shafts are now abandoned and the mine buildings mostly derelict. There is an unexpected exception, though, tucked away in a wooded valley leading down to the Tamar. For most tourists the name Cotehele is associated with the magnificent medieval house which stands on the west bank of the river near **Calstock** in Cornwall, the home of the Edgcumbe family for centuries, now owned by the National Trust and visited by thousands each year. But only a short walk away is the Cotehele copper and arsenic mine, also owned by the National Trust, but a very different

Arsenic and old copper – the engine house at the derelict mine on the Cotehele estate in Cornwall is now a holiday cottage

in the Wensum Valley in mid-Norfolk. Along one stretch of the river the excavators are still digging, the conveyor belts are still running, the gravel heaps are still growing. But just a few miles upstream is a group of older pits, which have had their gravel stocks exhausted. Over a million tons were extracted during the 1970s, with all the accompanying noise and dust and lorry traffic. But in 1982, the transformation work began and, six years later, the Duke of Edinburgh opened what is now one of the foremost wildfowl reserves in the country, on a par with Peter Scott's famous Reserve at Slimbridge.

It is on the site of an Ancient Saxon village, which has not totally disappeared. It had its own church, St. Margaret's, but by 1600 that was already a ruin, and the village of **Pensthorpe** was reduced to a manor house and a cluster of farm buildings – sitting on top of gravel, which remained undisturbed until thirty-odd years ago.

The gravel pits are now lakes, crowded with wildlife. The farm buildings have been converted into a visitors' centre, with the larger barns being turned into a shop, exhibition rooms and a viewing gallery, others into offices and lecture rooms. An old cattle shed, built on the site of St. Margaret's Church, has become a restaurant. Only the gravel on the entrance paths reminds the thousands of visitors – if they ever think about it – just how adaptable even a gravel pit can be...

Two watery adaptables which used to be a lot less peaceful: the Furnace Pond at Horsmonden in Kent provided power for an iron foundry...

...and former gravel workings near Fakenham in Norfolk have been transformed into Pensthorpe Wildfowl Reserve

have both initially ruined the landscape and subsequently enhanced it. There was a time when hammer ponds provided water power to drive hammers which beat iron into shape in rural foundries. There is an example at **Horsmonden** in Kent, in Furnace Lane, and it is still called Furnace Pond. But, instead of providing power for noisy metal-bashing, it is now a haven of peace for anglers and wildlife.

A similar transformation has taken place with old gravel pits, though new ones are being dug all the time to provide material for bigger, better, noisier roads. There are good before-and-after examples

Stately Adaptables

● ● ● ● ● ● ● ●

Castles, mansions, gatehouses, stables, even a game larder and a servants' privy

	Location	Old use	New use(s)
1	Beer, Devon: Bovey House	Tudor mansion	Hotel
2	Derby: Arboretum Lodge	Stately home	Photography centre and gallery
3	Gayhurst, Milton Keynes: Gayhurst House	Stately home	Private residences
4	Gunton, Norfolk: Gunton Hall	Stately home	Private residence
5	Hertford Castle	Castle	Council offices
6	Holme Lacy, Hereford and Worcester: Holme Lacy House	Stately home	Hotel
7	Ickwell Bury, Bedfordshire	Stately home	Yoga centre
8	Ilkley, Bradford: Denton Hall	Georgian mansion	Offices and training centre
9	Launceston, Cornwall: Eagle House	Stately home	Hotel
10	Melton Mowbray, Leicestershire: Stapleford Park	Jacobean mansion	Hotel and health club
11	Moor Park, Hertfordshire: Moor Park Mansion	Stately home	Golf and Country Club
12	Quidenham, Norfolk: Quidenham Hall	Stately home	Monastery; Children's hospice
13	Rutland Water, Rutland: Burley-on-the-Hill	Stately home	Private residence
14	Thornbury, South Gloucestershire: Thornbury Castle	Castle	Hotel
15	Woodhall Spa, Lincolnshire: Petwood Hotel	Mansion	Hotel
16	Yoxford, Suffolk: Satis House	Stately home	Hotel
17	Wilton Castle, Middlesbrough	Stately home	Industrial premises

Manners maketh man; manors maketh flats, hotels, offices...

'An Englishman's home', said James I's Lord Chief Justice rather grandly, 'is his castle' – and in his case, it just about was. Sir Edward Coke and his descendants created a castle-sized mansion and estate at Holkham in Norfolk which is still the family home today, more than three centuries after it was built. But, for the Cokes, times have changed, and for many landed gentry, an Englishman's home can now be part of a castle...

It has taken a great deal of ingenuity and enterprise for some of these great families to hang on to their castles at all. For some of them it has meant having lions in the park or lodgers in the parlour. Stables have been turned into souvenir shops, servants' kitchens into quick-serve cafés, and paddocks into playgrounds. Others have handed over their properties to the National Trust and share their tenancies with the tourists. A considerable number have given up altogether and sold off their stately homes to the developers – sometimes with disastrous results. But one or two of these sell-offs, happily, have

Burley-on-the-Hill in Rutland as it looked when the Earls of Nottingham lived there, and as it looks today. Not very different outside, but behind that facade it is now twenty-three sizeable homes

fallen into safe hands. A new breed of conservationist developer has arrived, who has managed to preserve the appearance and atmosphere of these cumbersome old piles while adapting them to new purposes – and still making a profit...

Burley-on-the-Hill, overlooking Rutland Water – not to be confused with Burghley-not-on-the-Hill, ancestral home of the Cecils – was the home of the Finches, Earls of Nottingham. **Gunton Hall** in Norfolk was the home of the Harbords, Earls of Suffield. Both great houses were built and extended over the centuries, regardless of cost. Both were extensively

Gunton Hall in Norfolk at its grandest, in 1879, before it was partially destroyed by fire. What remains has been divided into houses and apartments, and the game larder (right) is now a two-bedroomed cottage

damaged by fire within thirty-odd years of each other, near the turn of this century, and both deteriorated still further for lack of funds. Both have now been restored and adapted to provide elegant, but manageable, homes for twenty-odd individual families, where just one family lived before.

When Daniel Finch, the second Earl of Nottingham, built Burley at the end of the seventeenth century, Daniel Defoe took his mind off Moll Flanders to observe: 'I do not know of a house in Britain which excels all the rest in so many particulars, or that goes so near to excelling them all in everything.' It so happened that in earlier days the Earl had signed a warrant for Defoe's imprisonment, and maybe he didn't want him to do it again. But he was not exaggerating.

His Lordship had plenty of money to play with. As Secretary of State, a great many perks came his way, in addition to a substantial salary. And he wasn't starting from scratch. He already owned a house in London which he sold to William III to put

a down-payment on the Burley estate. That house is better known these days as Kensington Palace.

Even so, he cut down on architect's fees by getting some informal advice from Christopher Wren, then went ahead on his own. The result was a baroque fortress with the Earl's arms displayed on the imposing frontage, and wings on both sides linked by colonnades. Impressive it certainly was; cosy it was not.

While the Earl's descendants were trying to keep warm in this vast establishment, the Harbord family were, no doubt, doing much the same at Gunton Hall. Sir William Harbord was fifty years behind the Earl in building his country retreat, and he went in for Palladian rather than baroque, but this too was a vast mansion – and his son, the first Earl of Suffield, made it even vaster. He allowed forty thousand pounds for improvements to the house – a fortune in those days – and found the whole lot went just on the service buildings round the back.

This sort of shock is not unusual when householders are building extensions, but not quite on that scale. Most of us would have called it a day at that stage, but Lord Suffield just went on spending, and Gunton Hall, like Burley-on-the-Hill, just kept on growing. And both families just kept on trying to keep warm.

Both of them overdid it. Gunton Hall went up in flames in 1862, Burley in 1908. For the Suffields it was not entirely bad news, according to local rumour. The Prince of Wales had become a regular visitor to the hall, bringing with him his entire entourage, plus Miss Lillie Langtry and her lady friends, who were there – as one writer delicately put it – 'to entertain the Prince – and think of England...' The cost of entertaining this lot must have been prohibitive, and cynics have suggested the Suffields set fire to the place themselves to cut down on their hospitality bill. But that seems rather too extravagant a gesture, even for the Suffields.

The Finches also entertained distinguished guests at Burley-on-the-Hill, among them Winston Churchill, who was actually there when the house caught fire, but nobody has suggested that it might have frightened him away. On the contrary, he was much impressed by the blaze, and wrote enthusiastically: 'Until then I had no conception of the pure majesty of a great conflagration.' He described how chairs and tables burned like matches, floors collapsed, and the roof fell in: 'Every window spouted fire, and from the centre of the house a volcano roared skyward in a whirlwind of smoke.' He wrote as if the whole thing had been laid on expressly for his benefit...

Neither of the two great houses really recovered after their fires. Some restoration work was carried out at Burley, but it had another setback when the Government requisitioned it as a hospital during the last war, and did not hand it back until some years after it was over. By then it

Two features of Gayhurst House, Milton Keynes – the imposing front facade and the bizarre servants' lavatory, with Cerberus on top. The house is now an apartment, and 'The Dog House' is a cottage

was empty and not exactly in peak condition, and much of it remained unoccupied. In the 1990s it was bought by the enterprising Asil Nadir, who had plans to turn it into an hotel, but he was a little too enterprising and went bankrupt and the house went further downhill. Those parts not flooded because of the leaky ceilings were riddled with dry rot.

Meanwhile, Gunton Hall's condition grew even worse. A century after the fire, the last of the Harbords to live there, an elderly maiden lady, died in the only wing that was still habitable; the rest of the building was virtually derelict. As with Burley, it seemed to be heading irrevocably towards complete oblivion.

Enter the Master Adaptor, one Kit Martin, a property developer with an imaginative eye for converting enormous historic mansions into smaller manageable homes – which still looked like enormous historic mansions. He had a particular feeling for the servants' areas, generally the least attractive feature of a stately home. 'Eighteenth-century kitchens make extremely good Adaptables,' he told me.

He bought Gunton Park in 1979 and Burley-on-the-Hill thirteen years (and six adapted mansions) later. In each case he sliced up the main building into four or five substantial separate residences. At Gunton he left the central area, the seat of the fire, open to the elements – 'to preserve the romance of the ruins', as he put it, but it also provided an attractive open area at the rear of all the outward-facing residences.

The wings and stables were divided up into smaller apartments and cottages, and he had a great time at Gunton with the first Earl's over-expensive service buildings. One of them, the Audit House – if the Earl had any auditors they must have had strong nerves – is now a four-bedroomed house. So is the bottle and coal store,

which must have been able to contain an inordinate quantity of both. The brewery has become four cottages, and even the octagonal game larder, which could have contained enough pheasants to feed an army, is now an unusual two-bedroomed cottage with a round dining-room twenty-six feet across.

Kit Martin's system, at Gunton and at Burley-on-the-Hill, was to adapt the building in stages, so that the sale of one house or cottage would pay for the next, and any financial risk was minimised. He need not have worried. Every house and cottage and apartment he created out of these two mansions was snapped up before it was finished.

Mr Martin is not, of course, the only developer in the field of stately home Adaptables, nor, indeed, the first. In the early 1970s Gayhurst House near Milton Keynes was converted into **Gayhurst Court**, a complex of twenty-six flats and houses occupied by individual tenants. They are successors to some very remarkable characters who have lived in the original house over the centuries.

One of the earliest was Sir Everard Digby, who was hanged, drawn and quartered for his part in the Gunpowder Plot. Although he was a Catholic, he had been knighted by the Protestant James I. The King was so frightened of swords, it is said, that he shut his eyes while performing the ceremony, and instead of touching Sir Everard's shoulder with the blade he nearly put his eye out. Perhaps Sir Everard was still wincing at the memory when he agreed to join the plot against him, a couple of years later...

Gayhurst passed from the Digbys to the Wrightes, who lived there until it was leased in the 1850s to Robert, Lord Carrington, another memorable character. He was born Robert John Smith, but

Thornbury Castle near Bristol, built by the Duke of Buckingham in Henry VIII's time – the only Tudor castle in England which is now an hotel. Henry and Anne Boleyn spent their weekends here – but not necessarily in this bed

changed his name to Carrington when he succeeded to the barony. Among his slight eccentricities was the belief that his posterior was made of glass; the implications of this do not bear thinking about. After he died a journalist printed the story and, in classic style, Carrington's son horse-whipped the impertinent fellow on the steps of his club in St. James's. Not surprisingly, nobody referred to his lordship's glass bottom again.

In addition to this engaging story, Lord Carrington also left behind an eccentric little building, as part of his alterations at Gayhurst House. He engaged a well-known Victorian architect, William Burges, to include in his designs a circular five-seater outside lavatory for the menservants. For no obvious reason, this up-market privy was surmounted by a carved figure of Cerberus, the three-headed dog that guards the gates of Hades. Perhaps it was put there to discourage the servants from spending too much time in it.

When Gayhurst became an Adaptable, so did the privy. It now forms part of Number 12 The Mews, Gayhurst Court, which is occupied by Mr and Mrs Alan Lake. Its official name is Cerberus, but it

seems to be universally known as 'The Dog House'. Living as I do in Kennel House, I can sympathise...

Mr Lake agrees with me that the old toilet qualifies as an Adaptable in its own right. 'It is now our sitting-room, whereas previously the only sitting to be done was on one of the "thunderboxes" placed there for the use of the servants...'

As well as being split up into separate dwellings, stately home Adaptables can be very suitable for converting into hotels. There is no shortage of accommodation or parking space, they can look enormously imposing on picture postcards – 'our bedroom is in the second turret from the left' – and if there is any sort of royal connection they are irresistible to foreign tourists, who are prepared to endure the odd draught and the absence of lifts for the sake of sleeping where a crowned head just possibly lay, centuries ago.

The 'Queen Elizabeth slept here' tag is always a winner. Better still if it was Henry VIII, or one of his wives, or any combination of them. The ultimate is to find an hotel which was actually owned by him – and there are at least a couple. Imagine staying at an establishment which might once have had 'Prop: Henry Tudor' over the door.

Take **Thornbury Castle** near Bristol, for example; it has a pedigree second to none. The Staffords were Lords of the Manor for twenty-eight generations, and in 1511 the third Duke of Buckingham, as they later became, started building the present castle to replace the original manor house. Unfortunately, he fell foul of Cardinal Wolsey, always an unwise move, and was impeached, then beheaded.

It was at this stage, so it is said, that King Henry took over the castle and used it as a weekend retreat with his latest bride, Anne Boleyn. Alas, the castle may have had some sort of jinx on it because, in due course, she followed the Duke to the block.

The castle itself, however, survived, along with its carved coat of arms of the Staffords dated 1508, and its huge double chimney, said to be even larger than those at Cardinal Wolsey's Hampton Court (perhaps this one-upmanship was the Duke's undoing). Mary Tudor returned it to the Duke's descendants, but it remained unoccupied for three centuries. Eventually, it was restored in the 1850s and became a private residence again. It is now a very

superior hotel – the proprietors are the Baron and Baroness of Portlethen – where bedrooms are referred to as bedchambers, and there are no new-fangled pieces of plastic to unlock their doors, just enormous keys which any warder would be proud of. The catering, however, is not quite on the same scale as in the sixteenth century, when the Duke of Buckingham, one hectic Christmas Day, managed to entertain nearly six hundred guests to Christmas dinner.

Thornbury Castle claims to be the only Tudor castle in England adapted as an hotel. However, there are a fair number of Tudor mansions fulfilling that role. Bovey House at **Beer** in Devon, for example, was also owned by Henry VIII, and he presented it to the last of his

Charles II is said to have slept at Bovey House, near Seaton in Devon, but nobody is quite sure why or who with. Hotel guests using the Charles II bedroom will spot a reminder of him on the ceiling – the Boscobel Oak

wives, Catherine Parr, who fared much better than Anne Boleyn, and actually outlived him. As a bonus for collectors of royal resting-places, Bovey House has the Charles II bedroom, though it is not too clear when or why he slept there – nor with whom. If you fail to detect any royal aura, you can always enjoy admiring the splendid bedroom ceiling. Maybe Nell Gwynne enjoyed looking at it too...

Mansions do not have to be medieval to be massive, and the mansion which is now the Petwood Hotel at **Woodhall Spa** in Lincolnshire is more massive than most.

I counted as far as nine gables along the frontage, then gave up. But it is less than a hundred years old, built at the turn of the century for the daughter of the man who founded Maples, the furniture store. It was his craftsmen who built the oak staircase and provided all the oak panelling.

The house only stayed in the family for thirty years before becoming an hotel, but its main claim to fame arose after that, during the Second World War, when it was requisitioned by the RAF. Here you can sleep in the bedrooms once occupied by the pilots of 617 Squadron, the famous Dambusters. You may find yourself, however, in a period four-poster bed. Even the exciting aura of the Dambusters, it seems, has to be augmented by a flavour of the mock-medieval.

Not every proprietor of a stately home Adaptable has laid such emphasis on the past, genuine or artificial. Stapleford Park, near **Melton Mowbray** in Leicestershire, has every right to boast about its pedigree – a huge Jacobean mansion in grounds laid out by 'Capability' Brown, the home of the Earls of Harborough for generations.

Petwood Hotel at Woodhall Spa in Lincolnshire, in the days of horse-drawn mowers, when the grass was shaved more closely than the gardener's chin, and as it is today

Stapleford Park in Leicestershire was the home of the Earls of Harborough, then a 'with it' hotel owned by the 'King of Pizzas', now an outpost of Peter de Savary's up-market Carnegie Club

There are now once again butlers in traditional uniform; football shirts are definitely out. Instead of 'Staff Sauna and Solarium' on a blank door, there is a lavishly-equipped spa in the orangery with a swimming-pool, jacuzzi, and beauty therapy rooms. And the 'Do Not Disturb' signs, I imagine, really do say 'Do Not Disturb', although in this place nobody would dream of disturbing a guest anyway. And, oh yes: the hotel 'brochure' takes the form of a fifty-page glossy magazine, which has no mention of prices, of course, but it does have colour photographs throughout, taken by the Earl of Lichfield.

It is all, in fact, overwhelmingly magnificent. But, somehow, I have a sneaking nostalgia for the eccentric King of the Pizzas...

Somewhere between the eccentric brashness of Stapleford Park as it used to be, and the expensive sumptuousness it displays today, is **Holme Lacy House** in Hereford and Worcester, once the ancestral home of the de Lacys and the Scudamores, then a psychiatric hospital, now at the plusher end of Warners' Holidays, best known in the past for their holiday camps, but now into the stately hotel business.

This one is as stately as they come. Walter de Lacy, hero of the Battle of Hastings, was granted the estate by William the Conqueror and built the first

But for a period it was owned by an American, Bob Payton, known familiarly as 'King of the Pizzas', who decided to knock the stuffiness out of English country hotels.

He dressed his house staff in football shirts. His two dogs, Gunther and Gus, patrolled the house in woolly scarves, which were changed for silk ones when they dressed for dinner. A door that led nowhere was inscribed 'Staff Sauna and Solarium'. And guests might have been disconcerted to find that the 'Do Not Disturb' sign for their bedroom doors actually read: 'Go away – we're having too much fun!'

All that changed dramatically when the hotel was bought in 1996 by Peter de Savary, the one-time Americas Cup challenger and an energetic acquirer of stately homes. He spent three million pounds refurbishing Stapleford Park – including the odd fiver, no doubt, for blotting out all those facetious notices – and reopened it as an English 'outpost' of his Skibo Castle Carnegie Club.

Holme Lacy House, once the stately home of the Scudamores, looks little changed since sheep roamed the grounds, but it is now part of the Warners' Holidays empire

manor house. The de Lacys lived there for nearly three hundred years, then a de Lacy daughter married Thomas Scudamore, and the Scudamores were at Holme Lacy for another five hundred years or more.

The Scudamores were ardent Royalists, which was sometimes good news for them, sometimes bad. The good news came in Henry VIII's time, when John Scudamore was Usher to the Court and three times High Sheriff. More importantly, he was Receiver during the suppression of the monasteries, and picked up some extra land in the process. One of his acquisitions was the Dore Abbey estate. He not only confiscated the land, but demolished most of the abbey.

His grandson, the first Viscount, made amends by restoring and reroofing it for use as the parish church, but in his case his devotion to the monarch did him more harm than good. During the Civil War he was imprisoned by the Parliamentarians – who then in their turn proceeded to wreck much of his estate.

The present mansion was built by the second Viscount in 1673, and the family lived there until the turn of this century. In 1910 it was put on the market, and the

contents auctioned in a sale that lasted three days. The house stayed in private hands until Mrs Noel Wills, of Wills cigarettes fame, gave it to the local authority, and it was turned into a psychiatric hospital.

In 1981 it was back on the market again and, in due course, it was bought by an Australian who spent three million pounds trying to turn it into a five-star hotel, but the money ran out before he could finish it. Warners have completed the adaptation, with the help of another few million. It now looks as grand as it did in the days of the Scudamores – but they might be a little disconcerted by the fruit machines and the disco.

Eccentric owners of stately hotels these days are rather thin on the ground. Their predecessors, though, who owned the hotels when they were still homes, were better able to indulge their little oddities, at least until they ran out of money. I have a soft spot, for instance, for Mrs Clarissa Ricketts of Satis House at **Yoxford** in Suffolk. Even the name of the house is slightly unusual. Had it been adapted as a factory instead of an hotel, how splendid to be able to label its products 'Satis Factory'.

But Mrs Ricketts was unusual enough in her own right. In 1887 she gambled away all her money in Monte Carlo, plus a substantial sum borrowed from her friend, Lord North. She died soon after returning home, leaving curious instructions about her funeral. It had to be conducted after dark, by an undertaker who was a stranger to the district.

Inevitably, rumours began to circulate that she had not died at all. She was just trying to evade her creditors, and the coffin contained a bogus corpse. 'Mrs Ricketts is not dead, two fat pigs were buried instead', suggested one graffiti writer. Someone reported seeing her boarding a train, disguised as a man. Someone else claimed she had been seen in Egypt. But nobody ever found her, and the mystery – if indeed there was one – has never been solved.

Gambling has not always proved unlucky for stately homeowners. Eagle House, a very grand building in the heart of **Launceston** in Cornwall, was built with the winnings from a lottery ticket in 1767. Even in those days the national lottery was nothing new; it was first established a couple of hundred years before. A Mr Carpenter bought the ticket, and the prize was a thousand pounds – peanuts in today's terms, but a useful fortune then.

Mr Carpenter had given the ticket to his girlfriend, but he shrewdly avoided any possible argument by promptly marrying her, and they built the house together. Alas, later owners proved less lucky, and found Eagle House impossible to maintain as a private residence. It is now an elegant and successful hotel – so successful, in fact,

Satis House at Yoxford in Suffolk, now an hotel, was once the home of a woman gambler who lost her fortune in Monte Carlo. If it had become a factory instead, it could have labelled its products 'Satis Factory'...

that the proprietors have recently acquired another elegant Georgian house opposite, thus taking the adaptation a stage further. As for any current lottery winners who are thinking of building themselves a stately home – maybe that will end up in much the same way.

Or their houses may become a company property. Often it is only a big company which can afford the capital outlay and the maintenance costs of big old buildings and extensive grounds. But they can be worth it, for the prestige value as well as the space and facilities they can offer for offices, or conferences, or corporate hospitality.

Denton Hall near Ilkley in Yorkshire is a good example, a Georgian mansion built in 1768 by the same architect who designed Harewood House, and very similar to it but on a slightly smaller scale. It stands on the site of Denton Castle, which was once the family home of Sir Thomas Fairfax, the parliamentary general. But the family's luck ran out when Charles II was restored to the throne, and the estate was sold to the Ibbetsons, a more cautious family than the Fairfaxes in their politics, but rather less careful, it seems, with matches. The castle was burnt down in 1734 and the replacement went up in flames too. Thankfully, it was third time lucky for Sir James Ibbetson, and his mansion still stands.

It has one of those sweeping circular staircases which every hostess must dream of descending to greet her guests. Above it is a dome, the central feature of the house, and the builder, no doubt remembering Sir James's accident-prone ancestors, erected a plaque over the front entrance with the cautionary prayer:

Nor wrath of Jove, nor fire or sword I fervent pray
May this fair dome again in prostrate ruins lay.

The prayer was answered, and when the supply of wealthy squires finally ran out in 1976, along came Messrs N.G. Bailey and Company Limited, electrical and mechanical contracting engineers. Denton

Eagle House in Launceston, built with the winnings from a lottery for only a thousand pounds – but that was in 1767. It's an hotel now, and worth rather more

Denton Hall near Ilkley is now the headquarters of a contracting engineers'. The new 'squire' – the founder of the firm – lives in the coach house block

Hall now houses offices for the directors and staff, plus a residential management training centre. Much of its character and appearance has been preserved, but the old kitchen, for instance, has been converted into a tiered lecture theatre, and the coach buildings have become flats. One of them is occupied by the new-style squire of Denton, the founder of the firm, Mr Bailey.

Wilton Castle near Middlesbrough was rebuilt during the last century as a turreted stately home and looks little changed since, but it, too, is now owned by an industrial company, one of the biggest there is. And although it has not altered the appearance of the mansion, it has transformed the countryside around it.

When John Lowther swept away the ruins of the original thirteenth-century castle to build his new home, he also swept away the old village and rebuilt it out of sight, so his view of the open country would be uninterrupted. The present owners, Imperial Chemical Industries, have now covered that open country with the vast chemical works which dominates the landscape. ICI describes the view as 'the spectacular panorama of the Wilton site'; a less sympathetic guidebook describes it as 'Satanic beyond anything which William Blake could have imagined...'

The grounds around the house, however, are still intact, and a casual visitor might think it is still a traditional private residence, with the added benefits of a swimming-pool, sauna and gymnasium. It is, in fact, an up-market clubhouse for ICI staff and a guest-house for visiting business contacts. The former master bedroom, which has a spiral staircase conveniently linking it with the wine cellar, is now the guests' sitting-room. In the club bar is one of the few reminders of the Lowthers, the date 1887 which they inscribed over the fireplace when the last stage of their restoration work was completed.

ICI bought Wilton Castle from them in 1945. It sees nothing incongruous in its present role. 'The great country houses of Britain were always part of the world of business,' says its handsome brochure, 'focal points of the community but also in

Wilton Castle, near Middlesbrough, is now owned by ICI – who are also responsible for the 'spectacular panorama' at the rear. The original owners might have described it differently...

touch with the larger affairs of trade, commerce and matters of state – and always a place of hospitality for those with whom one had dealings.'

It is certainly true that the Lowthers made their fortune – enough to rebuild the castle – from the iron ore that was discovered on their land. But I wonder how the earlier owners might have viewed this Adaptable: the Bulwer family who were granted permission to build Wilton Castle by King John, the Cornwallises who succeeded them – one of whom commanded the British forces in South Carolina in the War of Independence – and Earl Lonsdale, the first Lowther to own the castle, who used his wealth to control nine parliamentary seats in the north of England as well as his own.

Actually, I don't suppose the Earl would have been too bothered. In his later years he went a little potty, decided he was a pauper and demanded parish relief – which was conveniently delivered to him in his drawing-room by his butler. After his death, a hundred thousand pounds in gold was discovered in the castle; I hope the parish got its money back – with interest.

While ICI may argue that their adaptation of Wilton Castle merely continues its ancient role in a modern context, I doubt that the golfers, who now use **Moor Park Mansion** in Hertfordshire as their luxurious nineteenth hole, would claim much of a link with the most famous previous owner of the estate, Cardinal Wolsey. Some of them may have a closer affinity with the man who built the present mansion in the eighteenth century, a Mr Benjamin Styles, who invested in the South Sea Bubble and was shrewd enough to cash in before it burst. No doubt some of the City stockbrokers who go golfing there at the weekend would like to achieve a similar coup.

Moor Park, near Rickmansworth in Hertford Shire, the Seat of the late Lord Anson.

The grounds were laid out by the ubiquitous 'Capability Brown', but when Lord Robert Grosvenor, the second Baron Ebury, inherited the estate he added a small golf course in the park for the entertainment of his guests. The adaptation became complete when Viscount Leverhulme laid out the present course in the 1920s and turned the mansion into a country club. Moor Park Golf Club has been a prestigious Adaptable ever since.

Ickwell Bury in Bedfordshire is not nearly as old as it looks. John Harvey's original manor house was burnt down in 1937, but Colonel G.H. Wells, of the brewing family, built another one just like it, in what is described as 'free neo-Georgian'. Only the stables are the genuine

Moor Park Mansion in Hertfordshire as it was in 1770, and as it is now. Cars are parked instead of deer, and the gentlemen in the foreground would now be carrying golf clubs

Ickwell Bury in Bedfordshire was built by a rich brewer, but its present occupants have a rather different interest – it is now a Yoga centre

Quidenham Hall in Norfolk, once the home of the Earls of Albemarle, is now a carmelite monastery – with a children's hospice in the coach-house

article, built in 1683 and still boasting a rare turret clock by Tompion, who lived in the village. Long before that, Ickwell Bury was a priory, and it has now reverted to a meditative role; it is the centre of the Yoga for Health Foundation.

There is much meditation, too, at **Quidenham Hall** in Norfolk, ancestral home of the Keppels, Earls of Albemarle. The family themselves were more military than meditative. One of them was the admiral who commanded the British fleet at the Battle of Sebastopol; another, much younger, died in Flanders in the Great War while leading his company against the German trenches – his battered tin helmet was placed above his memorial in the parish church.

For the past fifty-odd years, however, Quidenham Hall has been given over to meditation and prayer. It is a Carmelite monastery, tucked away from the world behind one of those seemingly interminable flint walls which wealthy Norfolk landowners used to erect around their estates to keep out the peasants.

In recent years there has been another Adaptable at the hall. The old coach house, which was used for a time as the

monastery guest-house, has been converted into a children's hospice, the first in the county. The archways used by the coaches have been bricked up, but its original purpose is still apparent. Fortunately, the Keppels must have kept a fair number of coaches, because there is enough space inside to provide roomy accommodation for half-a-dozen children at a time, with extra rooms for families and all the equipment and fittings required to help them live their sometimes very short lives to the full. The hospice follows a simple philosophy: 'There's still a lot of living to do.'

This adaptation of auxiliary buildings at former stately homes is fairly common, but more frequently it is done after the stately home itself has gone. One of the most imposing examples is the former gatehouse at **Hertford Castle**, which now houses the offices of East Hertfordshire District Council. It could be mistaken for a castle itself.

There is just a lawn now inside the imposing curtain wall, but the buildings which used to stand there were, at various times, a royal fortress, a royal residence, and a royal prison. King Alfred's son Edward built the first fortification to defend London from the Danes. The Danes never took the castle but, surprisingly, the

Hertford Castle as it was in Victorian times, and the castle gatehouse in its present role, incorporated into council offices – the latest of a number of adaptations

The Arboretum Lodge in Derby was once the grand entrance to England's first custom-built public park; now it is a photographers' co-operative

Dauphin of France did, in 1216, when he was called in by the barons to team up against King John. Edward III used the castle as a luxury prison for the assorted kings he captured, from John of France to David II of Scotland. Queen Elizabeth – inevitably – slept here, and so did Charles I, but he got bored with it and gave it to the Earl of Salisbury, whose descendants still own the estate.

However, by the time the Salisburys took over it was already 'ruinous and decayed', except for the gatehouse, and they never occupied it. They let the gatehouse to various wealthy tenants, who added another wing or two when they had the odd bag of gold to spare. The Marquess of Downshire, for instance, who lived there in the 1750s, built a new porch, altered all the windows, remodelled the rooms in what was then the very with-it Georgian style, and added a south wing. It was about then, I suppose, that the gatehouse

graduated to the rank of castle, and it is still called Hertford Castle – though it saw service as a college, a junior school and a private house before the Corporation converted it into offices in 1911.

The Arboretum Lodge in **Derby** is not quite such a grand gatehouse as the one at Hertford, but it was the entrance to something which, in its day, was unique. It was built in 1840 for the first landscaped area in Britain specifically created for public use; in other words, our first public park. The benefactor was a Mr Joseph Strutt, whose statue looms over the lodge in a massive pillared niche. Mr Strutt himself cannot be blamed for this display of ostentation; the Park Management Committee put it there, thirteen years later.

Originally there were two lodges, but only one survives, and that was getting in a sorry state when the Derbyshire Historic Buildings Trust took it over, a few years ago. The frontage, with Mr Strutt's statue, remains unchanged, but the arboretum behind it has been converted into a photographers' cooperative called 'Arbor'. Where exotic plants used to flourish, photographs are now developed in nine darkrooms. Part of the building has become an exhibition gallery, where the more successful products of their labours can find – as so many Adaptables have, in their own way – a safe Arbor...

Other stately homes became health-care or educational Adaptables; they feature in separate chapters.

Consecrated Adaptables

● ● ● ● ● ● ● ● ●

Churches, chapels, meeting houses, citadels

	Location	Old use	New use(s)
1	Bradford: Sheik's Restaurant	Church	Indian restaurant and night-club
2	Burgh-le-Marsh, Lincolnshire: Bishop Tozer's Chapel	Chapel	Flag workshop
3	Cheddington, Dorset: St. James'	Church	Street-organ workshop
4	Chipping Norton, Gloucestershire	Salvation Army citadel	Theatre
5	Derby: St. Michael's	Church	Offices and library
6	Doncaster	Chapel	Nightclub
7	Gosport, Hampshire: The Little Church	Church	Health and beauty centre
8	Halifax, Calderdale: The Playhouse	Methodist chapel	Theatre
9	Harrogate, North Yorkshire: St. Luke's	Church	Flats
10	Holt, Norfolk: Holt Warehouse	Methodist chapel	Warehouse
11	Huddersfield, Kirklees: Lawrence Batley Theatre	Methodist chapel	Theatre
12	Keighley, Bradford	Methodist chapel	Muslim centre
13	Kenninghall, Norfolk: The Particular Pottery	Baptist chapel	Pottery
14	Kirkby Stephen, Cumbria	Chapel	Youth hostel
15	London:		
	St. George's Theatre, Tufnell Park	Church	Theatre
	Former Mission Church	Church	Sports hall
16	Manchester: Arts Centre, Victoria Park	Church	Performing arts centre
17	Newtown, Southampton	Church	Sikh temple
18	Norwich, Norfolk: Puppet Theatre	Church	Puppet theatre
19	Oxford: Lincoln College Library	Church	Library
20	Preston, Lancashire: Red Rose Radio	Church	Radio station HQ
21	Rotherham: Congrational Church	Church	Theatre
22	Stebbing, Essex: Friends' Meeting House	Meeting place	Community hall

Nothing new about conversion: it was their business

Twenty years ago the conservationists had little doubt which group of buildings were in the greatest danger of redundancy, with a grim fate awaiting them unless they could become successful Adaptables.

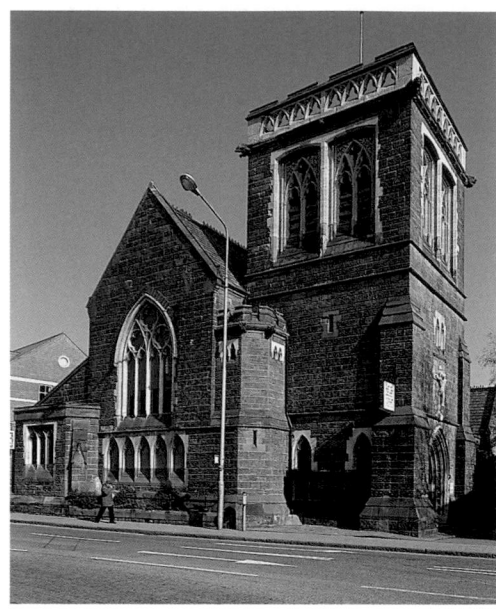

St. Michael's in Derby was made redundant in 1977. A firm of architects specialising in church conversions kept this one for their head office

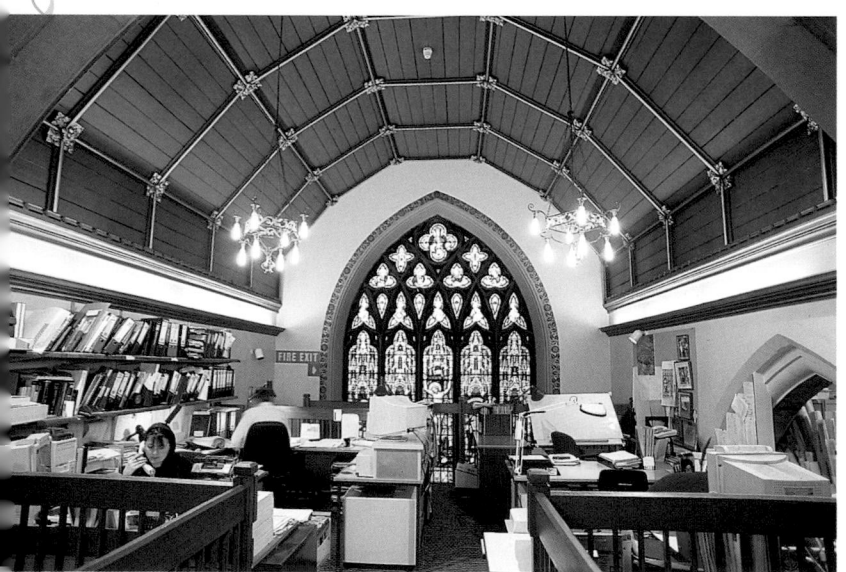

'Closure, abandonment and demolition threaten churches and chapels of all denominations on an alarming scale,' wrote a sombre Marcus Binney, chairman of Save Britain's Heritage, in 1976. 'Unless positive steps are taken, there is a real danger that the second half of the twentieth century will be remembered as an age of destruction of religious art and architecture comparable to the ravages of the Reformation and the Civil War...'

Ten years later his successor, Sophie Andreas, was just as depressed. 'Of all types of historic building under threat at the present time, none is more at risk than churches. The losses of fine buildings both in town and country have been devastating, far outweighing the numbers of country houses demolished since the war.'

But there was a glimmer of hope. She was writing in a SAVE publication, *Churches – A Question of Conversion*, and its theme was to illustrate, in effect, how churches and chapels could become Adaptables.

Since then an impressive variety of new uses have been found for old churches. Many, like redundant barns, have been turned into residences – not always with much sensitivity, so far as the conservationists are concerned, but at least they still serve a useful purpose. Others have simply been stripped of furnishings and decorations and turned into public halls. But some have demonstrated great ingenuity in devising new roles and ways of achieving them.

They range from flats and offices to libraries and theatres, from night clubs and Indian restaurants to squash courts and swimming-pools. There are radio stations, a puppet theatre, a street-organ works, a flag-making factory. One Methodist chapel even became a Muslim centre.

A good many successful church Adaptables are inevitable in the big towns, where there are more activities requiring premises. This is also where a lot of our less attractive, less historic, and less architecturally important churches can be found, so there are fewer restrictions on how they can be altered, or the uses to which they are put.

St. Michael's Church in **Derby**, for instance, was made redundant in 1977, and for three years it was left to the vandals and the elements. The Council for the Care of Churches was not too worried about it – 'of very slender merit, architecturally speaking' – and even its supporters agreed that its chunky tower was 'more of a fortification than an eloquent symbol'. It was, in fact, a fairly typical product of the 1850s.

In 1980 it was rescued by a firm of architects specialising in church conversions and, in this case, they converted it for their own use. They inserted two more floors and turned it into open-plan offices, occupying the first floor themselves and letting the floors above and below. The chancel became a library, with shelves made from redundant pews, and a reception area was created in the tower, with the choir stalls providing seats for the visitors and the lectern acting as a bookstand. It still has the original timber screen, but small windows were inserted in it to provide more light. The bell-ringing chamber above it, and the old vestry, were both adapted as conference rooms. Most of the stained glass, including the great east window, has been preserved, the memorial plaques were set in the walls, and the original metal chandeliers were hung in the lobby.

The conversion was completed in 1982, after only six months' work. From the outside there is little to indicate the transformation that has taken place inside – which, perhaps, is one sign of a successful Adaptable.

The same applies to St. Luke's Church at **Harrogate** in North Yorkshire, although if you look a little closer you will spot the new entrance that has been created in the north wall, and there is a new row of skylights in the roof. St. Luke's was one of the first churches to be successfully adapted into flats, and one of the few which looks little changed as a result. The carved heads beside the entrance, incidentally, look as if they have always been there, but they were actually taken from the main body of the church.

Twenty-nine small flats have been created inside, on four floors, and they proved so popular that all of them were sold before the conversion was complete. Half of them were bed-sitting-rooms, the others had a separate bedroom. They were even fitted into the tower and the vestry.

The only vacant space is inside the spire, which was originally going to be removed, but it is a distinctive landmark in Harrogate and the planners said it had to stay. As a sort of bonus, the architects added some extra little decorations on the roof, known as crockets. They are really there to conceal the vent pipes from the bathrooms and kitchens.

St. Luke's in Harrogate still looks like a church – except for those skylights in the roof

In contrast to the high-density adaptation of St. Luke's, All Saints' Church in **Oxford** High Street has had very few additions internally – except for bookcases. Since 1975 it has been the library of Lincoln College.

The church's links with the university go back three hundred years, when it was built to designs by the then Dean of Christ Church. There was some connection at one time with Lincoln College, which lies just behind it, but the college had its own chapel seventy years before All Saints' was built, and nobody is quite sure what the connection was. The church was closed in 1972, but for once there was no need to look far to find a new use for it. The college's existing library, which was built in 1906, had become inadequate for its purpose, and the redundant church was right on the doorstep.

Outside, there was little change. Inside, the main alteration was to raise the floor by nearly six feet, to make room for a muniment room and a Senior Library in the semi-basement below. Eighteenth-century panelling and bookcases were brought from the old Senior Library, and other woodwork from the college and the church was used for tables and desks. At the east end, the reredos that used to be behind the altar is still in place.

St. Paul's Church at **Preston** in Lancashire has also become a centre for the dissemination of information, but through a different medium. In 1982 it became the headquarters of Red Rose Radio, the local commercial station. The church was built in the 1820s, a great barn of a place without a tower or spire, just twin pinnacles at each end. After it became redundant in 1973 it was empty for fourteen years; the only interest shown in it, apart from by local vandals, was from a company proposing to use it as a furniture

All Saints' Church in Oxford is now the library of nearby Lincoln College. It incorporates eighteenth-century panelling and bookcases from the old Senior Library

design centre. But they wanted to cut a loading bay into the west wall and, although the church almost looked like a warehouse already, the planners drew the line at that.

Then along came Red Rose Radio, and the church now houses three studios, with open-plan offices at gallery level. There is little indication of its new use from the

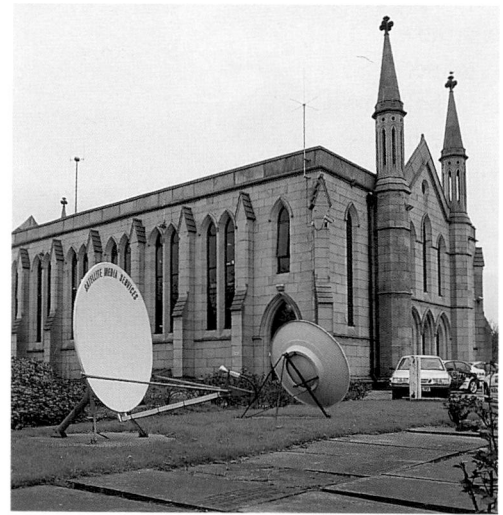

The satellite dishes outside St. Paul's in Preston are not an attempt by the Vicar to make direct contact with the Heavenly Host; the church now houses the studios of Red Rose Radio

outside, apart from the satellite dishes beside it, but the war memorial which used to stand in front of the building was taken round to the rear in two pieces and re-erected there.

Norwich is known as the City of Churches – one for every Sunday of the year, it was said, and one pub for every day – but, inevitably, several of them have become redundant over the years. In the early days they were just allowed to fall into ruin, and little is left except, perhaps, a scarred tower or an ivy-covered wall. Some thirty still survive of the original fifty-two, but not all in their original roles.

In more recent times, the Adaptables amongst them have become a Scout hall, a 'drop-in' centre, an ecclesiastical museum, a warehouse, and so on. But perhaps the most unusual church Adaptable in the city is St. James's, Pockthorpe, which, for the last sixteen years, has been the Norwich Puppet Theatre.

Not much is known about its very early history, but the registers date from 1553 and the rood-loft was even older – its panels were painted, or even repainted, in 1479. The screen had quite an adventurous time before it was finally removed. In the nineteenth century it was dismantled and sold, and its twenty-four panels depicting bishops and saints were split up among various private owners. Somehow, in 1917 the panels were retrieved and set in a new frame in the church – only to be taken away again with the rest of the fittings when the church became redundant.

The wall plaques and ledger slabs are mostly seventeenth and eighteenth century, and they include a slab in memory of a former Lord Mayor of Norwich, Henry Hearne, who held the office in 1673 and died seven years later. His remains, and those of many others, presumably, still lie in the church.

Norwich used to have a church for every Sunday of the year, but many have had to find new uses. St James's, Pockthorpe, has become a puppet theatre; a couple of its star performers like to pose outside

In 1987, a local Methodist minister, the Reverend Jack Burton, wrote quite an epic poem about the medieval churches of Norwich, past and present. St. James's features in verse ninety:

*Its small west tower supported by the
  nave
Saint James Pockthorpe hid once in
  narrow lanes;
But 'progress' made an age its willing
  slave –
With roundabouts, and great highways
  for chains!
Exposed to view, St. James stands
  awkwardly,
And muses, sadly, on its history.*

It does, indeed, stand beside a busy roundabout on the inner ring road, but these days it can feel more cheerful. After a period as a night shelter – and some interesting visitors still turn up looking for a bed – it was adapted as the only theatre of its kind in Norfolk. It had a problem in its early days, when audiences assumed they would have to sit on hard pews, and indeed some newcomers still expect to do so but, in fact, it has a tiered auditorium with tip-up seats for two hundred. There is also a coffee-shop and bar; when the church was adapted, there was not the ban on selling alcohol which often applies to former Anglican churches.

The theatre has been so successful that an extension has been built on to it, the walls flint-clad to match the church. It contains the Octagon Studio, with workshops and a gallery and seating for fifty. The season lasts most of the year; when the puppets are not performing in the church or the studio, they are touring local schools. Even if St. James's muses sadly on its history, it can look forward optimistically to its future.

St. James's is very small by city church standards, which perhaps is appropriate for puppets. Larger churches of all denominations have been converted into full-size theatres and concert halls with full-size performers. In **London**, for instance, there was the Anglican church of St. George's at Tufnell Park. Built in the 1860s, it was criticised by traditionalists because of its 'auditory' design, with the congregation ranged in a semi-circle round the altar. 'Thoroughly suitable for Cushing's American Circus,' commented one irate Victorian, who probably had little time for circuses either.

However, when it became redundant after the last war, this layout made it an ideal Adaptable for Elizabethan-style performances 'in the round', and it became the St. George's Theatre.

Nonconformist churches, which favour that kind of layout anyway, have been particularly popular for conversion into

theatres. In **Halifax**, the former Methodist New Connexion Chapel became the Playhouse, a notable centre for amateur drama, with theatre billboards each side of the doorway instead of Bible tracts. In **Rotherham**, after its only theatre was flattened in 1957 to make way for Woolworth's, the hundred-year-old Congregational Church became an Adaptable and was converted into a civic theatre; the box office and workshops were in the Sunday school buildings next door. And in **Manchester**'s Victoria Park, the Edwardian

Places of worship which are now places of entertainment: in Halifax the Methodist New Connexion Chapel has become the Playhouse...

...and at Chipping Norton in Oxfordshire the Salvation Army Citadel is also a theatre, recently refurbished with the help of the National Lottery

First Church of Christ Scientist became a performing arts centre.

Even in smaller towns this kind of adaptation has

Two rather more unlikely church conversions: the imposing United Reformed Church in Bradford is now an Indian restaurant...

taken place, involving all kinds of church buildings. Even a Salvation Army Citadel at **Chipping Norton** in Oxfordshire has been converted into a two-hundred-and-thirty-five-seat theatre, after spending a less happy period as a furniture warehouse. It started with a tiny stage, but in recent years a grant from the National Lottery has paid for it to be enlarged, and covered the cost of buying the house next door to use as dressing-rooms and offices.

Drinks are banned in what is now the auditorium, but the theatre does have a recently refurbished bar with murals by the artist Graham Rust, a distinction it shares with the Marquess of Hertford's home at Ragley Hall in Warwickshire, though the themes of his paintings there are rather different.

Some denominations impose rather stricter regulations on the sale of alcohol in their former premises, particularly the Methodists, but a former Unitarian Chapel at Devonport in **Plymouth** became the Old Chapel Pub, and a former Congregational

...and the distinctly unimposing Congregational Chapel in Doncaster has become a night-club

The Temple Street Methodist Church in Keighley changed its religion to become a Muslim centre

Chapel in **Doncaster** ended up the same way. The most striking licensed Adaptable in this field must be the former United Reformed Church of St. Andrew's at Westgate in **Bradford**. The conversion took place after it was gutted by fire. The imposing Doric facade with its four great pillars remains unchanged, but the church notice-board outside was adjusted to display menus, under the building's new title, 'Sheik's'.

Inside, the ground floor was transformed into an Indian restaurant, with ornamental plants around the font, and what have been described as 'elements abstracted from Indian architecture'. Meanwhile, the first floor became a night club.

The change of use from Nonconformism to Indian is taken a stage further at **Keighley** near Bradford, where the Temple Street Methodist Church became a Muslim centre. The Church of England is not always too keen on this sort of thing; and not far from Keighley at Dewsbury it turned down a similar bid by the local Sikh community. The redundant church was demolished instead.

One of the rare Anglican exceptions was St. Luke's Church at **Newtown** in Southampton, which was sold to the Sikhs for use as a temple – but only after the local argument had got as far as the General Synod.

Churches have looked more kindly on sporting and recreational uses. Some of them, in fact, are used in that way while they are still active churches. Once they become redundant, their size and loftiness make them particularly suitable for badminton and squash, providing there are no objections to the interior being stripped.

It has happened to church Adaptables as varied as a former mission church in **West Kensington**, built by Harrow School, which became a sports hall in the 1960s, and Queen Street Methodist Chapel in **Huddersfield**, said to be the largest Wesleyan Mission in the world when it was built in 1819, with seating for nearly two thousand. When it closed in 1970 it had a period as an arts centre, and very recently it has returned to the arts world as the Lawrence Batley Theatre, with the main auditorium in

the chapel, a smaller Cellar Theatre, and a restaurant and bar in the south wing where the superintendent minister used to live.

However, for a period in the 1970s it was converted into a squash club called the Ridings. It was not entirely devoted to promoting fitness and good health; under the squash courts, thirty players could wander down into the Catacombs – not caves, but a night club.

The health and fitness regime does not allow for such temptations at the Miracles Swim School and Health and Beauty Activity Centre near **Gosport** in Hampshire. It was a private church built in 1937 for the National Children's Home estate next door, which closed in the 1980s. The Little Church, as it was known locally, was designed to look more at home on the shores of the Mediterranean than the banks of the Solent, with white rendered walls and pantiled roofs. Now the inside looks just as unusual as the exterior, with a swimming-pool under the organ gallery, two gymnasia, a ladies' hairdressing salon, and a beauty salon rejoicing in the title of Heavenly Bodies.

However, it has retained its stained-glass windows, the pews and pulpit have been put to use in the various rooms, and the organ still

The Continental-style 'Little Church' near Gosport in Hampshire is now even more exotic, with a swimming-pool under the organ

plays – although it is now enclosed in glass and operated by a computer...

The Miracles offers special-rate Healthy Awaybreaks using the Figure-Shaping Suite and the Calories Countdown Centre, with its Shapemaster calorie-burning machine. Actual miracles presumably come extra.

In most small towns there is not much scope for such exotic church Adaptables. They are more likely to become storerooms, or shops, or a combination of both, like **Holt** Warehouse in Norfolk, a converted Wesleyan Methodist Chapel. Its former congregation might be impressed to know that it reached the top three out of six hundred entries for the *Draper's Record* independent retailer awards. The chapel even features on the information super-highway. But casual passers-by may not realise it is an Adaptable – with its elegant shop front, it only looks like a chapel from the first floor up.

It is rather less common to find a chapel converted into a youth hostel, but at **Kirkby Stephen** in Cumbria they have

managed to fit over forty beds into the old chapel in Market Street, and still leave room for some of the original pews. They have also kept the oak beams and the stained-glass windows.

Out in the countryside the uses of church Adaptables are even more limited. In some fortunate cases there may be a need for a communal hall – plus the funds to carry out the conversion. One recent example is the former Friends' Meeting House at **Stebbing** in Essex, one of the oldest in the country. It was built in 1674, soon after Charles II permitted Dissenters to have their own meeting-places.

The last time it underwent major restoration was probably more than two hundred years ago. A bill has been found dated 1794 for a hundred bricks, eighteen bushels of lime, a bushel of horsehair and four days' labour by an unknown number of bricklayers. The total was £10 10s 5d. This time the bill was over £30,000 to restore the windows, walls and doors, and lay a new oak floor. Happily, the Friends' Meeting House found a new friend in the National Heritage Lottery Fund, which footed ninety per cent of the bill.

Another good friend to rural church Adaptables has been COSIRA, the Council for Small Industries in Rural Areas. It has helped to finance their conversion into workshops, where a surprising range of goods can be produced. For instance,

A former chapel at Kirkby Stephen in Cumbria is now a youth hostel

but a flag factory in a converted chapel is quite unusual too.

There is no mistaking the origin of the Baptist Chapel at **Kenninghall** in Norfolk; the path to the entrance is still lined with tombstones, and the design of the building is typical of its kind. But, while the exterior is largely unaltered, the interior is now a pottery. The gallery, which used to take the overflow congregation, displays the work of David Walters, a South African-born potter who uses the chapel as his studio. The pulpit which still dominates one end of it now houses a fax machine.

Mr Walters came to England with his wife and family in 1988 and acquired the old chapel, which had been disused for many years, together with the adjoining house and stables – and, of course, the graveyard. He had no difficulty in devising a name for his pottery; the Nonconformists the chapel belonged to had stricter rules than some, and were known as Particular Baptists; the chapel is now the Particular Pottery. It must be a very handy trade name if a customer in a shop enquires vaguely: 'Do you have anything in Particular?'

St. James's Church at **Cheddington** in Dorset produces street organs – baby brothers of the kind of organ the church was once more accustomed to – and Bishop Tozer's Chapel at **Burgh le Marsh** in Lincolnshire turns out flags – not the stone variety, but the sort that are run up flagpoles.

The Bishop's Chapel does not actually look much like a church except, perhaps, for the little bell turret at one end, though even that is more reminiscent of a village school. And, indeed, it was originally a school on the ground floor, with the chapel above. Since it became an Adaptable the flags are manufactured where the schoolroom used to be, and the proprietor and his family live upstairs. The village is mainly famous, incidentally, for its five-sailed windmill. Lincolnshire windmills liked to be at least one-up on the average –

Bishop Tozer's Chapel at Burgh le Marsh in Lincolnshire has become a flagmaking factory – that must be one of theirs on the pole

The Particular Baptist Chapel at Kenninghall in Norfolk is now the Particular Pottery – but you still have to pass the gravestones to reach it

Travelling Adaptables

• • • • • • •

On *stagecoaches, canals, sailing barges, railways*

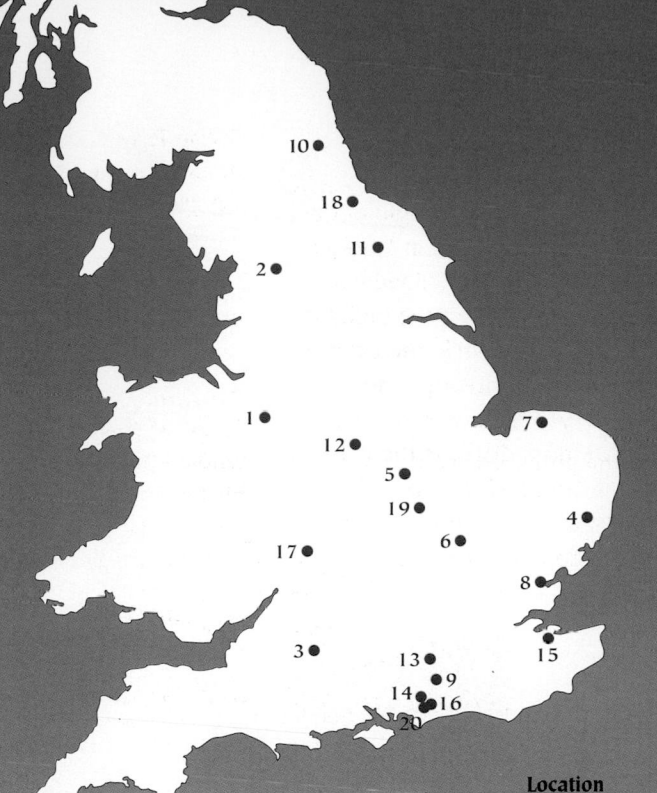

	Location	Old use	New use(s)
1	Bunbury, Cheshire: Bunbury Locks	Canal stables	Boat builder's workshop
2	Clapham, North Yorkshire: Station House	Railway station	Living accommodation
3	Devizes, Wiltshire	Railway carriages	Private residence
4	Framlingham, Suffolk	Railway station	Motor cycle showroom
5	Leicester: Gallowtree Gate	Thomas Cook HQ	Shop and hairdresser
6	Leighton Buzzard, Bedfordshire	Industrial railway	Passenger railway
7	Little Walsingham, Norfolk: Orthodox chapel	Railway station	Orthodox chapel
8	Maldon, Essex	Sailing barge	Training ship
	The *Thalatta*	Sailing barge	Educational sailing boat
9	Newbridge, West Sussex	Canal warehouse	Guest-house
10	Newcastle-upon-Tyne	Car ferry	Night club
11	Nunnington, North Yorkshire: Ryedale Lodge Hotel	Railway station	Hotel
12	Shardlow, Derbyshire: Clock Warehouse	Canal warehouse	Bar and restaurant
13	Sidney Wood, Surrey: Lock House	Canal workshop	Private residence
14	Singleton, West Sussex	Railway station	Winery; private residence
15	Sittingbourne, Kent	Industrial railway	Passenger railway
16	Slindon, West Sussex	Railway carriage	Thatched cottage
17	Tewkesbury, Gloucestershire:		
	House of the Nodding Gables	Stage coach depot	Offices
	Hop Pole Inn	Coaching inn	Pub
18	Thorpe Thewles, Stockton-on-Tees	Railway station	Visitors' centre
19	Weedon, Northamptonshire	Tollhouse	Hotel
20	Yapton, West Sussex	Canal office	Estate agent

It's the end of the line: all change!

Road transport in England started with the Romans and their chariots – unless you count the Ancient Britons plodding along the Icknield Way with their sledges, wishing someone would invent the wheel. Neither of them left behind anything which qualifies as an Adaptable, and it was only when turnpikes were introduced, roads were brought back up to Roman standards, and long-distance travel became simpler, that specialised buildings were needed to serve road travellers.

The obvious ones which were purpose-built in considerable numbers were the tollhouses, for taking the money at the turnpike gates, and the coaching inns, for taking more money to provide fresh horses and sometimes not-so-fresh accommodation. Many of both still survive, and very picturesque they look too. But in general, tollhouses are still houses and coaching inns are still inns; only the tolls and the coaches have gone.

There are exceptions, of course. Some of the coaching inn Adaptables are in another chapter, and as an example of a tollhouse Adaptable there is the Crossroads Hotel at the junction of the busy A6 and

The tollhouse at the Weedon crossroads in Northamptonshire has been expanded into an hotel, but the original little building is still recognisable on the corner

A45 trunk roads at **Weedon** in Northamptonshire, which incorporates the building erected by the Daventry and Southam Turnpike Company. The original tollhouse has been blended so skilfully inside that no one would guess, for instance, that the ladies' toilet opening off the restaurant used to be part of it, but from the outside the difference in the architecture is quite distinctive. Perhaps the landlord could be tempted one day to have a Turnpike Bar, or even a Tollhouse Loo, just to keep the memory alive.

Another building which was in the travel business in those days, but had quite a different role, is just as difficult to identify. **Tewkesbury** in Gloucestershire is full of buildings more obviously associated with the coaching era, not least the Hop Pole Inn, where Mr Pickwick warmed his coat-tails, so Dickens recorded, in front of the fourteenth-century fireplace. Not far away in the High Street is the House of the

Nodding Gables, which has one gable leaning gently sideways, as if nodding off to sleep. It now houses the offices of a building society, but it was once the depot and ticket office for the stage coaches which served the town. Mr Dickens might well have noted that Pickwick bought his ticket there, to give added authenticity to the story – but perhaps even Dickens, like Homer and gables, can sometimes nod...

While coach travellers were enjoying faster travel on better roads, the most popular way of shifting goods in bulk was by river or canal. In the middle of the eighteenth century there were about a thousand miles of navigable rivers; in the next hundred years the canal-builders added another three thousand miles to the waterways system. Then the railways arrived and the canals began to decline. As trade dwindled, buildings became redundant; then the canals themselves started to dwindle, with just short stretches left for boating and fishing.

In some cases, a canal Adaptable has survived where the canal itself has disappeared. **Sidney Wood** in Surrey used to be on the route of the old Wey & Arun Canal, part of an ambitious project in 1810 to create an inland waterway system linking London with Portsmouth and the English Channel. The idea was to avoid the hazard of attack by the French as the vessels sailed round the Kent and Sussex coast, but by the time the link was complete, the Napoleonic Wars were over, and the cost and time involved in negotiating all the locks meant that most goods were still sent by sea.

The Wey & Arun Canal closed in 1871, and although in recent years a preservation trust has restored lengths of it for recreational use, other sections have virtually disappeared. One such section passed through Sidney Wood. It was not the most direct route the canal could have taken, but that would have meant digging through pheasant country, and the local landlord said it would upset the birds. The detour meant an extra mile-and-a-half of canal, and an extra fifteen thousand pounds on the cost, but at least the pheasants were happy – until the shooting season began.

In the heart of Sidney Wood is the building which used to house the main workshop of the canal company, where lock gates were built or repaired, along with other canal equipment. Now the canal is derelict, the nine locks in the wood have disintegrated, and the workshop has been

In the days of horses and carts the House of the Nodding Gables in Tewkesbury's main street was a ticket office for stage coaches. The coaches have gone, but the gables still nod

When the Wey & Arun Canal linked the Wey and Arun rivers, this was its main workshop, in Sidney Wood. Much of the canal has disappeared, but Lock House survives, as a private residence

adapted as a private residence, much extended and improved – but it is still called Lock House.

At the southern end of the Wey & Arun, at **Newbridge** in West Sussex, where it linked up with the navigable River Arun, a building survives which is made more recognisable in its original role by the continued presence of the water beside it. Before the canal was built, this marked the end of the line for river traffic heading up the Arun Navigation. Cargoes were unloaded on the wharf and stored in the warehouse to await collection. When the canal was opened, traffic came from both directions and the warehouse was busier still. William Cobbett passed by on one of his Rural Rides in 1823 and was much impressed: 'a grand receiving and distributing place,' he noted.

The coming of the railways and the closure of the canal soon changed all that,

and the great wooden hoist wheel at the top of the open wooden staircase on the warehouse no longer functioned. It was fortunately retained, however, as a striking feature of the Old Wharf Guest House, and a sympathetic owner kept the waterway dredged to improve the view for his guests.

In contrast, much further south on this ill-fated waterway system, at **Yapton**, there is another canal Adaptable which is virtually impossible to identify, because there is no trace of the canal anywhere near it, except for the nearby Canal Road. The Portsmouth & Arun Canal was the final waterway on the route to the sea, linking the River Arun with Chichester Harbour. It was the last link in the chain to be completed, and the first to be broken. Chichester still has its canal basin and a stretch of the canal itself, but between the River Arun at Ford and the junction at Hunston there is little to be seen except a footbridge at Yapton, which used to span the canal but is now marooned in a housing estate.

Beside Canal Road, however, there is a rather ordinary-looking single-storey building, now occupied by an estate agent. This was the canal office, and it stood by the canal turning-basin, the busiest section of the canal. When it was abandoned the basin was filled in and levelled; it is now the village playing field.

Even on canals which still exist and remain in active use, there are old

Where the Wey & Arun Canal used to join the River Arun, the warehouse on the old wharf has been adapted as a private hotel

The village playing field at Yapton in West Sussex used to be the turning basin for the Portsmouth & Arun Canal. When the canal was abandoned the basin was filled in; the nearby Canal Road is the only reminder

buildings which have lost their original purpose. In most cases it is because commercial traffic has virtually ceased and the canal is mainly used by holiday craft. On the Trent & Mersey Canal at **Shardlow** in Derbyshire, for instance, there is the imposing Clock Warehouse, a massive canal Adaptable sitting astride an arm of the canal, named after its distinctive clock high up on the gable.

It was built when the canal was opened in 1780 by a company floated by Josiah Wedgwood, who wanted a safe and convenient route to send his pottery from Staffordshire to Hull, for onward export to Russia. Because the locks above Burton were designed only to fit narrow boats, the cargoes had to be trans-shipped at Shardlow. The Clock Warehouse was at the centre of all this activity, and remained so until, in due course, the railways took over.

In 1986 the redundant warehouse was bought by a brewery, which converted part of it into a restaurant overlooking the canal, and created a traditional bar on the ground floor opening on to a sitting-out area beside the great wooden hoist which used to load and off-load the barges. They retained the clock on the gable and the proud notice beneath it: 'Navigation from the Trent to the Mersey.'

The old place is now owned by a different brewery, which has enlarged the restaurant, refurbished the bars and provided extra facilities for youngsters. Josiah Wedgwood might find it a little disconcerting, but the holiday-makers, whose boats have taken over from the pottery barges, find the Clock Warehouse a useful place to fill their pots instead of trans-shipping them.

At the other end of the scale in canal-side Adaptables there is the long, low building which stands near **Bunbury** Locks in Cheshire, on what used to be the

Chester Canal and is now part of the Shropshire Union Canal. The locks themselves are twice the width of usual ones, built to accommodate the big barges carrying local salt and cheese on their way to the River Dee at Chester. The barges were hauled by relays of horses, and the long, low buildings used to be the stables, where the horses spent their leisure hours. When horse-drawn barges gave place to motor-powered holiday cruisers, the stables managed to keep up with the times, and were adapted to build the cruisers.

While commercial transport was changing on the canals, coastal transport was changing, too, though rather more slowly. The old sailing barges were being replaced, and those that have survived rely

The Clock Warehouse at Shardlow in Derbyshire was where Josiah Wedgwood's pottery was trans-shipped. Now it is a restaurant and bar, and any pots are only there for the beer

At Bunbury Locks in Cheshire the barge-horses' stables have been adapted to a more modern form of canal transport – building cruisers

The sailing barge Thalatta, based at Maldon in Essex, now carries schoolchildren instead of cargoes, for educational trips under sail

The Sittingbourne & Kemsley Railway in Kent was built to carry logs and wood pulp between two papermills; now it carries ten thousand trippers a year

mostly on holiday-makers who enjoy the novelty of sail. A small handful of Norfolk wherries still function in this way, and all around the East Coast there are sailing barge Adaptables which are now used for holiday charter work, or as training ships, or holiday homes. **Maldon** in Essex, for instance, has quite an assortment of them, ranging from one old barge which is now a training ship for the Sea Rangers, to the sailing barge *Thalatta*, built in 1906 to carry one-hundred-and-fifty-ton cargoes around the coast, now adapted by the East Coast Sail Trust to provide schoolchildren with five-day educational trips under sail. The former cargo hold has been converted into living quarters, with wooden sea chests and hammocks to give a genuine flavour of 'yo-ho-ho' – without the bottle of rum...

A rarer form of a waterborne Adaptable is the redundant car ferry at **Newcastle-upon-Tyne**, just below the High Level Bridge – one of the many bridges which now cross the Tyne and carry the cars instead. The proprietors made the best of things – and turned the car ferry into a night club.

This was one of the few transport redundancies which was not directly caused by the railways. Horse-drawn traffic on the roads and the slow-moving traffic on the canals and around the coasts were the principal, and most obvious,

victims. Ironically, many of the branch railway lines have now succumbed, in their turn, leaving behind a new generation of transport Adaptables: converted railway carriages, railway stations, railway track beds and, in some rare cases, the railways themselves – those which were built for a specialised purpose, to carry a particular kind of goods traffic, and instead are now carrying tourists, on lines which never took passengers before.

For instance, the **Sittingbourne & Kemsley** Light Railway in Kent was built to carry logs and wood-pulp one way, and paper and newsprint the other, between two paper mills and a wharf on the River Swale in the Thames estuary. In the mid-sixties road transport took over, but with the cooperation of Bowaters, who owned it, and the Locomotive Club of Great Britain, two miles of the line between the two mills was handed over to local enthusiasts, and they have been running the line ever since, carrying people instead of paper.

It is a slightly bizarre tourist attraction. The main features of the track-side scenery are a travellers' camp, a rubbish dump, a sewage works and a car-breakers' yard, with a stretch of bleak marshland to provide a brief rural flavour, before the second paper mill is reached. It is the

Much the same could be said for the **Leighton Buzzard** narrow-gauge railway in Bedfordshire, which started life during the First World War, carrying sand from the quarries just outside the town to the nearest main line, the London & North Western Railway. For half a century the tipper trucks were hauled through the sand-pits by little diesel engines, until it was decided that road transport would be cheaper, and the humble industrial railway looked doomed.

But, again, the local enthusiasts came to the rescue. They found antiquated railway carriages to replace the tipper trucks, and quaint old steam engines to replace the less attractive diesels.

One of them is a wood burner which began life in the Cameroons. Now they run regular services, no longer through the quarries but through the housing estates which have replaced them.

The line ends at what used to be the Stonehenge Brickworks, where the railway workshops were built originally as stables for the horses which hauled the brick trucks – another unlikely transport Adaptable. The German prisoners-of-war who erected them left behind a rather daring gesture of defiance, which presumably nobody spotted at the time; the stones in one wall are laid in the form of a phallic symbol...

With most railway Adaptables, though, the adaptation has been the other way. Former railway equipment and buildings have been converted to other uses. The English countryside has large numbers of former railway stations, for instance, which have been adapted as living accommodation of one kind or another – sometimes when the railway they stand

The Leighton Buzzard railway was built during World War I to carry sand from the quarries. Now the quarries are housing estates, but it still attracts tourists

Clapham Station – the one in North Yorkshire, not South London, and a lot quieter. The trains still run, but the station building is now a private house

epitome, in fact, of an industrial railway. And yet, since it became an Adaptable, it has attracted over ten thousand passengers a year with an annual turnover of more than thirty thousand pounds – and it is difficult to say who enjoys it most, the volunteers who work on it or the customers who pay on it. I once dubbed it the MUESLI Line, not only because it provides so much simple, healthy enjoyment, but also because it has the Most Un-Exciting Surroundings – and Loves It...

enquiries about the cost of a return ticket to Leeds, or the time of the last train to Lancaster. But on the whole, Clapham Station is just as peaceful as its London namesake is noisy. The last real excitement there was nearly forty years ago, when the Royal Train spent the night in a nearby siding, and Prince Philip actually nodded at the stationmaster next morning when it set off for Leeds.

Other disused stations have been adapted as pubs or small hotels, but in these cases the actual lines have generally disappeared. Ryedale Lodge at **Nunnington**, also in North Yorkshire, is one example. All that is left of the track bed is a grassy strip set with cherry trees, but it does provide a useful path for guests, down to the river nearby. The station is a mile or more outside Nunnington village which is, no doubt, one reason it was closed during the Beeching purge of the 1960s, along with the rest of the line, but it does mean the hotel guests now enjoy a very unrailway-like atmosphere in the heart of the countryside. The old station building has been extended into the

Nunnington Station in 1926, when the Gilling-Pickering railway was functioning in North Yorkshire. The platform is still recognisable, but the building has been enlarged into the Ryedale Lodge Hotel

beside is still in use. For example, there is Station House at **Clapham** – not the South London Clapham, which might be a little too noisy for even the most devoted rail enthusiast, but Clapham in North Yorkshire, a rural station on the branch line which still operates between Leeds and Lancaster.

Twelve trains stop at the little station each day, but the passengers buy their tickets on the train these days, and the ticket office is now the bathroom of Station House, while the old parcels office is the dining-room. But strangers can still get confused, and the occupants of Station House, Eric and Vera Feasey, often answer

Singleton Station, when Edward VII used it to attend Goodwood Races (far right). When the station became a winery, the outsize gents' toilet block (right) was used as the wine store

Framlingham Station in Suffolk, in the days when trains were running (top right), and in its present role as a showroom for classic motor-cycles

forecourt at the front and onto the platform at the back, so it no longer looks much like a station, but the platform itself is still easily recognisable, just outside the dining-room windows.

You can enjoy a good selection of wine at former stations like Rydale Lodge, but at **Singleton** in West Sussex the wine has actually been produced on the station – in the former waiting-room, which Edward VII used when he went to the races at Goodwood or stayed at West Dean Park. Ian and Andrew Paget leased the station from the West Dean estate and planted a vineyard on the hill behind it – the first in the district since Roman times. After the wine had been made it was bottled on the premises, too, then stored in the building which used to house the lavatories and the barber's shop, said to be the largest gents' toilet block ever built for a country station. Here again, no doubt, King Edward was a regular patron – it was probably built that size for his benefit.

Wine-tastings used to be held in the booking hall, but alas, not any more. The vineyard no longer functions, and the station buildings are now let as a private

residence. Singleton station has seen the last of its summer wine.

On the other hand, **Framlingham** Station in Suffolk is still well stocked with a different kind of specialised British product – classic motor cycles. The station was built when the branch line was opened in 1859, the celebrations being slightly marred when a porter fell off the platform in front of the inaugural train. Fortunately, the driver stopped the train in time, but the hapless porter happened to be the leader of the town band, and a celebratory concert had to be cancelled while he recovered from the shock.

Nothing quite as dramatic ever happened at Framlingham Station again, and the last regular passenger train left in 1952. The line still kept functioning, however, thanks to Framlingham College, which ran special trains for London-based pupils at the beginning and end of each term. The public was allowed to use the school trains, too – though it could hardly have been the most relaxing of journeys.

The branch finally closed in 1965, and twenty years later Andrew Tiernan took over the station, and still uses it as a showroom for his classic motor bikes. He has despatched them to customers as far afield as Australia and Japan from

Framlingham Station – but not, of course, by rail.

Perhaps the most striking station Adaptable is at **Little Walsingham** in Norfolk, familiar to thousands of pilgrims who flock to the shrines there each year. But they no longer arrive by train – the line closed in the 1960s. Even so, the railway station still sees a great many pilgrims, because it is now the Orthodox Chapel of St. Seraphim of Sarov, much visited by Orthodox Christians from other parts of Britain, as well as abroad. The only clue to its new identity, from the outside, is the little gilded dome on the roof but, inside, it has been quite transformed. The old waiting-room is divided by the iconostasis, the screen which separates what is now the chancel from what is now the nave.

Incidentally, although the original track has long since disappeared, a train still runs on one section of the old track bed, between Walsingham and Wells. It does carry passengers, but these passengers sit just two abreast in little carriages and trundle through the Norfolk countryside for four miles, seated only a foot or so above

the track and passing the old station platforms virtually at eye level. This is, in fact, the longest $10\tfrac{1}{4}$-inch gauge railway in the world, and in its small (narrow-gauge) way it has brought new life to a redundant railway line.

Most disused track beds are either left to revert to a natural wilderness, or built over, or adapted as footpaths – which does qualify them, because people now walk or

The station at Little Walsingham in Norfolk has finished up as the Orthodox Chapel of St. Seraphim of Sarov…

…and Thorpe Thewles station in County Durham is the starting-point for the Castle Eden Walkway – along the old railway bed

cycle on them instead of sitting in trains. A typical example is the Castle Eden Walkway in **Durham**, a walk of over six miles along the route of the Castle Eden Branch Railway, closed in 1966. The line was built for the mundane and rather grimy task of carrying coal from the Durham Coalfield to Middlesbrough; it is recorded that farm produce, livestock and passengers were also carried, presumably in that order of priority.

In spite of its industrial purpose the line passes through some very pleasant countryside; indeed, it is known as the Cuckoo Railway, not because the locals thought it was crazy to build it, but because of its rural surroundings. The walkway links a newly created country park with Hurworth Burn Reservoir, passing through one of the last ancient woods in Durham. The starting point is at **Thorpe Thewles** Station, where the waiting-rooms and the stationmaster's house, as in many cases of track-bed Adaptables, have themselves been adapted as a visitors' centre.

Another fairly common railway Adaptable is the railway carriage. It can often be a ramshackle affair, just used as a store or a garden shed, but it can also make quite an attractive home. At **Slindon** in West Sussex, for example, there is a

railway carriage Adaptable which has been given a thatched roof – an interesting contrast in architectural eras and styles.

Ronald and Pat Thomas's home near **Devizes** in Wiltshire looks, at first sight, like an ordinary tiled house, except for the excessive number of identical small windows. It is actually two railway carriages converted into one residence, and the windows date back to the 1860s when the carriages were built. They had an unusually short life on the railway, perhaps no more than fifteen years, so for once Dr Beeching cannot be blamed for their redundancy. They finished up on their

Railway carriages in new roles: a thatched 'cottage' at Slindon in West Sussex...

...and a much grander double-carriage bungalow near Devizes in Wiltshire

current site in 1922, and were sold in the 1930s for a modest £250.

Mr Thomas bought them ten years ago for the rather higher sum of £68,000 – and he has been offered a lot more than that since. Railway carriage Adaptables, in fact, can be a good investment – if the carriages come in pairs, are set far enough apart to create a living-room between them, have partitions removed to make spacious rooms, then are renovated, refurbished, insulated, given patio doors and a built-on dining-room, and are sold with two acres of land...

Finally, a railway Adaptable which is a reminder, not so much of the railways as the man who provided it with thousands of its passengers, and whose name will always be associated with travel, first by rail and now by all forms of transport, worldwide. The headquarters of Thomas Cook & Son was at Gallowtree Gate in **Leicester**, and although his offices became an Adaptable and are now occupied by a shop and a hairdresser, there is no mistaking its original role.

The friezes on the wall illustrate the story of the firm's first fifty years in business, from the day Thomas Cook organised his first excursion to Loughborough in 1841. Ten years later he arranged for over 165,000 people to visit the Great Exhibition from the Midlands.

After that he had only one out-and-out failure – when he arranged transport up the Nile in the hope of rescuing General Gordon in Khartoum.

There are two other buildings in Leicester associated with Thomas Cook which also became Adaptables. The red-brick Italianate villa he built for his retirement, and where he died in 1892, is now the headquarters of Leicester Red Cross, and the public hall, where he often spoke on the subject of temperance, is now the public lending library. But the phrase he added to the English language, 'a Cook's tour', still remains unaltered and is in common use today. Who knows – someone may even arrange one to see Timpson's Adaptables...

The transport connection is not too obvious – until you spot the frieze on the wall. This was the original Leicester headquarters of Cook's Tours

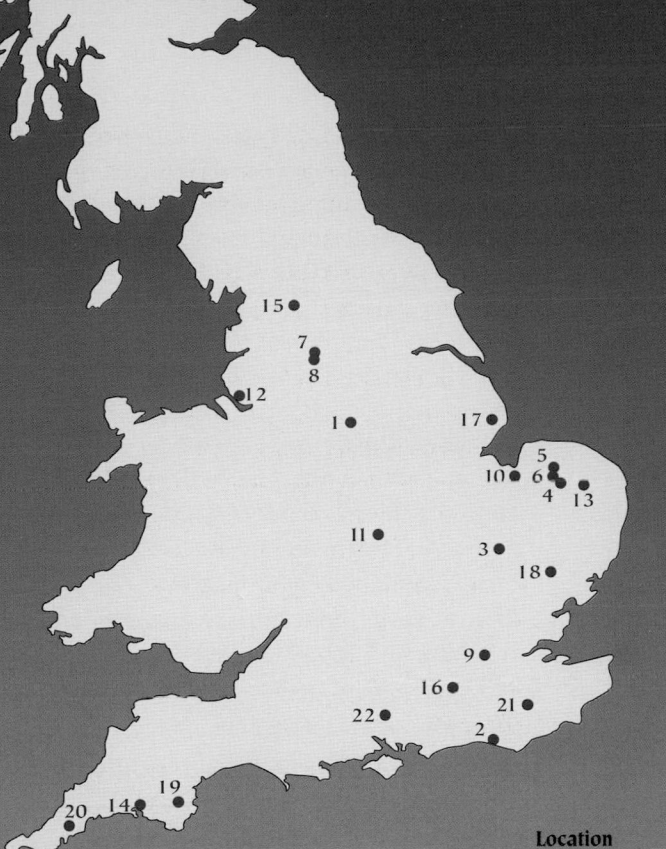

High Street Adaptables

● ● ● ● ● ● ● ●

Banks, corn exchanges, town halls, public buildings large and (very) small

	Location	Old use	New use(s)
1	Bakewell, Derbyshire	Town hall	School; shops
2	Brighton: 'Flowers of Convenience'	Public lavatory	Florist's shop
3	Cambridge	Public lavatory	Cycle hire shop
4	East Dereham, Norfolk: Exchange Cinema	Corn hall	Cinema and pub
5	Fakenham, Norfolk	Fire station	Tyre and exhaust fitters
6	Great Ryburgh, Norfolk	Public lavatory	Hairdressing salon
7	Halifax, Calderdale: Piece Hall	Cloth hall	Antique and craft centre
8	Heptonstall, Calderdale	Cloth hall	Private residence
9	Kew, Richmond upon Thames	Public lavatory	Private residence
10	King's Lynn, Norfolk: Entertainment Centre	Corn exchange	Skating rink; public hall; entertainment centre
11	Leamington Spa, Warwickshire: Polish Centre	Town hall	Police station; Polish centre
12	Liverpool: The Trials Hotel	Bank	Hotel
13	Norwich, Norfolk: Anglia Television Centre	Agricultural hall	Entertainment centre; Television centre
14	Plymouth, Devon: The Bank	Bank	Pub
15	Settle, North Yorkshire: National Westminster Bank	Saddler's shop	Bank
16	Shere, Surrey	Fire station	Public lavatory
17	Spilsby, Lincolnshire	Town Hall	Petrol station and shops
18	Sudbury, Suffolk	Corn exchange	Library
19	Totnes, Devon: Barclays Bank	Private residence	Dancing school; bank
20	Truro, Cornwall	Assembly rooms	Household goods emporium; garage; offices
21	Tunbridge Wells, Kent: The Pantiles	Assembly rooms	Post office and shops
22	Winchester, Hampshire: Lloyds Bank	Guildhall	Bank

I know a bank whereon the right time tolls...

There was a time, within fairly recent memory, when a job in a bank, or a Post Office, or local government administration, was virtually a job for life. And the majestic buildings which offered this safe employment also seemed pretty secure. But banks have amalgamated, Town Halls have been rationalised, Post Offices have been cut back, and the buildings themselves have sometimes become redundant, too, and qualified as Adaptables.

In earlier years of expansion it worked the other way. Banks, for instance, were looking for new or bigger premises. There was not always the time, or the site, to put up a custom-built one, so they took over what was available already. Barclays Bank at **Totnes** in Devon, for instance, occupies a splendid private house which was built in 1585 by a wealthy local merchant, Nicholas Ball, who made a fortune trading in pilchards and became mayor and local MP. The facade bears the date and notes Mr Ball's initials – appropriately N.B.

Unfortunately, he died within a year of building the house. Events moved rapidly, and four months later his widow (and his house) were taken over by Thomas Bodley, a writer, a diplomat – and a very fast worker. Apparently, Mrs Ball already had another suitor – she too must have moved fast – but, according to a contemporary account,

The ornate frontage of Barclays Bank in Totnes, built in 1585 by a pilchard magnate, later the home of the founder of the Bodleian Library at Oxford

Bodley was playing cards in the company of his rival when he realised she would be on her own. 'Finding this opportunity, he entreated the gent to hold his cardes till he returned, courted and obteined his desyre. Soe, he played his game, while another held his cardes...'

Bodley used part of his wife's inheritance to re-found the library at Oxford University and gave his name to it – though perhaps it should be the Ball Library as much as the Bodleian. When he and his wife died the house passed through various hands; early in the last century it was a dancing school and seminary for young ladies. It started its first career as a bank in 1896, when the privately owned Naval Bank took it over. The partners became insolvent when the value of securities slumped at the outbreak of the Great War and, in due course, the premises were bought by Barclays, who now occupy the adjoining house as well. Nicholas Ball's parlour is now the manager's office, where clients may, perhaps, occasionally gaze up at its splendid sixteenth-century ceiling in delight – or despair...

There are other, more modest, examples of banks taking over the private premises of individuals who have made names for themselves in other spheres. In **Hertford**, for instance, Barclays occupy the birthplace of Samuel Stone, who did not make his own name so much as the name of his home town. Mr Stone was one of the first to emigrate to the American colonies and in 1636 he founded Hartford, Connecticut – pronounced the same as Hertford, of course, but spelt phonetically to make life a little easier for the locals.

There have been two more examples of this kind of bank Adaptable at **Settle** in North Yorkshire, though one did not last very long. The Reverend Benjamin Waugh

Sir Edward Elgar never lived here, he just visited, but the National Westminster Bank at Settle in North Yorkshire still thinks he's worth a plaque

was born in a saddler's shop behind the Market Place in 1839. Like Samuel Stone, his name may not be immediately familiar, but the seeds he sowed, like Stone's, have continued to blossom. Waugh was the passionate social reformer and philanthropist who founded the London Society for the Prevention of Cruelty to Children in 1884. Today, it is better known as the NSPCC.

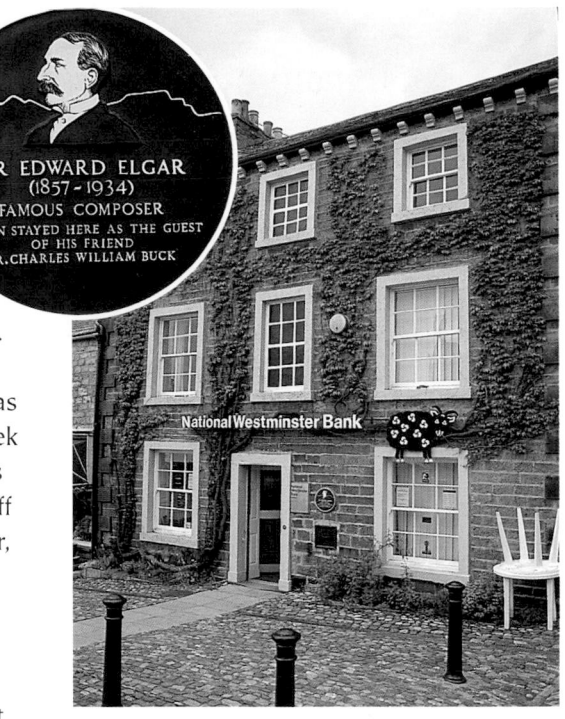

When the saddler's shop closed it was used as a bank on one or two days a week by the predecessor of the Trustee Savings Bank. However, the unfortunate bank staff found that the stench of untanned leather, which still pervaded the premises, was quite overwhelming. No doubt, many Victorian employers would have issued clothes-pegs to put on their employees' noses and told them to get on with it, but the bank proved more benevolent. The smelly old shop was demolished, and a very bank-like bank was built on the site, with just a plaque, instead of a pong, to recall its history.

When Lloyds Bank took over the Guildhall in Winchester, the ground floor was open-sided – not too secure for a bank. They filled it in, but kept Queen Anne, the curfew bell, and the rather ostentatious clock

There is also a plaque on another bank in Settle, the National Westminster, but this is the original building, and still looks like a rather elegant town house. It was the home of a local doctor, Charles William Buck, but it is not his face that appears on the plaque. It depicts, instead, his friend Sir Edward Elgar. Dr Buck was, in fact, only famous by association, but the bank thought it worthwhile to record that the distinguished composer frequently visited him in what is now their Settle branch. If their positions had been reversed and the doctor had visited Elgar, the plaque might just have read: 'Buck stopped here.'

At **Winchester** in Hampshire, Lloyds Bank aimed for something rather higher than a saddler's shop

They still look like banks, but they offer a rather different service. 'The Bank' in Plymouth is now a pub...

...and a much more grandiose bank in Liverpool has become the Trials Hotel. Perhaps appropriately, the vast banking hall where lots of brass changed hands is now the Brasserie

or the home of a country doctor. It occupies the imposing building which used to be the Guildhall, built to replace a former one in 1911. Originally, it had an open-sided ground floor – not really suitable for banking purposes from a security point of view. Other features, however, have been retained. The statue of Queen Anne, a gift to the City from one of its MPs, still stands in its niche at first floor level, beside an exact replica of a gift from another MP – they had many ways of winning votes in those days. The replica is the clock which projects rather ostentatiously over the pavement and bears the arms of the Marquis of Winchester – presumably an influential friend of the donor.

The Guildhall turret still surmounts the building, and when the bank took it over, it continued the medieval tradition of ringing the curfew every weekday at 8 p.m., the signal to *couvre-feu*, or cover the fires – a necessary precaution when most buildings were made of wood. These days, however, the curfew has rung for some branches of the banks themselves, and even larger establishments have become Adaptables.

'The Bank' at **Plymouth** in Devon, for instance, was originally just that, and indeed, it still looks like one, but it too was fated to become an Adaptable and found itself converted into a public house.

The Trials Hotel in **Liverpool** still looks like a bank too, but a much grander one; the sort of imposing neo-classical pile which Victorian bankers used to favour. It has arched windows and balustrades on the outside, and ornate ceilings and

marble columns within. It still sees plenty of bankers, but they come there to stay or to wine and dine. The enormous banking hall is now the Trials Brasserie...

Town halls, those other imposing reminders of past prosperity, have also succumbed over the years, and now serve more humble roles. At **Spilsby** in Lincolnshire, for instance, the two-hundred-year-old Town Hall, in the middle of the market place, has been adapted as a

The old Town Hall at Spilsby in Lincolnshire traded politics for petrol to become a service station and car showroom

The former fire station at Fakenham in Norfolk is now a car repair workshop...

...while the one at Shere in Surrey has finished up as a public lavatory

petrol filling station, and petrol pumps were installed in its elegant archways. In the 1960s the owners made various improvements, and the ground floor became a car showroom, with offices and a meeting hall on the floor above. A shoe repair shop was tucked into one corner.

Incidentally, another kind of public building at **Fakenham** in Norfolk, which had a certain similarity to Spilsby Town Hall – large bays along the front – also finished up in the motor trade. The red brick fire station was built early this century and served the town well until a larger, and more modern, station made it redundant. These days, instead of fire engines, the bays contain repair pits and hydraulic lifts, for cars being fitted with exhaust pipes or tyres – but the words 'Fire Station' and the date '1911' are still proudly carved in the stonework of the facade. It

has fared rather better, in fact, than the redundant fire station at **Shere** in Surrey, which the local authority has converted into a public lavatory.

At **Bakewell** in Derbyshire, the old Town Hall was built in 1602, with the upper floor as a combined town hall and courthouse, and an almshouse below, so even then it was a multi-purpose building, and it has served a variety of other purposes since. For fifty years, in the last century, it housed the Lady Manners School. Services were held there for a time

while the church was being rebuilt. In 1885 the Working Men's Club was established on the upper floor, while the fire engine was housed below together with the butter market. At some stage there was a fish shop, too. All these activities had gone by the 1960s, and in 1991 the building started a new life as a china and crystal shop. Alas, in 1997 it was empty again, awaiting yet another adaptation.

The Town Hall at **Leamington Spa** in Warwickshire, where Napoleon III was entertained during his period of exile in the town, had a long spell as a police station before it was put on the market in the early 1970s. Leamington had acquired a considerable number of foreign residents since Napoleon III, and the Polish community was so substantial that it was able to raise the £10,000 needed to move into the Town Hall – not to take over the

town, of course, but to use it as their community centre. One of their adaptations was to turn the CID department into their church, and at the grand re-opening of the Polish Club, a former police chief visiting his former office was heard to comment: 'I bet I've heard more confessions in here than you have...'

As well as town halls and banks, the builders of imposing corn exchanges and agricultural halls must have believed that their splendid edifices would serve the same purpose indefinitely. They built them big, they built them to last. Unfortunately, the corn traders moved on and did their deals elsewhere, and there are corn hall Adaptables in a great many market towns throughout the country, particularly in the grain-growing areas of East Anglia. You will find them thinly disguised as bingo halls, or cinemas, or licensed clubs; their elegant facades obscured by posters and show-cases and advertising slogans.

The Corn Hall in **Dereham**, for instance, looked very grand when it was

opened in 1857, with a high arched entrance flanked by pillars, and a statue of 'Coke of Norfolk', a famous local landowner and agriculturist, perched on the roof. In 1950, almost symbolically, the statue was struck by lightning during a summer thunderstorm and toppled off its plinth, never to be replaced. The building itself survived, but only as the Exchange Cinema, with an outside staircase attached to its elegant frontage for the benefit of the projectionist. These days the lower floor has been converted into a pub.

But, occasionally, a real effort has been made to preserve their original appearance, even though the interior has been transformed. The most recently completed example is the Corn Exchange at **King's Lynn**, which was built in 1854 and has been an Adaptable, stage by stage, over the past ninety years. The first major adaptation took place in 1909, when the Borough of King's Lynn proudly announced that it had converted the building into 'a most up-to-date Roller Skating Rink' – and explained why.

Leamington Town Hall did a stretch as a police station before becoming the Polish Centre...

...and Dereham Corn Exchange in Norfolk became a cinema and pub. A statue on the roof of Coke of Norfolk, a noted agriculturist, was struck by lightning – perhaps symbolically – before it all happened

'Roller skating has now for some time been recognised as the most popular and exhilarating form of pastime and amusement, giving both pleasure and profit to old and young.' It was, of course, the profit the Borough had

King's Lynn Corn Exchange in Norfolk as it is today, a multi-purpose entertainment centre, and in its days as a roller-skating rink. Unlike Coke at Dereham, the statue of Ceres, Goddess of Agriculture, has survived it all

in mind, and it reported, after ten weeks, that it had been attended by 'some thousands'. To attract a few more, it pointed out that the special floor of rock maple was 'the largest uninterrupted floorage within a radius of fifty miles, regularly kept in a perfectly cleanly and skating condition by means of our patent surfacing machine.'

That was not the only innovation. 'It is lighted with the Electric Light throughout, including some hundreds of Coloured Electric Incandescent Lights, giving the most brilliant lighting and spectacular effect, and the Skating is enlivened by the Grand Orchestraphone, which is electrically driven and lighted, rendering the skating almost noiseless.'

But interest in roller skating flagged, and all these amazing new devices could

not save the rink. In subsequent years it became just another public hall, its condition slowly deteriorating. Only its imposing colonnaded facade, which Pevsner lightheartedly described as 'jolly and vulgar', remained unscathed, though the statue of Ceres, the Goddess of Agriculture, perched on top of it seemed to look increasingly apprehensive.

Then, in the 1990s new funds became available, and over four million pounds was spent on the most recent adaptation of the Corn Exchange, creating a multi-purpose entertainment centre, with new technology again playing a vital part, enabling the seven hundred seats to be folded away automatically to provide standing room for twelve hundred. 'Acoustic baffles ensure excellent sound quality', says the 1997 equivalent of that 1909 publicity leaflet, trying to compete with the excitement of the Orchestraphone, 'and with a technical specification to match, any event can easily be accommodated, from classical concerts to

Behind the statue-less, but still ornate frontage of Sudbury's former Corn Exchange in Suffolk there is now a county library

conferences, craft fairs to comedians' – anything, in fact, except roller skating.

Another former Corn Exchange, at **Sudbury** in Suffolk, took on a literary, instead of a sporting or theatrical, role when it became redundant in the early 1960s. It was threatened, at first, with demolition, but the conservationists stepped in to save the elegant early-Victorian building with its elaborate stone-columned facade. A building preservation order was put on it and in 1967 it was bought by West Suffolk County Council for adaptation as a branch library. It opened a year later.

The frontage is virtually unchanged, but at the back there is an extension with accommodation for children and the librarian (not in the same room). There are also facilities for mobile libraries to load and unload. A gallery has been added to the main hall, providing space for twelve thousand books.

The Agricultural Hall in **Norwich**, opened by Edward VII when he was Prince of Wales in 1882, and perhaps the most majestic of the Adaptables in this category, also disseminates knowledge, but in a

rather different way. Sceptics might say it is not a true Adaptable at all, since it still deals with corn in some of its output, but it is, in fact, the headquarters of Anglia Television and, although the facade that towers over Bank Plain is almost unaltered, the rear has been transformed into a modern television complex, ranging from a giant communications dish to a glassed-in staff restaurant.

It was not the first adaptation of the old building. Although it was erected primarily for the farming community, it also housed circuses, pantomimes, banquets, fairs and film shows. Visiting luminaries ranged from Prime Minister Gladstone, trying to keep all the voters happy, to the legendary Blondin walking another kind of tightrope, in his case literally. It was suspended between the balconies of the hall, and he crossed it carrying a trumpeter on his back. Gladstone, of course, blew his own...

When Anglia took over the Agricultural Hall in the late 1950s, the front part of the building was divided into offices, and the main exhibition hall was converted into studios. To make them soundproof, a virtually separate building made of reinforced concrete was erected inside the

Heptonstall Cloth Hall, like many others in Yorkshire, became redundant years ago, when the weaving trade declined. It is now an anonymous private house

shell of the old one. The space between the new ceiling and the iron and glass roof was used to store scenery.

One gallery of the old hall has survived, in the form of a corridor, giving access to the control rooms above the studios, so that, in the midst of this very modern complex, you find yourself walking past the original elegant girders supporting the Victorian roof. They have been picked out in equally elegant royal blue and gold, just in case you think they have been left there by mistake.

The northern weavers' equivalent of the corn exchanges and agricultural halls of the south are the cloth halls, and those that survive have become Adaptables, too.

by the time the Rochdale Canal was opened in 1804, diverting what was left of Heptonstall's industry to Hebden Bridge, in the valley below. The rows of weavers' cottages no longer house weavers, Weavers Square is occupied for the most part by tourists, and the Cloth Hall was adapted as a private residence.

It may be some consolation to the shades of all those Heptonstall weavers that **Halifax** Cloth Hall, which took over much of their business, became an Adaptable too. It was the last of the cloth halls to survive, under its better known name of the Piece Hall – confusing to foreigners from the South who heard the name and associated it with some pacifist organisation. It referred to the pieces of cloth sold by the weavers, who traded from the little rooms opening off the colonnaded galleries around the central courtyard. In due course, the weavers moved out and the antique dealers, booksellers and craft shops moved in.

The comparable public building in **Bradford** is the Wool Exchange, built in the 1860s in a style described as 'Venetian Gothic, freely treated'. It was redolent of Victorian prosperity, from the top of its one-hundred-and-fifty-foot clock tower, decorated with serpentine marble, to its imposing foundation stone, laid by the then

CULTURAL HALL ROLLER SKATING RINK & STAFF. NORWICH.

Norwich Agricultural Hall had a number of roles, including a garlanded roller-skating rink, before it became the headquarters of Anglia Television

One of the earliest to become redundant was the hall at **Heptonstall** in Calderdale, a hillside village which was once a thriving weaving town of four thousand people. Its Cloth Hall, dating from the sixteenth century, was built of distinctive masonry, much paler than the dark stone buildings around it. The cloth trade had already begun to switch to more accessible Halifax

79

The famous Assembly Rooms at Tunbridge Wells, where Beau Nash was Master of Ceremonies, has now been absorbed into a row of shops

Prime Minister, Lord Palmerston. Its main hall has pillars of red Aberdeen granite, and its hammerbeam roof is rather astonishingly claimed to be 'one of only two of its kind in the country, the other being Westminster Abbey'.

These days, however, the Wool Exchange deals in books instead of wool. It was adapted in 1996 by Waterstone's.

The other great gathering places for townsfolk in the eighteenth and nineteenth centuries were the Assembly Rooms; no genteel community could be without one. The most genteel of all, perhaps, were the Assembly Rooms in **Tunbridge Wells**, in the famous Pantiles. Before the pantiles were laid they were known as the Walks, and got off to an inauspicious start when the youthful Duke of Gloucester, son of the princess who later became Queen Anne, slipped and hurt himself while walking on the unpaved path.

The town fathers promised to put matters right, but local government moved as slowly then as it sometimes does today, and when Princess Anne returned the

following year she found nothing had been done. Only under increased pressure – again, little changes in local government – did they get the pantiles laid before the following season – but Queen Anne never returned. It was not until the Georgian dandy 'Beau Nash' took over as Master of Ceremonies at the Assembly Rooms in 1735, after her death, that Tunbridge Wells quite recovered, and he continued to preside there until his own death in 1761. In due course, his elegant empire qualified as an Adaptable, and became a Post Office and a row of shops.

Assembly Rooms in other parts of the country suffered a similar fate, as elegance gave way to economics. A typical example is at **Truro** in Cornwall, built in the 1780s and, in their time, the only Assembly Rooms to include a theatre. Just to stress the point, the architect incorporated plaques on the facade, depicting the heads of Shakespeare and Garrick, and they still stare at each other just under the gable looking, perhaps, a little dazed at the changes which have taken place below.

A century after they were opened, the Assembly Rooms were brought with a jolt into the world of commerce, and became a household goods emporium. In the 1950s the building housed a car repair business, and its future looked unpromising, to say the least, but the Ancient Order of Foresters acquired it, restored it, and turned it into offices, before selling it again. For several years now it has been occupied by the estate agency offices of General Accident, who lease it from the present owners, a duo as well-known to the present generation as the two who are on the plaques under the gable. Instead of Shakespeare and Garrick, it might be appropriate to substitute Mr Marks and Mr Spencer.

Finally, from the ostentatious grandeur of town halls, corn exchanges and assembly rooms to the humblest public building of them all – so humble that, in many cases, it barely shows its head above the ground. Yet, it offers a vital facility to the community; it is more than just a convenience, it can often be an enormous relief...

Our first municipal public lavatory was opened in the City of **London** in 1855, on the pavement outside the Royal Exchange – or rather, underneath it, since it was the first underground public lavatory, too. The nation was given its first opportunity to spend a penny, and it was duly appreciative. The idea caught on and, in the years that followed, nobody could have believed that public lavatories would ever become redundant. How could the demand dry up?

It was not lack of demand, but of public funds that thinned their numbers. In the 1980s and 1990s, according to a public-spirited group called All Mod Cons, up to a third of Britain's public lavatories were shut by local authorities because they could not afford to maintain them. Newcastle-upon-Tyne, for instance, was left with two of them for a population of 276,000; Wigan had just one for over 300,000. Like other, much grander, public buildings, public conveniences were becoming a financial inconvenience – and a large proportion of the public was left crossing its legs...

This has presented a real test of ingenuity for the adaptors. When a lavatory qualifies as an Adaptable, what can you convert it into? In **Cambridge** there was an additional problem: two redundant lavatories were both listed buildings, so the outside appearance had to remain unchanged.

For some time they were left empty – vacant is, perhaps, the more appropriate word. So their appearance, inevitably, began to alter anyway, and for the worse. Then along came the delightfully named Cambridge Recycles, who not only sell and

Truro's former Assembly Rooms, which incorporated a theatre, sold household goods before becoming an estate agents' office. To this day, Shakespeare and Garrick on the front wall gaze at each other in disbelief

A new use for a Cambridge public convenience that no longer functions – it hires out bicycles so you can make a dash for one that does

'Flowers of Convenience' in Brighton – a most fragrant Adaptable

hire out cycles, but have proved they can recycle buildings, too. They adapted one lavatory first as a cycle hire shop, perhaps on the principle that, for anyone expecting to find it still working and having an urgent need, cycles could offer a handy method of getting to one which did. Whatever the reasoning, it worked. Early in 1997 they adapted a second redundant lavatory in the same way; both establishments have seen a steady through-flow ever since.

The most ambitious lavatory Adaptable must be in **Kew**, in south-west London, built by the council in 1905 for ladies coming off the river boats or visiting the nearby fairground. It could have been quite a tourist attraction in itself, a mock Tudor affair with solid brick walls and imitation beams, a jolly little cupola with a yacht as a weathervane, and Doulton tiles let into one wall bearing the inscription in ornamental lettering: 'Ladies' Lavatory: Hot & Cold Water'. All the toilets and washbasins were still in working order when it came on the market in 1993; even a small safe used by the attendant still had a piece of imitation jewellery in it, labelled 'Lost Property'.

The little building fetched £60,000, surely a record price for a redundant ladies' loo – though it did include the fake jewellery. The buyer, Mr Frank Webb, has spent another £20,000 converting it, retaining the glass and pine partitions, but removing the solid slate ones. 'An awful lot of unladylike graffiti had been scrawled over them,' he explained – but he did take photographs before they went. He has built a first floor and made other internal changes, but the elegant 'Ladies' sign is still over the door – and when desperate ladies are deceived by it, Mr Webb lets them use his...

There are other examples of lavatory Adaptables being given a new lease of life, ranging from the Boar Inn at **Great Ryburgh** in Norfolk, where the redundant outside toilet has become a unisex hairdressing salon, to the menservants' lavatory at Gayhurst Court in Buckinghamshire, mentioned on page 37, which is now a cottage known as 'The Dog House'. But the award for the most appropriate choice of a name for a born-again loo must surely go to **Brighton**, where a former public lavatory owned by the council has been adapted as a florist's shop. There could have been some coy comparison of the perfumes to be enjoyed there, past and present, but it is called simply: 'Flowers of Convenience.'

Licensed Adaptables

• • • • • • • • •

*Coaching inns,
village locals, city pubs –
and a boatmen's brothel*

	Location	Old use	New use(s)
1	Ashburton, Devon: Church's	Inn	Ironmonger's shop
2	Barleythorpe, Rutland: Barleythorpe Stud	Inn	Horse-owners' HQ
3	Brough, Cumbria: Post Office	Posting inn	Post office
4	Burford, Oxfordshire: The George	Coaching inn	Shops; offices and homes
5	Dunchurch, Warwickshire: The Old Lion	Packhorse inn	Private residence
6	Jackfield, Shropshire: The Severn Trow	Inn and brothel	Guest-house
7	King's Lynn, Norfolk: The Hulk	Inn	House; Quaker meeting-place
8	Kirkbymoorside, North Yorkshire: Mr Towler's	Inn	Chemist's shop
9	Newcastle-upon-Tyne: The Wheatsheaf	Inn	Billiard Hall; Music Hall; Disco
10	Parkgate, Cheshire: Mostyn House School	Inn	School
11	Romsey, Hampshire: Working Men's Conservative Club	Inn	Working Men's Club HQ
12	Saffron Walden, Essex: The Old Sun	Inn	Private residences; Book and antique shop

Royals and regicides, highwaymen, trowmen; they'll never drink there again

Historic inns and public houses seem to make reluctant Adaptables. Even though they may have lost their original role a century or more ago, their names still persist, if not on a sign outside the door then at least in the memory and the folklore of the locals. The inns may have long since been converted into houses, or shops, or even a Quaker meeting house, but to those whose forebears once used them or talked about them, they are still the Old Sun, or the Old Swan, or in the case of the Quaker meeting house, rather less attractively, the Old Hulk.

The George at **Burford** in Oxfordshire, for instance, still looks like a coaching inn from the road, with its high gables and central archway leading to the former stables at the rear. But it has not been an inn for nearly two hundred years. In 1800 the two elderly sisters who ran it, daughters of the previous

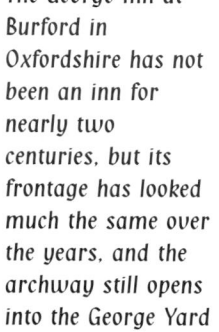

The George Inn at Burford in Oxfordshire has not been an inn for nearly two centuries, but its frontage has looked much the same over the years, and the archway still opens into the George Yard

landlord, were bought out by the owner of the main competitor in Burford, the Bull. He ran both establishments for a few months, but as so often happens with buyouts and mergers, the George was declared redundant and closed down for good.

The next time it is mentioned in the local records, there is a stonemason's business in the yard. Today, the frontage has been divided into shops and offices, and the two rows of nineteenth-century cottages, which were built in the stable yard, have been modernised by a housing trust as sheltered accommodation.

But to those who remember its history, it is still the George, the inn which was there before the Tudors, and reputed to be one of the weekend retreats of Charles II and Nell Gwynne. There is certainly a connection between them and Burford. When Nell called her infant son 'a poor bastard' in front of the king, and said she had no other name to call him, Charles promptly created him Earl of Burford, a title the lad still retained when he later became the Duke of St. Alban's.

Nell Gwynne's other link with the town was also probably forged at the George.

The Old Lion at Dunchurch in Warwickshire was a rendezvous for the Gunpowder Plotters. It is now a private house called – predictably – Guy Fawkes House

Her house in Windsor, one of her royal 'perks' and still bearing the proud inscription, 'In this historic house Nell Gwynne lived', was named Burford House.

The notorious Dunsdon brothers, the improbably-named Tom, Dick and Harry, were regulars at the George in the 1780s. They were highwaymen by profession, and in 1784 two of them returned for a final visit – they had just been executed in Gloucester jail and their bodies were on their way to Shipton Down, where they would be hung in chains...

There is no reminder of the Dunsdon brothers now, except for the archway through which the carter drove his wagon with the two corpses on board. Nor can anyone point with certainty to the rooms where Charles and Nell dallied. But, in Burford they are not forgotten.

At **Dunchurch** in Warwickshire there is a pub Adaptable which also had some famous patrons, perhaps the best-known group of conspirators in English history. Dunchurch was a handy place for such a rendezvous – it was the junction where the roads from London, Holyhead, Oxford and Leicester met, and indeed, it still lies on the A45 trunk road, which used to bring some of the heaviest traffic in the Midlands through the village until it was bypassed by the M45 motorway.

On 5 November 1605, a group of Catholic dissidents gathered at the Old Lion, once a packhorse inn, to await the arrival of the leading figures in the Gunpowder Plot. If they brought the news they were hoping for, the successful blowing-up of the House of Commons and the death of James I, they were ready to lead a full-scale rebellion to restore a Catholic to the throne.

But, of course, it did not work out that way. The plot had failed, Guy Fawkes had been captured, and his fellow plotters in London were fleeing for their lives. Their leader, Robert Catesby, took four of them to his home at Ashby St. Ledgers in Northamptonshire, where they picked up a colleague, Robert Winter, then rode the final ten miles to the Old Lion.

As one account described their arrival: 'The six fugitive conspirators, all bespattered with the mire of November high roads, with dejected looks and jaded aspect, arrived in due time to tell their tale.'

About thirty people were gathered at the inn. When they heard the news, some made a run for it straight away. Most of them said they would stay with Catesby, still vainly hoping they could launch a rebellion. At ten o'clock that night they rode off to Warwick, trying to raise more forces on the way. Sheriff's men caught up with them at the home of one of the conspirators near Stourbridge in Staffordshire, and Catesby and most of the other ringleaders were killed. Robert Winter, who must have wished he had never left Ashby St. Ledgers, escaped with a crossbow bolt in his shoulder, but was captured two months later. None of them ever returned to the Old Lion again.

After playing its part in this notorious little slice of history, the inn sank back into obscurity, and nobody knows exactly when it ceased to function. At the time of the plot it was part of the Catesby estate, and no doubt, after the death of Robert Catesby, much of the property was confiscated, so the Old Lion may have changed roles as well as hands at that time.

During the last war the Home Guard used the building as their headquarters, and it was about that time that the splendid old timbers on the front of the house were covered with pebble-dash. Their restoration was due to an unlikely benefactor, the English Electric Company, which acquired Guy Fawkes House, as it was now known, as part of the Dunchurch Lodge estate in 1954. The company had the pebble-dash stripped off to reveal the original frontage, which is how it remains today. It is privately occupied and has been for the last century or more.

The Old Swan at **Romsey** in Hampshire retains a memento of a more successful uprising of the seventeenth century, the Civil War. An elegant wrought-iron bracket on the front of the building was reportedly used by General Fairfax to hang one of his soldiers found guilty of robbery and murder. A plaque on the wall below the bracket records the event. The Swan is now occupied by the Working Men's Conservative Club.

General Fairfax seems to have spent a fair amount of time during his campaign in pubs, which have since become Adaptables. When he was in Devon, for instance, he made his headquarters, for a while, at the former Mermaid Inn at **Ashburton**. This time he did not even leave behind a bracket as a reminder, and the Mermaid itself has not been an inn since early in the last century. At one stage it was a bakery, then in the 1850s a Mr Chalker converted it into

an ironmonger's shop, and it has filled that role ever since, currently under the name of Church's. But in the gazetteers it is still the name of Fairfax which is primarily associated with it.

The Wheatsheaf in **Newcastle-upon-Tyne** achieved lasting fame in the 1860s, but not under that name. It was taken over by the former landlord of the Royal Hotel, John Balmbra, who put his own name on the front of the building, and every Geordie knows of Balmbra's, the place 'aw tyuk the bus frae' to go to Blaydon Races.

Like other pubs in the city at that time, he brought in singers and entertainers to attract more custom, but none of his rivals could find the equal of George 'Geordie' Ridley and the song he launched in

The Swan at Romsey in Hampshire has left its former role as an inn – and a place of execution – firmly in the past

Mr Church's shop at Ashburton in Devon was once an inn, and a headquarters of General Fairfax during the Civil War

Balmbra's. He had written it himself, in his own phonetic spelling:

Aw went to Blaydon Races, 'twas on the ninth
of Joon,
Eiteen hundred and sixty-two on a summer's
afternoon.
Aw tyuk the bus frae Balmbra's, and she was
heavy laden,
Away we went along Collingwood Street, that's
on the road to Blaydon...

Ridley died two years later, but his song – they called it 'Tyneside's National Anthem' – lived on, and so did Balmbra's. The room where he sang it was enlarged and became the Oxford Music Hall, better known to the regulars as the Geordie Music Hall, and one of the first of its kind. It had a soaring arched ceiling with panelled walls, and alcoves along one side for those who could afford a shilling for a 'private box'.

Eventually, however, the competition from the Variety Theatre became too strong, and Balmbra's went through its first adaptation, as a billiard hall called, rather grandly, the Carlton Hotel.

On the centenary of the Blaydon Races in 1962, the billiard tables were cleared out and it was re-opened as a music hall, with as much period flavour as possible. Two ornate lamp standards on the pavement outside were still lit by gas, even though the rest of the street had long since been converted to electricity.

In 1981 the traditionalists got a nasty jolt. Balmbra's – the name was still over the door – had its second adaptation. The old music hall was transformed into a pub disco. The local paper reacted colourfully: 'Ye've gorra be joking, bonny lad!' The chairman of the Northumbria Tourist Board put it more formally: 'We are very disappointed. It is sad to lose part of the city's heritage.'

Balmbra's music hall in Newcastle was immortalised in 'Blaydon Races'. A new proprietor made it a pub disco and called it 'Gaslight and Lazer' – but Balmbra is back

Five years later, even the name was altered, and another shudder went through the old-timers. Its new manager, Atilla Boyla (they must have thought his first name all too appropriate) rechristened his now ultra-modern pub: 'Gaslight and Lazer'. They looked on him a little more kindly, however, when the 125th anniversary of the Races came round a year later, and Atilla (now Atilla the Fun) changed the name back to Balmbra's and joined in the local celebrations.

The White Swan at **Brough** in Cumbria survived much longer before changing its role. It was an important posting inn during the last century, when up to sixty stagecoaches a day passed through the little town on their way between London and Glasgow. There were extensive stables and other buildings at the rear, which used to be linked by a tunnel. The White Swan was the main change-over point for mail being carried between the two cities, and by coincidence it continued to handle the mail after becoming an Adaptable. For the past twenty years or so, it has been the local Post Office.

The Old Sun Inn at **Saffron Walden** in Essex is another picturesque pub Adaptable, but it started life even earlier as a fourteenth-century 'hall house', with a central open hall and two side wings, and that made it easily convertible into two private houses. They became a fully-fledged Adaptable for the first time during the 1700s, when they were combined into one again, as the Sun Inn. It only continued as such for about a hundred years, and the last landlord moved out in 1870, but it is still known to everyone locally as the Old Sun Inn.

The inn's first known owner was a Mr Gibson, and even when it was divided into private houses again – five of them this time – it stayed in the Gibson family until it was acquired by the National Trust. In the 1960s the lease was sold to John and Paul Lankester, who carried out its final adaptation as a books and antiques shop. Their family runs it still.

The most striking feature of the Old Sun Inn's splendid seventeenth-century pargeting is the portrayal of Tom Hickathrift, the Wisbech giant killer, and the giant that he killed. Visitors sometimes find it disconcerting that they are the same size, and some experts have even suggested they are really the two giants Gog and Magog. Why should Tom

Hickathrift be featured, they argue, so far from his Cambridgeshire home? But then Gog and Magog spent most of their lives in London, doing duty as porters at the Royal Palace, and London is just as far from Saffron Walden as Wisbech.

There is, in fact, a logical reason for the similarity in size of the two figures. According to legend, Tom was well over seven feet tall, able to uproot trees with his bare hands and carry a wagon-load of corn on his back. So there was probably little to choose, in terms of size and

The White Swan at Brough in Cumbria was an important posting inn on the mailcoach route between London and Glasgow. It is still involved with mail, as the local Post Office

The Sun Inn at Saffron Walden in Essex still has its splendid pargeting, but these days it is a book and antique shop. As for the figures standing over the archway – opinions vary...

strength, between him and the giant. But when they met, Tom was shrewd enough to use a wheel from his wagon as a shield, and the axle-tree as a club, and that is what he could well be holding here. The giant is armed only with a stave – and looks, understandably, apprehensive. Neither Gog nor Magog specialised in wagon wheels or axle trees, so this seems pretty conclusive. In the argument between the experts, as in his argument with the giant, Tom Hickathrift seems to have won the day.

King's Lynn in Norfolk is much closer to Hickathrift country – he was carting beer from there to Wisbech, it is said, when the giant tried to block his way. So the name of a pub Adaptable at Lynn, close by the quayside, seems singularly appropriate. But the Hulk was not named after that hulking young drayman; it was a seafarers' pub, used by the whalers who sailed from King's Lynn to the waters around Greenland. Unlike the other pub Adaptables so far, it was still functioning within living memory, though the whalers had long since departed. Then it became a private house, and ten years ago it was acquired by the Society of Friends. Slightly incongruously, the rooms where they hold their Quaker meetings still have some of the stained glass in the windows from its days as a Victorian pub, elegantly inscribed 'Smoking Room' and 'Bar Parlour'.

There is a former inn at **Kirkbymoorside** in North Yorkshire which has retained a different kind of distinctive feature after becoming an Adaptable, which would normally have been withdrawn – its licence. It is now Towler's chemist's shop, but Mr Towler is still permitted to purvey wines and spirits, as well as aspirin and Alka-Seltzer, and they can be consumed on or off the premises – though few customers actually crack open

a bottle in the shop... Incidentally, the local doctors' surgery, where Mr Towler's customers get their prescriptions, was also an Adaptable. It started life as the village school.

At **Parkgate** in Cheshire there is another variation on this theme, a former inn which is now a school. In the eighteenth century, when the town was the principal port for exporting Cheshire cheese and Macclesfield silk, the George Inn on the Promenade was the favourite overnight stop for passengers waiting to sail to Ireland. Handel stayed there in 1741 before embarking for Dublin to attend the opening performance of his *Messiah*, and other names in the hotel register ranged from Nelson and Lady Hamilton to John Wesley – on different nights, naturally. Then the River Dee silted up, the sea retreated, and ships went to Liverpool instead. The fortunes of the George declined, and the building was adapted and enlarged to become Mostyn House School.

When most inns close, the reason is generally lack of local support, but the Horse and Groom at **Barleythorpe** in Leicestershire was closed for precisely the opposite reason – it was supported too enthusiastically. In the early years of

The inscription on the door is misleading – the bar parlour of the former Hulk Inn at King's Lynn in Norfolk is now the meeting place of the local Quakers

From bed and board to blackboard – at Parkgate in Cheshire the George Inn has become Mostyn House School

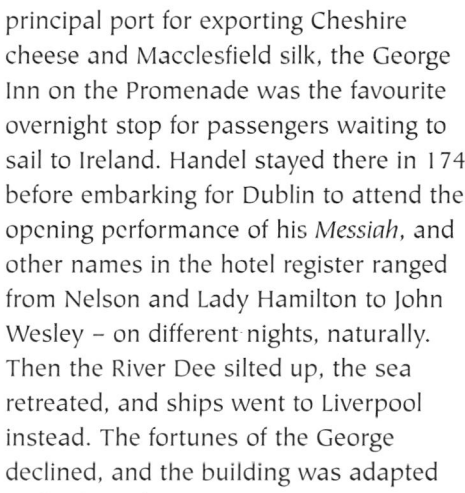

this century it was owned by the fifth Earl of Lonsdale, who indeed owned most of the village. He was known as the Yellow Earl, not a suggestion of cowardice but just his favourite colour. He designed yellow livery for his carriages and his servants; even the gardeners had yellow cardigans and pushed yellow wheelbarrows.

The Earl's principal interests were hunting and boxing. He gave his name to the Lonsdale Belt, and he was Master of the Cottesmore until he was in his sixties. But above all he was a firm master of his staff as well as his horses. When a new and expensive hunter refused to jump a fence, he ordered his groom to shoot it. And it was this same unrelenting approach which forced the Horse and Groom out of business. Lord Lonsdale decided that his staff were spending too much time there – so he closed it down.

Until quite recently there were elderly villagers in Barleythorpe who remembered drinking at the Horse and Groom, but the old pub has been so thoroughly adapted it is difficult to identify today. Even the occupant of the adjoining cottage, who has lived there for over thirty years, has no recollection of it – though he knew a man who did. It is actually No. 31 Main Street, but the equestrian connection still exists; it is part of the headquarters of the Barleythorpe Stud.

If the Horse and Groom had offered the same services as the Severn Trow, another pub Adaptable at **Jackfield** in Shropshire, Lord Lonsdale might have had even greater difficulty in extricating his staff – and possibly a riot on his hands if he had tried to close it. It was built late in the eighteenth century on the banks of the Severn, within a stone's throw of the famous iron bridge, during the early days of the Industrial Revolution, and it served the various bodily needs of the trowmen. It

had its own brew house – and certain other facilities.

These trowmen were the so-called 'men of iron' who handled the trows, the distinctive flat-bottomed sailing barges peculiar to the River Severn because of its very shallow stretches. They took iron, pottery and coal down the river, and the boats were then hauled back upstream against the current. There were boarding-houses dotted along the river where they stayed overnight, and the Severn Trow is thought to be the last one to survive.

It had a forty-foot dormitory for the men to sleep in, and individual cubicles for other activities. It had been empty for nearly seventy years when the present owners, Jim and Pauline Hannigan, took it over in 1984, but happily, it had not been vandalised and many of its original features survived – including one relic from the cubicles which is not kept permanently on display.

The Severn Trow did, in fact, have another unofficial title, and although the dormitory and the cubicles have given place to en suite bedrooms and four-poster beds in its new role as a comfortable guest house, it is still known locally as the Boatman's Brothel...

The Severn Trow at Ironbridge used to provide rather special personal services for the boatmen. It is a very respectable private hotel now, but the locals still have a name for it...

Industrial Adaptables

● ● ● ● ● ● ● ● ● ●

*Power stations, factories, mills, warehouses –
and four gasometers*

	Location	Old use	New use(s)
1	Baldock, Herts: Kaysor Bondor's	Stocking factory	Supermarket
2	Caldeck, Cumbria	Blanket factory	Working men's club; hen-house; clog factory
3	Leeds	Wool warehouse	Offices
4	Londesborough, East Yorkshire	Laundry	Village hall; wartime prison
5	London: Bankside Power Station	Power station	Art gallery
	Battersea Power Station	Power station	Entertainment centre
	Bryant & May's, Bow	Match factory	Apartments
	Gasometers at St. Pancras	Gas tanks	Undecided
6	Lowestoft, Suffolk	Flour mill	Private residences
7	Manchester: Bottoms Mill, Summerseat	Textile mill	Flats
	Britannia Hotel	Warehouse	Hotel
8	Market Harborough, Leicestershire: Symington's	Corset factory	Offices and library
9	Norwich, Norfolk: Whitefriars Mill	Textile mill	Print works; factory; offices
10	Olney, Milton Keynes: Bucks Lace Industry Building	Lace factory	Luxury apartments

Council offices in a corset factory – what goes in a gasometer?

Industrial Adaptables can be an enormous challenge to the ingenuity of a developer. There are the comparatively straight-forward ones, of course. Smallish factories or mills are not too difficult to convert into offices or flats, but larger ones generally look so forbidding, and are often in such

The familiar outline of Battersea Power Station in South London, long since redundant but a difficult building to adapt...

insalubrious surroundings that, even if they could be made habitable, few people would fancy moving in.

And then there are the blockbusters, massive structures on the scale of **Battersea Power Station**, which has stood empty since it stopped operating in 1982. Unattractive though it may look to the average eye, its exterior has been Grade II listed by the preservationists, so no one can disturb it. The first proposal was to convert it into a massive indoor theme park, but the money ran out. The current plan is to turn it into an entertainment centre, incorporating a multi-screen cinema as well as two hotels. Perhaps they could also

...but Bankside Power Station in another part of London has fared rather better – as the New Tate

rig up helter-skelters around those four great chimneys...

Another giant London power station has fared rather better. **Bankside** was designed in 1947 by Sir Giles Gilbert Scott, whose previous creations had ranged from Liverpool Cathedral, when he was only twenty-one, to the famous red telephone kiosk, which made its debut in 1926 and is still much preferred by many of us to the draughty, fragile glass boxes that have largely replaced them.

Bankside Power Station was not one of his most beautiful designs, but it was big, and solid – which, perhaps, is why it took sixteen years to complete. It remained in use for just eighteen years before being decommissioned. That was the bad news. The good news, so far as being an Adaptable was concerned, was that somehow it had missed being listed. Even so, it was yet another sixteen years before the Tate Gallery took it on as the New Tate. No doubt, Sir Giles would have wished they had decided to put a New Tate there in the first place; he could surely have designed a much more attractive building for it.

No solution has yet been found for, perhaps, the trickiest industrial Adaptable of all. What on earth do you do with four enormous gasometers behind **St. Pancras Station**, that have recently been decommissioned? London and Continental Railways, who want to build their Channel Tunnel link across the site, were in no doubt at all: knock 'em down. English Heritage, however, wanted them preserved.

A major problem for any adaptor: one of the four giant gasometers behind St. Pancras Station in London. Any ideas to English Heritage please

Bryant & May's match factory in east London has been converted into a massive complex of flats and apartments, including the water towers, but the familiar 'BM' logo is still preserved

Observe, they said, the elegance of the colonnades, with capitals which are Doric at the bottom, Ionic in the middle, and Corinthian at the top – let alone the latticework on the interbracing, embossed with white roses; definitely not your average gasometer.

A compromise was reached. The gasometers would be taken to pieces, packaged up and put into storage until somebody could think what to do with them. London and Continental Railways are footing the bill. Their spokesman commented resignedly: 'What is five million pounds in the face of a three billion pound project?'

Surprisingly, ideas have already been put forward for adapting these huge, apparently useless chunks of Meccano. A multi-screen cinema seating two thousand people, an indoor sports centre, water sports – nothing is too unlikely for the English Heritage think-tank.

Back in the hard world of profit and loss, it has proved more practical to base an Adaptable on matches than Meccano. At **Bow** in East London a massive factory complex, which was used for over a century for manufacturing matchsticks, has been transformed into over eight hundred 'exclusive' apartments. The two enormous water towers now contain penthouse flats, and the original chimney-stack has been preserved as a decorative feature in what is now a leafy courtyard.

Some of the buildings on the eight-acre site originally produced candles; the road at the back of the premises is still called Wick Lane. In the 1860s it was taken over by Bryant and May, and switched from candles to the matches which light them. The company moved out to Aylesbury in 1976 and the buildings were let, primarily for storage. They were finally bought by property developers, and the conversion was completed around 1990 – but the Bryant and May emblem is still preserved there, in concrete.

Developers tackling another massive industrial Adaptable, at **Summerseat**, near Bolton, had the additional problem of its name. Bottoms Mill is not exactly a gift to an advertising copywriter, but they bravely preserved the name as well as the building, keeping the facade unchanged, but converting the interior into fifty-five flats.

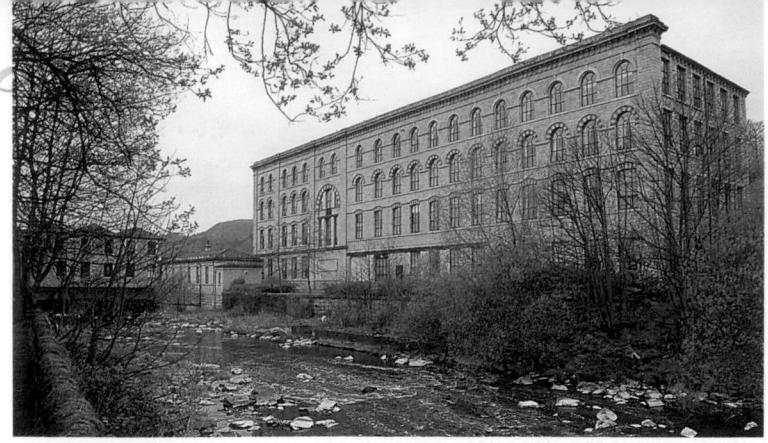

Bottoms Mill at Summerseat near Bolton could have had a more enticing name, but it has been successfully adapted into flats, served by the defiantly named Bottoms Restaurant

It used to be the Watts Warehouse – and what a warehouse it was. Its elaborate exterior is now matched by its elaborate interior, to make it one of Manchester's most imposing hotels

The old weaving shed, an Adaptable in itself, was defiantly named Bottoms Restaurant.

In the centre of **Manchester** there is a much grander industrial Adaptable, the Britannia Hotel, converted in the 1980s from a warehouse – but what a warehouse the Watts warehouse was! It was built in 1858 by Samuel and John Watts, who might almost have had its later adaptation in mind, because this must have been the Lancashire cotton industry's most elaborate workplace.

They incorporated Venetian and Egyptian, Dutch and Elizabethan. Each floor had a different decorative style, from Egyptian granite on the ground floor to an imitation of the Galerie de Glacés at Versailles

on the fourth. The roof was almost entirely plate glass, a startling innovation for any building in the 1850s, let alone a cotton warehouse. When it was built, a local historian described it as 'a structure fit for kings, which many a monarch might envy', and the list of distinguished visitors in its warehouse days would have done credit to any luxury hotel. They included Prince Albert, the Maharajah of Jodhpur and King George V. Perhaps it was not for nothing that the Watts family claimed descent from the first King of England.

The S. & J. Watts Building continued to function as a warehouse after the company had become part of the Courtauld Group, but in the 1970s it came on the market, and there was a plan to turn it into offices. When that failed it was taken over by the Receiver, and there was talk of demolition. Lady Eleanor Campbell-Orde, a surviving member of the Watts family, led a campaign to save it and finally, in 1979, it was bought by Britannia Hotels.

They spent five million pounds converting it into a 362-bedroomed hotel, with assorted bars and restaurants, two discos and an indoor swimming-pool. Egon Ronay describes it rather unenthusiastically as 'a peculiar mix of rather gaudy, gilt-decorated public rooms and simply decorated bedrooms; fancier suites are split-level and bedecked in flowered prints.' Prince Albert, the Maharajah and George V may well have preferred it as a warehouse...

A wool warehouse in another northern city centre was also provided with lavish trimmings, rather in the style of a Moorish

in terminal decline, with hundreds of weavers falling out of work. A number of local worthies got together in an effort to help them. They set up a joint stock company and built spinning mills, where cheap yarn could be provided for them. The idea was not entirely philanthropic – the more the weavers could earn for themselves, the less would have to be provided from the Poor Rate which these gentlemen had to pay.

They built two mills, the second one much larger than the first and erected on the site of a former White Friars priory. The Whitefriars Yarn Mill took nearly three years to build and was completed in 1839. Unfortunately, not enough money was left to equip it fully, and it was not long before all the floors were let for other uses. By the 1870s the yarn mill was virtually an Adaptable; as well as producing yarn it was also manufacturing piano parts.

It was bought for the first time by its present owners, Jarrold & Sons, in 1904, but instead of using it for their own printing and publishing activities, they let the mill to Caley's, a local chocolate-making company which was then branching out into a new field. Thus the old yarn mill became their box and cracker-making department.

Never mind the minarets, it was just a wool warehouse in Leeds. Then it became offices – but the minarets are still there

palace, with minarets at the corners. It was built in **Leeds** in 1878 and saw service as a warehouse for around a century. Then it became another up-market industrial Adaptable and was converted into offices, but the Moorish flavour was carefully preserved. If a minaret suffered damage, it was replaced during the restoration work with a fibreglass replica.

The English textile industry was not confined entirely to the north of England. For over three hundred years a large proportion of the weaving trade was centred on **Norwich;** the name of the nearby village of Worstead will always be associated with it. But, by the 1830s, it was

The Whitefriars yarn mill in Norwich had a period as a cracker and boxmaking factory, before it went into printing and publishing – as Jarrolds

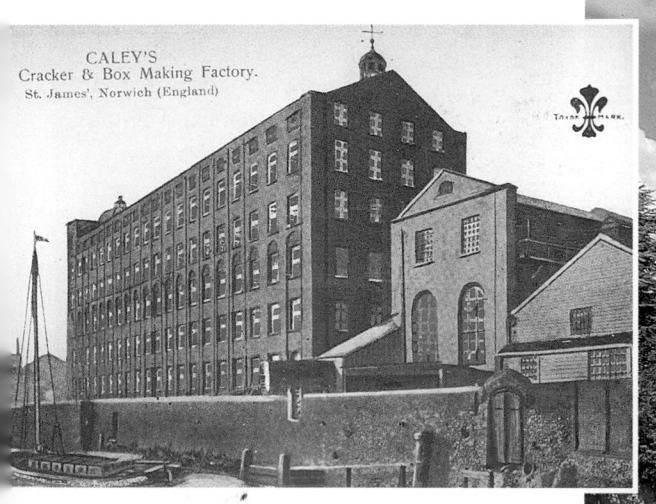

Its next adaptation was in 1920, when Jarrolds sold the mill to the Ministry of Works. Like its original owners, the intention was to help provide work for the unemployed; not redundant weavers, but disabled ex-servicemen, who had no trade they could return to. This time the idea worked. The Government Instructional Factory, as it was called, taught a wide range of trades, from carpentry and plastering to tailoring and watch repairing.

The Ministry ran out of trainees in 1933, and Jarrolds bought back the mill. There have been various refurbishments over the years, including a major one in 1990, but the lofty exterior is virtually unchanged, towering over the River Wensum and the smaller industrial buildings that have grown up around it. In a way, perhaps the Whitefriars Mill has reverted to the use it was originally intended for. It is still spinning yarns, but the yarns are used to create books – not cloth – including this one...

Another factory involved in the clothing trade has had a much more radical adaptation, but again the facade has been preserved – and a very grand facade it is too. The three great archways over the entrance are flanked by pillars and surmounted by a classic-style portico, embellished with stone scrolls and curlicues. A frieze runs along the top, depicting pairs of winged lions with human heads, facing each other with a paw resting nonchalantly on a shared urn. And all this for a stocking factory...

When Kaysor Bondor moved into **Baldock** in Hertfordshire they decided their factory would look as elegant – from the front anyway – as the mannequins who advertised their stockings and underwear. It stood on a large open site on the edge of the town, the first building to catch your eye as you drove into the main street along the old London road. It was, in fact, an ideal position for a supermarket, and when Kaysor Bondor moved out, Tesco moved in.

The shoppers who pass under the open archways are now protected by a modern transparent cover. Shopping trolleys weave among the parked cars, and on my last visit a kind of bouncy castle by the entrance was advertising burgers made of meat substitute. High above all this, the winged lions are still exchanging glances, but it was difficult to tell whether the expressions on their human faces indicated amusement or disdain...

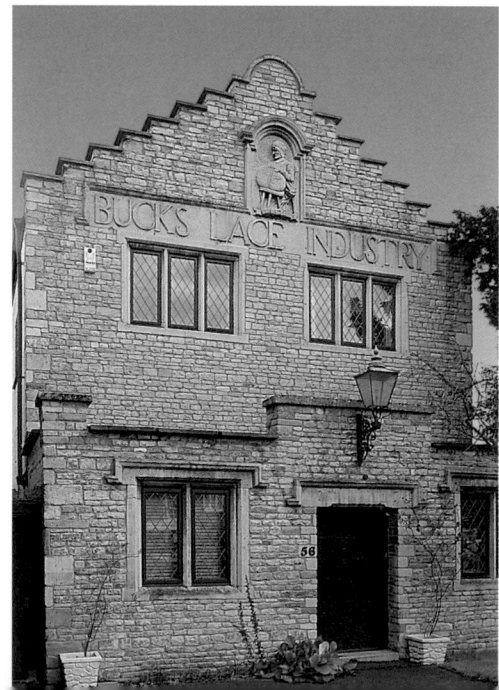

Smaller industrial Adaptables in market towns and villages are generally quite different in character from their big brothers in the more heavily populated areas. They may not be so imposing, but they have their individual flavour and they often reflect the industrial past more clearly. Nothing could be clearer, for instance, than the inscription carved on the stone facade of a stepped-gable building in **Olney** High Street near Milton Keynes, scene of the famous annual pancake race on Shrove Tuesday. The many hundreds of visitors which the event attracts can hardly miss the name 'Bucks Lace Industry', with a bas-relief of a bonneted lady working away with her bobbins.

It was built in 1928 by a Mr Harry Armstrong, of Stoke Goldington, in a rather quixotic attempt to revive the flagging handmade lace industry, for which Olney was famed, and which had fallen victim to a change in fashion and the economic climate. Lace was never actually made at the Bucks Lace Factory, in spite of its name and the lady with the bobbins. It was brought in from the surrounding towns and villages to be packaged and despatched around the world. But Mr Armstrong's dream failed to survive him, and for a time the building was used for making lampshades, no doubt to the confusion of the bonneted lady on the facade. This modest industrial Adaptable is now a block of luxury apartments, but it would be nice to think that the residents have a few lace curtains in their windows, if only to make her feel at home again.

There is a rather different decoration at an industrial Adaptable in **Market Harborough** in Leicestershire. The town owes much of its prosperity to the Symington family, who built the red-brick Victorian factory behind the church in 1898. This was, in fact, a corset factory,

but it gained a special place in the history of ladies' underwear because this was where the liberty-bodice was first produced. Many families have financed Foundations of other kinds, but few can have provided so much comfort to so many ladies.

Sadly, fashions changed for Market Harborough's liberty-bodices, just as they did for Olney's handmade lace, and the factory was switched to soap and groceries. In 1980 it became a fully-fledged Adaptable by being converted into council offices and a library. But a reminder of those liberating days survives, the splendid little Symington Statue of Liberty – the bodice, that is.

At **Caldbeck** in Cumbria there is little to indicate that the old blanket mill ever produced blankets. Since then it has had a slightly bizarre variety of uses, ranging from a working men's club to a hen-house, but its current products are rather more specialised than blankets. Since 1973 it has been the home of a firm making clogs.

In a former laundry at **Londesborough** in East Yorkshire, there are still the white

No, he has not taken off his shoes to rest his feet. The old blanket mill at Caldbeck in Cumbria has been put to a new use with an old craft, clogmaking

Market Harborough's corset factory looked grand enough to be council offices or a library – and that is what it became

An unlikely mural in the former estate laundry, now the village hall, at Londesborough in Humberside. It was painted by German prisoners of war

The old flour mill at Lowestoft in Suffolk, before and after its conversion into flats

tiles around the walls as a reminder of its original use, but it is the murals above the tiles which really catch the eye, and they have as unusual a history as the laundry itself.

It was built for the workers and their families on the Londesborough estate during the second half of the last century to coincide, so it is said, with a royal visit: perhaps the squire wanted to make sure the maids had clean aprons. It was designed in the same style as the estate houses around it, and from the outside it looked more like a village hall than a laundry, which is what it eventually became. By 1910, the village's dirty washing was being dealt with in another building down the street, and the laundry assumed the rather grand title of the Concert Hall.

In 1945 it had a different role. German prisoners of war spent some time in it, and they were the amateur artists who painted the murals on the walls. Legend has it that the brushes they used were made from their own hair. Although the building has since been used

for various village activities, from stage shows to badminton, the murals have mostly survived. A local historian wrote of them, with muted enthusiasm: 'Although rather theatrical, with Londesborough Hall portrayed in various Georgian Regency scenes, they show the men had a certain talent.'

Unfortunately, some of the paint has begun to flake off, which prompted an attempt to restore one of the murals, a romantic young couple in Regency dress. The result was to make them look rather different from their neighbours – the young man, for instance, looks uncommonly like Clark Gable in *Gone with the Wind* – but then the restorers did not have the benefit of brushes made from their own hair…

Finally, at **Lowestoft** in Suffolk, there is an old flour mill which was once owned by the first mayor of the town, William Youngman. In 1996, as an industrial Adaptable, it became part of a one-and-a-half million pounds housing project to create twenty-four flats and seven houses. The original timbers and brickwork, and the old sack house have been restored, and when the complex was officially opened, an old mill-wheel was unveiled by the leader of the Council, Bob Blizzard. More importantly, perhaps, he summed up what industrial Adaptables are all about.

'This is part of Lowestoft's heritage,' he said in his speech at the ceremony. 'If we want to preserve a building like this, we have got to find a new use for it.'

Which takes us back to those gasometers behind St. Pancras Station…

Scholastic Adaptables

Schools, institutes,
study centres,
American colleges

	Location	Old use	New use(s)
1	Abberley, Hereford and Worcester	Stately home	School
2	Bathford, North-East Somerset: Old School House	School	Hotel
3	Bicester, Oxfordshire: Chesterton Manor	School	Private residence
4	Bowes, Durham	School	Café; houses
5	Cholmondeley, Cheshire	School	Bar and restaurant
6	Cornwell, Oxfordshire	School	Village hall; estate office
7	Cowan Bridge, Lancashire	School	Cottages
8	Grantham, Lincolnshire: Harlaxton Hall	Mansion	American university
9	Grassington, North Yorkshire: Town Hall	Working Men's Institute	Cinema, Town Hall
10	Helmsley, North Yorkshire: Duncombe Park	Stately home	School; stately home
11	Herstmonceux, East Sussex: Herstmonceux Castle	Mansion	Observatory; international study centre
12	Ingleborough, North Yorkshire: Ingleborough Hall	Shooting lodge	School; children's home; education centre
13	Ironbridge, Shropshire: Youth Hostel	Working Men's Institute	Youth hostel
14	Letchworth, Hertfordshire: Cloisters	School for Psychology	Masonic lodge
15	Llanyblodwell, Shropshire: Post Office	School	Post office
16	Lyme Regis, Dorset: All Hallows' School	Manor house	School
17	Milton Abbas, Dorset: Abbey House	Stately home	School
18	Penrith, Cumbria: Dame Birkett's School	School	Private residence
19	Sawston, Cambridgeshire: Sawston Hall	Stately home	Language centre
20	Siddington, Cheshire: Thornycroft Hall	Manor house	Greyhound Association centre; children's home; educational centre
21	Snigs End, Gloucestershire: Prince of Wales	School	Pub
22	Stowe, Buckinghamshire: Stowe School	Stately home	School
23	Tissington, Derbyshire	School	Tea-shop; kindergarten

For some, school's out; for others, it's moved in

William Edward Forster is not a name which immediately rings bells, but it ought to – particularly school bells – because it was Mr Forster's Education Act of 1870 which gave rise to so many of those Victorian schools in our villages. His Act set up locally elected Boards with the authority to build schools, appoint the staff and supervise standards, and they effectively filled any gaps left by the Church of England, which was in the field rather earlier.

The Old School House at Bathford, near Bath, is now an hotel. There used to be separate wings for the boys and girls; now guests can mingle...

...and at the former village school at Cholmondeley in Cheshire, they can drop in for a drink

Mr Forster's schools are generally easy to spot. The 1870s were not exactly the heyday of imaginative school architecture, and there seemed to be a standard design of red brick walls, slate roofs, lofty ceilings and tall chimneys. The same design and materials were used, regardless of the character of the rest of the village.

When farms were mechanised, transport improved and families became smaller, many of these buildings were no longer required. Their outward appearance was not easy to disguise, but internally there have been ingenious adaptations of the standard classrooms and assembly halls, and even the standard cloakrooms with their standard rows of pegs – though most adaptors drew the line at the standard outside lavatories.

Any sign which says 'The Old School House' generally means a private residence, but the larger schools can be adapted for other purposes, and the Old School House at **Bathford**, just outside Bath, for instance, is now an hotel. This is a pre-Forster school built by the Church in 1837 on the site of an old tithe barn. The boys' and girls' classrooms were discreetly separated by the teacher's accommodation, but segregation no longer applies, and mixed couples can now occupy the bedrooms which have been created where the classroom used to be. General discipline, in fact, is considerably more lax.

When Clough Williams-Ellis, of Portmeirion fame, designed the school at Cornwell in Oxfordshire, he typically hung the bell inside the chimney. It is no longer a school, but the bell is still there

But one school rule still applies: the hotel is entirely non-smoking.

The **Cholmondeley Arms** in Cheshire, close by the castle and deer park of the Marquess of Cholmondeley, was another Victorian schoolhouse. It continued to function as a school until 1982. Now the lofty school hall, shaped like a cross, has been curtained off to form a bar and two dining areas, and although there are still school chairs they are new ones, bought to match the pine tables, instead of the battered originals.

Snigs End School in Gloucestershire owed its existence, not to the Church of England nor to William Edward Forster, but to an Irish MP called Feargus O'Connor. He founded the Chartist movement in the 1840s, which had the entirely praiseworthy object of reforming parliamentary elections, by the introduction of secret ballots, fairer constituencies, the abolition of property qualifications for MPs, proper salaries for them, and universal suffrage. All of these reforms eventually came about, but O'Connor and the Chartists backed a loser as well – the idea of cooperative land management. They founded model villages by buying up tracts of agricultural land in the south, selling shares in them to townsfolk, mainly from the North, dividing

Snigs End School in Gloucestershire is now a pub – though the Chartists who founded the village would hardly approve

the land into smallholdings and running a lottery among the shareholders to select who should live in them.

The villages were supposed to be self-supporting but, unfortunately, they were often established on land with poor soil, in areas with no accessible markets for their produce, and cultivated by people with little idea of how to grow anything anyway.

Snigs End was one of five such villages, with another just down the road at Lewbands, and the others in Oxfordshire, Worcestershire and Hertfordshire. All of them were disasters, and O'Connor finished his days in an asylum.

He did, however, leave one sound feature of these villages behind. Each one had an excellent school. Snigs End was founded in 1847 and failed by 1853, but the buildings were sturdily built and well laid out, and the biggest in the village was the school, which continued to function. Like many others, it consisted of two bays

101

for the boys' and girls' classrooms, separated by the teacher's premises. And again, like many others, it eventually became redundant. O'Connor might be disconcerted to discover that today his segregated school has become the village pub, the Prince of Wales – particularly as the sale of alcohol was banned in all Chartist settlements.

Cornwell, just across the Oxfordshire border, was also created by a remarkable character, nearly a hundred years later. Clough Williams-Ellis, the architect best known for his slightly bizarre Italianate-Welsh village of Portmeirion, enlarged the manor house at Cornwell and completely rebuilt the village. That included the school, which he remodelled in neo-Georgian style, with a curved end, a hipped roof, and tall narrow windows. The only clue that it was a school was the bell-cote – unexpectedly inserted, in typical Williams-Ellis style, inside the chimney-stack. The school eventually became the village hall, and is now the estate office – but the bell still hangs in the chimney.

A rather different eccentric built the village school at **Llanyblodwell**, originally in Wales, but since 1573 in Shropshire. The Reverend John Parker was not a professional architect, just the local parson, but he designed and built the church and the school, and both buildings are startling monuments to his originality.

The church has a separate tower and broach spire, a hundred feet high, rather like a rocket waiting to be launched. Inside the church he painted every available wall with his favourite texts, and filled all the floor space with carved bench pews, a carved screen, a carved organ case and pulpit, and carved galleries. Church and tower are linked by a brick arch bearing the inscription: '1855–1856. From Lightning and Tempest, from Earthquakes and Fire, Good Lord deliver us.' So far, He has.

The school with its teacher's quarters is not quite so distinctive and, although it has a spire, its design is more orthodox. But this substantial pile of red sandstone is impressive enough, with its massed ranks of gables and chimneys. And the good parson could not resist the opportunity to inscribe yet another text, this time on the Gothic lintel over the front door: 'That the soul be without knowledge, it is not good. Even a child is known by his doings whether his work be pure.'

The building and its sombre warning still survives, but the school became the village Post Office, and the living quarters are privately occupied.

The village school at **Tissington** in Derbyshire owed its existence to a memorable Lady of the Manor, Frances Fitzherbert. The Fitzherberts have been

An even more elaborate village school at Llanyblodwell in Shropshire, built by a rich Victorian parson, became an Adaptable too – and stayed that way

Lady Frances Fitzherbert's rather grand village school at Tissington in Derbyshire became a tea-shop, but now it has gone full circle

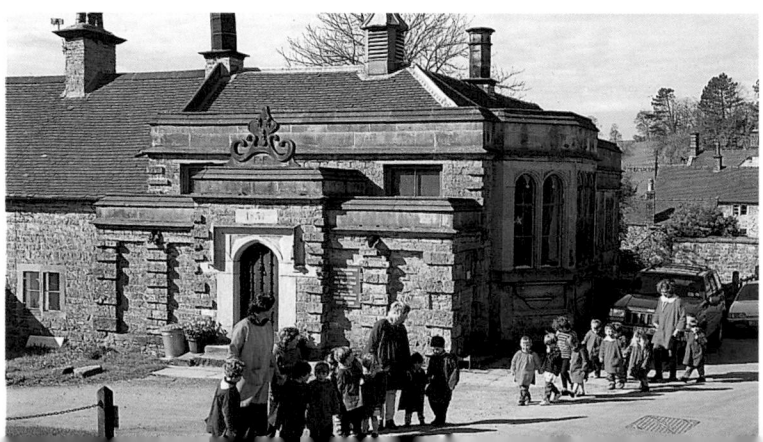

The Brontë girls attended Cowan Bridge School in Lancashire – and two of them died of consumption. It is now a terrace of cottages – and much healthier

squires since the sixteenth century, and Frances Fitzherbert built Tissington Hall in the early 1600s, but most of their improvements to the village were made between the 1830s and 1860s, by Sir Henry and his wife Frances. Her initials, F.F., with the family coat of arms, are over the door of the school which she built in 1837 to mark Queen Victoria's coronation.

In due course it became a tea-shop, which might have been a shrewd conversion, because Tissington is much visited by tourists on the Derbyshire well-dressing circuit. The tradition is actually

Another former school with a bad record, now private residences. It was the one at Bowes in County Durham on which Charles Dickens based Dotheboys Hall

said to have started there, back in the fourteenth century, and on Ascension Day all its five wells are decorated with biblical scenes made of thousands of flower petals. They remain an attraction until the petals fade or fall, and all the visitors who came to see them should have appreciated a cup of tea in Frances Fitzherbert's school.

Alas, the petals only survive for three or four weeks, and I suppose there is a limit to the number of cups of tea you can

sell in that time. The tea-shop closed – but Lady Frances would probably be happy to know that this particular school Adaptable has come full circle. It is in use as a kindergarten again.

The former village school at **Cowan Bridge** in Lancashire might well be a tourist attraction in itself. It was opened in the 1820s by the Reverend William Carus Wilson as a school for the daughters of impoverished clergymen, 'so they would be equipped to earn their own living' – and this was where the Reverend Patrick Brontë sent his four young daughters.

They could hardly have been grateful. Conditions were harsh, the food inadequate, the sanitation positively dangerous and, by 1825, so many pupils were ill that the school was temporarily removed elsewhere. It was too late for some of the victims, including the two elder Brontë sisters, Maria and Elizabeth. They returned home to die of consumption, aged just eleven and ten. Charlotte and Emily were, fortunately, removed by their father before they too succumbed, and he educated them at home.

The school was refounded at Casterton a few miles away, and has had a happier record since.

Part of the original building at Cowan Bridge has been converted into cottages, but its role as a school lives on in Charlotte Brontë's *Jane Eyre*. Lowood in the book is based on her miserable schooldays there. I suppose it could be argued that the school fulfilled its purpose, as originally defined by its founder: it played its part in equipping Charlotte and Emily to earn their own livings...

Another north-country school immortalised in a Victorian classic has been through a rather more drastic adaptation. When Charles Dickens stayed at the Unicorn Inn at **Bowes** in County

Durham (formerly in the North Riding), he watched young boys being decanted from the stagecoaches, many of them from distant parts of the country, to attend one of the many tyrannical boarding schools or 'boy farms' in the vicinity. It is thought that Dotheboys Hall is based largely on one of these establishments, run by a Mr William Shaw, who became the model for Wackford Squeers. One of the pupils at Shaw's Academy, nineteen-year-old George Taylor, became the unhappy Smike. His grave, like that of his headmaster, is in the churchyard.

After the publication of *Nicholas Nickleby* Shaw's Academy had to close. In due course, it became a café, no doubt happy to cash in on its notoriety. It has now

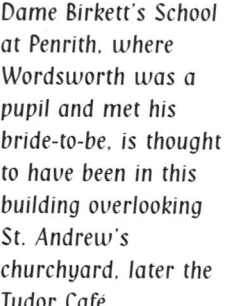

Dame Birkett's School at Penrith, where Wordsworth was a pupil and met his bride-to-be, is thought to have been in this building overlooking St. Andrew's churchyard, later the Tudor Café

been converted into a row of attractive terraced homes, where I hope the residents fare rather better than their unfortunate young predecessors. They are not allowed, however, to forget the dismal origins of their homes. The building is known throughout the village – and, indeed, there is a carved wooden notice on the wall to confirm it – as Dotheboys Hall.

Another school in the North with literary connections has been adapted so skilfully that nobody seems quite certain where it is. As a very small boy in the 1770s, William Wordsworth attended Dame Birkett's School at **Penrith** in Cumbria with his sister Dorothy. So did the daughter of a Penrith tobacconist, Mary Hutchinson, whom he later married. The young Wordsworths stayed with their grandfather, William Cookson, who was a mercer in the town. It is known that his house stood on the site of a draper's called Arnison, and it is also known that Wordsworth's cousin, John, lived in one of a pair of houses designed by Robert Adam in 1791, which later qualified as Adaptables and were converted to become Penrith Town Hall.

However, there is less certainty about Dame Birkett's School. One reference book says, rather vaguely, that 'it was possibly the building overlooking St. Andrew's churchyard.' The town guide is a little more precise; it says the school 'is believed to have been' in a Tudor house to the south-west of the church. It would seem that only Dame Birkett – and of course William Wordsworth – could provide us with the definitive answer.

The former Audley House Preparatory School near **Bicester** in Oxfordshire had a rather different significance for John Patterson, founder of the dating agency 'Dateline'; his children were pupils there when it closed. So he bought it, adapted it as a private house, renamed it Chesterton Manor, and lived there himself until his death early in 1997. One of the old classrooms became his kitchen-cum-dining-room, and was probably unrecognisable to his children, but they were certainly familiar with the coat pegs which he retained in the cloakroom, and the original toilets, which still functioned. 'You just have to crouch a little,' he used to say.

Other types of educational establishment have also become redundant over the years, because of changing social patterns. Many of the Working Men's Institutes which were set up by Victorian worthies to benefit their inferiors are no longer needed, and as most of them were constructed in heavily built-up or industrial areas, they were just absorbed into the buildings around them. But some of those in more picturesque locations were able to become Adaptables.

The Literary and Scientific Institute at **Ironbridge**, for instance, was provided for employees at the nearby ironworks who

wanted to improve themselves, in the days when this corner of Shropshire was leading the way to the Industrial Revolution. The iron bridge itself, the first in the world, and the former factories and foundries around it, now form part of a vast open-air museum, and the imposing institute has become a youth hostel. Instead of providing food for the mind, it holds a 'Heartbeat Award' for its healthy menus.

There used to be a Mechanics' Institute at **Grassington** in North Yorkshire. These days this rural community might seem a little short on mechanics but, in 1855, when the institute was provided by the Duke of Devonshire, the term covered a wider field. It was actually for the benefit of the lead miners and textile workers who lived in the area. It had a library and other basics of adult education, on similar lines to the institute at Ironbridge and many others. The locals were so grateful that they renamed it the Devonshire Institute, but that was forty years later, when the philanthropic Duke was not around to appreciate it.

The institute was built on the site of the redundant pinfold, where stray sheep and cattle were kept. In

The rather grand Literary and Scientific Institute at Ironbridge is now a youth hostel...

...while the rather less grand Mechanics' Institute at Grassington in North Yorkshire went up-market and became the Town Hall

due course it became redundant too, and in the 1920s, enlarged and adapted, it became a cinema. That, too, outlived its usefulness, and today it has resumed a rather more dignified role as Grassington Town Hall.

At the other end of the educational scale there was the Cloisters, an elaborately designed 'School for Psychology' at **Letchworth** in Hertfordshire. It was created by an heiress called Annie Jane Lawrence in 1905. She installed the green-veined marble fountain in the front hall to represent spiritual growth. There was accommodation for twenty students in the cloisters, and the building was surmounted by an impressive octagonal tower.

The School for Psychology at Letchworth in Herts, with its green-veined marble fountain representing spiritual growth. It became a Masonic Lodge – probably the only one with a green-veined marble fountain

Although she spent a great deal on the school, Annie Jane spent very little on herself. In the 1950s she said she was still living on ten shillings a week. That might have made her an interesting study for her psychology students, but by then it was too late. The Cloisters closed down in 1948 – and became a Masonic Lodge.

Educational adaptations have not all been one-way. Although there is this strong trend to close small schools in the countryside, there are also examples of big new ones being opened – in some cases, very big indeed. These, of course, are mostly privately run, and often specialise in particular fields of education. As you might expect, the Adaptables involved are about as grand as you can get.

The best-known example, perhaps, is **Stowe School** in Buckinghamshire, one of the youngest of England's great public schools. Since 1923 it has occupied the seventeenth-century ancestral home of the Dukes of Buckingham and Chandos. Some of the greatest names in English architecture were involved in building it: Robert Adam, Vanbrugh, William Kent and Grinling Gibbons. 'Capability' Brown followed Kent in laying out the four hundred acres of grounds, decorated with thirty temples and other assorted follies and today owned by the National Trust.

It is all taken very much for granted now, but it must have been quite bizarre for the young pupils of 1923 to make their way to school by walking past the Temple of Ancient Virtue, the Congreve Monument and the Temple of British Worthies, with its sixteen busts of historic figures from King Alfred through to Alexander Pope. Then they entered the massive house with its nine-hundred-foot frontage, to live and study in premises which were more used to footmen than fags, and where the only use for chalk was to polish the ballroom floor...

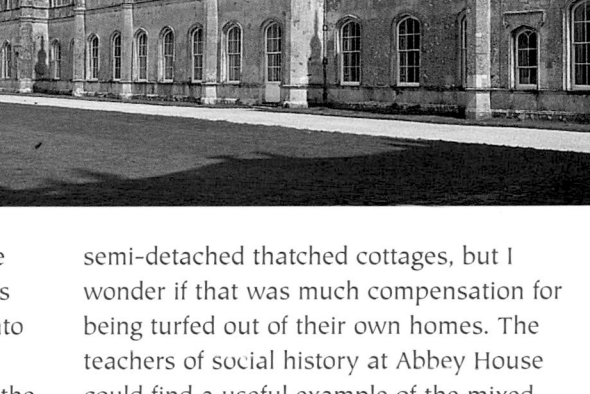

Abbey House at Milton Abbas in Dorset, now a school, was built by the Earl of Dorchester, seen with his wife in this sculpture. The Earl knocked down the village to improve the view – now the pupils can enjoy it too

The imposing entrance to Stowe School, formerly the ancestral home of the Dukes of Buckingham and Chandos. New boys must find it rather daunting

The same may have applied, although to a lesser degree, at **Milton Abbas** in Dorset where the imposing Abbey House, built by James Damer, Earl of Dorchester, in the 1770s on the site of a medieval abbey, also became a public school. Again, the grounds were laid out by 'Capability' Brown, but in this case they have been largely converted into playing fields. However, the splendid ornamental lake has been left intact, on the site of the original village, which the Earl completely demolished to improve his view.

He built a new 'model village' for the displaced inhabitants, well out of sight of his new house. It has very attractive little semi-detached thatched cottages, but I wonder if that was much compensation for being turfed out of their own homes. The teachers of social history at Abbey House could find a useful example of the mixed blessings of eighteenth-century feudalism, here on their own doorstep.

The boys who attend school at **Abberley Hall** in Hereford and Worcester have something rather different to look at, instead of the classical follies of Stowe or the ornamental lake at Milton Abbas. The hall was built in the mid-nineteenth century by the Moilliets, an Anglo-Swiss banking family, but it was soon acquired by the more down-to-earth Joneses, who made their money in the Lancashire cotton industry. In 1883 John Joseph Jones built an ornate clock tower on a prominent site outside Abberley, where everyone could see it. It was in memory of his father, but sceptics say he also wanted to impress his more illustrious neighbour, the Earl of Dudley at Witley Court.

When John Jones' Abberley Hall in Hereford and Worcester became a school the coach house was adapted as the school chapel – but nobody could do much about Jones' Folly

It is unlikely the Earl was much impressed, because he had no need to worry about keeping up with the Joneses – he had far more grandiose extravagances in his own garden. But, in the end, Abberley Hall had the last laugh, because Witley Court was turned into a ruin by a disastrous fire in 1937, while the hall still stands, albeit as an educational Adaptable. A preparatory school moved there from Blackheath in 1916 and has been there ever since. Among other changes to the buildings, the old coach house was converted into the school chapel.

The clock tower also still stands, and can be seen for miles – and heard for miles too. Its twenty bells are tuned to play over forty different peals. It is known, inevitably, as Jones's Folly.

A grand Victorian manor house which stands outside **Lyme Regis** in Dorset might well have been called Peek's Folly. Henry and Margaret Peek spent their honeymoon at Lyme Regis in 1848, and were so taken with the place that they built this vast pile on the hillside above it, with arched entrance ways, mullioned windows, mock-Tudor porch and mock-medieval tower, surmounted by a top-heavy clock house apparently perched on stilts. Inside the house is a mock banqueting hall, its ceiling as lofty as a fair-sized church.

As it turned out, 'mock' was the operative word in its other sense, because Henry Peek, while very rich, was 'in trade', and the society folk who patronised Lyme Regis did more than just patronise the Peeks; privately they mocked them, too. They were, in fact, just as supercilious as Jane Austen portrayed them in *Persuasion*. She knew all about them, because she lived in Lyme Regis while writing the book.

Mr Peek spent a quarter of a million pounds on the mansion and estate, a considerable fortune in those days, and I hope he felt it was all worthwhile, in spite of his chilly reception. Alas, judging by the portraits of him and his wife which still look down from the grand staircase, I rather doubt it.

In 1938 his descendants sold the place, and it is now the home of All Hallows School, which was formerly in Honiton. In very recent times it played host to the BBC's *Antiques Roadshow*, the programme where even society folk queue up to find out what their family heirlooms are worth – from experts in 'the trade'. I wish I could have seen Henry Peek's portrait while all that was going on; could I have detected a mocking smile?

Duncombe Park in North Yorkshire is that rarity, a stately home which became a school – then became a stately home again

Henry and Margaret Peek spent their honeymoon at Lyme Regis and liked it so much they built themselves a mansion nearby. But neither the Peeks, nor their mansion, really caught on. It is now All Hallows' School

Not every stately home that becomes a school stays that way. Duncombe Park at **Helmsley** in North Yorkshire had been the home of the Duncombes since 1689, when Sir Charles Duncombe bought it from the impoverished Duke of Buckingham. Alexander Pope was pretty sour about the sale: 'And Helmsley,' he wrote, 'once proud Buckingham's delight, Slides to a Scrivener of a City Knight.' But Sir Charles actually had a distinguished pedigree. One of his forebears was a Chancellor of the Exchequer, another was Ambassador to Sweden, and a third, Sir Saunders Duncombe, introduced a revolutionary

form of transport into England – the sedan chair…

Sir Charles's descendants became Earls of Febersham, and they occupied the great house until the First World War, when the Earl was killed in the Battle of the Somme. Duncombe Park became an Adaptable and was leased to a girls' school, and normally the story would end there. But in 1986, after three generations' absence, the present Earl and his family decided to move back into their ancestral home, restore the buildings and grounds, and open it to the public. For once a stately home educational Adaptable was re-adapted as a stately home.

Ingleborough Hall in North Yorkshire has been through three stages of educational adaptation, becoming more specialised each time. It was the home of the botanist Reginald Farrer, who introduced a hundred new plants into Europe, and wrote a few hundred thousand words about them. It was originally a

shooting lodge, extended by the Farrers and occupied by the family until the 1930s.

The first change of use happened in the last war, when a preparatory school from Broadstairs in Kent was evacuated there. Then came a period when the old West Riding Council took it over as a home for delicate children, and finally it was developed into an Outdoor Education Centre for Yorkshire schools.

One of the most historic stately homes to be adapted for special educational purposes is **Sawston Hall** in Cambridgeshire, an Elizabethan mansion which for centuries was the home of the Huddlestones, a distinguished Roman Catholic family. In 1553 they gave sanctuary to Mary Tudor, who was being pursued by the supporters of Lady Jane Grey. Mary eluded them with the Huddlestones' help, and they had their home burnt down as a result – but when Mary became Queen she had it rebuilt for them, complete with its secret priest's hole in the tower. These days it is the Cambridge Centre for Languages.

Thornycroft Hall at **Siddington**, near Macclesfield in Cheshire, has been through a succession of adaptations, and two changes of name, between the time the Thornycroft family vacated it earlier this century and its current educational use.

The Thornycrofts were Lords of the Manor from the days of Edward I, when William de Siddington gave the manor as a wedding present to his new son-in-law, for a yearly rent of sixpence. The manor was called Thornycroft so, to confuse the genealogists, the son-in-law took over the name as well.

The Thornycrofts never did much to qualify for the history books. One chronicler calls them simply 'an undramatic family'. They did not even remain a family, in a blood-line sense. In 1817 the male line came to an end with the death of Edward Thornycroft. He bequeathed the estate, after the death of his sisters, to a friend of his, the Reverend Charles Mytton, on condition he took the family name. He also left him the eighteenth-century mansion, which he had improved and enlarged.

The Mytton Thornycrofts occupied the hall until early this century. After they left it continued as a private residence, then

took on an unlikely role in the 1930s when it was acquired by the Greyhound Association. From the sporting it then switched to the spiritual; in 1952 it was bought by the Pallotine Order of German Nuns, who converted the fifty-roomed mansion into Cheshire's largest residential home for children, renaming it Pallotti Hall.

The sisters moved out in the 1970s, and the hall went on the market again. This time, however, the purchasers had more in common with their predecessors. It was bought by Opus Dei, a Catholic organisation which encourages people in all walks of life to seek holiness while following their own trade or profession.

Opus Dei rechristened the hall as Siddington Manor and turned it into an educational and conference centre. The name has since been changed back, but its activities continue. As well as religious retreats, the educational side has expanded from seminars and lectures to include courses in a separate 'hospitality training centre' – a rather grand title perhaps for a catering college. So if the Thornycrofts returned they could be sure of a warm welcome and a decent meal – but they would have to get used to having a little chapel in their family home. On the other hand, in their much earlier days, when it was common practice in stately homes, they probably had one anyway…

Finally, two incredibly grand buildings which are now international educational centres, disseminating wisdom to students from across the Atlantic. The first to undergo this dramatic adaptation was **Harlaxton Hall** in Lincolnshire, three miles outside Grantham. It was built in 1837, and one critical admirer has written: 'Any louder trumpet-blast for the Victorian age's fanfare would be deafening.' Another, equally impressed and appalled, commented: 'It is a huge thunderous caricature of the Elizabethan mansion, a nightmare-ish blown-up Burghley.'

Harlaxton is, indeed, so utterly over the top, with its vast assortment of pinnacles, gables and turrets surmounted by a domed tower, that one can't help wondering if Walt Disney was somehow involved. But it was actually created, over a period of fifteen years, by a trio called Anthony Salvin, his assistant James Deeson, and William Burn, under the patronage of George de Ligne Gregory, who acquired the estate in 1823. Mr Gregory did not want this 'prodigious pile' – another apt description – to reside in, and who can blame him. He had it built to house his art collection. When he died the collection passed to another family – 'leaving the vast echoing galleries, halls and corridors as empty as they are today.' Writers just can't stop marvelling at the place.

But that was in 1980, and they are empty no longer. Perhaps, not surprisingly, the Americans found Harlaxton irresistible. It is now part of the University of Evansville, USA. Goodness knows what sort of impression the American students get of the English way of life…

Thornycroft Hall at Siddington in Cheshire has had three different roles and two different names this century. It is now an education centre run by the Catholic organisation Opus Dei

Harlaxton Hall in Lincolnshire, with its bewildering array of pinnacles and turrets, is now home to part of the University of Evansville, USA

The other 'prodigious pile' to become part of a transatlantic university, though this time in Canada, is far more venerable, and a genuine historical gem. **Herstmonceux Castle** in East Sussex was built in 1441, not as a castle but a fortified mansion, and it remained in the same family for over 250 years. It was sold in 1708 for the fairly reasonable sum of £38,215, but it hardly proved to be a bargain, because less than seventy years later it was declared beyond repair. Much of the interior was demolished and it became an ivy-covered ruin, a great attraction for Victorian sightseers.

It was more than a century before the cavalry came riding over the hill to save it, in the form of Lieutenant-Colonel Lowther. He started a major repair programme in the 1930s, and it was continued by Sir Paul Latham. After the last war the castle caught the eye of the Admiralty, not as a potential naval base, but as a new home for the Royal Observatory. The Observatory was best known to the general public for supplying the 'pips' for the Greenwich time signal, but its primary purpose was to improve navigation by observing the heavens – which was becoming increasingly difficult through the polluted atmosphere and bright lights of East London.

The Admiralty bought the castle in 1946 for £75,000, and the first great adaptation took place. It was an observatory for forty years until the work was moved to Cambridge, and Herstmonceux was sold to a developer in 1989 for £8 million, having increased its value – on paper at any rate – a hundred times over.

But the developer, it seems, had not done his sums too well. Two years after the purchase he went bankrupt. Unabashed, the receivers nearly doubled the price again, and put it on the market for £15 million.

The next purchaser was rather more shrewd. Dr Alfred Bader was a refugee from Nazi Germany who had made good – very good indeed. He spent some time after the war at Queen's University in Montreal, where he was made very welcome and met his wife. As a not inconsiderable gesture of gratitude, Doctors Alfred and Isabelle Bader bought Herstmonceux and five hundred acres around it, for the rather more realistic price of £3.6 million, and presented it to the University as an international study centre, 'where students of Queen's can broaden their horizons and look to Europe for new ideas and inspiration.'

A lot more money had to be spent, and is being spent still, on restoring and converting the castle, but the first students arrived in 1994 and the centre was officially opened a year later. One of England's oldest buildings has thus become one of the newest educational Adaptables – right at the top of the range.

Herstmonceux Castle in East Sussex is part of Queen's University, Montreal. The 1840 etching shows it during its period of decline

Herstmonceux Castle

Military Adaptables

• • • • • • • • • •

Fortifications and other military establishments

	Location	Old use	New use(s)
1	Aldeburgh, Suffolk	Martello tower	Signalling station; billet; private residence; lookout tower; tourist attraction
2	Bridport, Dorset: The Chantry	Watchtower	Guardhouse; chantry; private residence; holiday accommodation
3	Cardington, Bedfordshire	Airship works	Aircraft hangar; RAF training centre; fire research station
4	Dacre, Cumbria: Dacre Castle	Fortified tower	Private residence
5	Egmere, Norfolk	Control tower	Private residences
6	Great Yarmouth, Norfolk: Royal Naval Hospital	Military hospital	Cavalry barracks; civilian hospital; private residences
7	Jardwick Hill, Devon: Telegraph Cottage	Signal station	Private residence
8	London: Admiralty Arch, Trafalgar Square	Naval HQ	Undecided
9	Martlesham Heath, Suffolk	Airfield	Private residences, pub and playgroup
10	Sandwich, Kent: The Barbican	Fortified gateway	Toll-gate; private residence
11	Sedgeford, Norfolk: The Magazine	Arms store	Private residence
12	St. Merryn, Cornwall	Airfield	Holiday centre
13	West Mersea, Essex: Two Sugars Café	Pill-box	Café
14	Winchester, Hampshire: Peninsula Barracks	Military barracks	Private residences

First it was swords into ploughshares...

Ever since Offa dug his dyke and Hadrian built his wall, military fortifications and ancillary buildings have played their part in English history, and then become redundant. Of the very early ones, little is left, certainly not enough to qualify as an Adaptable. Not many people could devise a new use for a ditch or a ruined wall, even if English Heritage would let them.

Norman castles are probably the earliest military buildings to survive in any numbers, and most of them can only be used as museums or tourist attractions; they are too basic, or too battered, to serve any other useful purpose. But some of the smaller defences that were built around towns and strongholds have proved a little more versatile, in particular, the gatehouses and towers which formed part of the protective town walls.

After eight or nine hundred years, nobody can be quite certain what they first looked like, what their original uses were, and how many other careers they had before they took on their current role. But it seems a fairly safe bet, for instance, that the Chantry at **Bridport** in Dorset, before it was a chantry, formed part of the defensive wall of the early-thirteenth-century harbour. In those days Bridport was a sizeable port with an inshore harbour, and the Chantry would have overlooked it. The solid construction indicates it was probably a defensive watchtower. Another theory is that it served as a lighthouse, but if that was its primary object, the massive masonry seems a little excessive.

Nowadays, it is difficult to picture it being used for either of those purposes, because by the eighteenth century the harbour had silted up, the town expanded southwards, and the watchtower-lighthouse now stands in a suburban street surrounded by rows of houses.

Its earliest name adds to the confusion. Before it became the Chantry of St. Katherine in 1368 it was known as 'Dungeness'. There is no connection with that vast expanse of shingle on the Kent coast; in this case Dungeness is probably

What was the original use of the Chantry at Bridport in Dorset – a defensive watchtower, a lighthouse, or a jail? Experts were uncertain in 1875, when this watercolour was painted, and they are none the wiser now

linked with dungeons, because yet another theory about the Chantry is that it was once a local guardhouse or prison. Quite possibly it was both, plus a watchtower and lighthouse as well, before the records confirm it was being used as a chantry, occupied by a prior who not only chanted but kept pigeons in the loft to augment his meat supply.

Henry VIII saw off the prior and the pigeons during the Dissolution. The history of the Chantry becomes obscure again for a century or so, until it became a dwelling house. In 1979 it fell empty and was looked after by the local Civic Society, until the Vivat Trust leased it in 1985 and converted part of it into holiday accommodation.

The gatehouses of town walls can make quite convenient Adaptables. At **Sandwich** in Kent, for instance, where there have been defensive fortifications since Roman times, the ramparts built on the line of the old town walls still stand, and so do the town gates. The Barbican, as the name suggests, was once the main fortified gateway, guarding the approach across the river. More recently it acted as a toll-gate, then it became a private house.

During the Border raids in the early fourteenth century, when the Scots and the English regularly invaded each other to steal cattle and thump the local peasantry, a line of fortified pele towers was built on the English side of the border for protection against the Scottish marauders. One which still stands, almost unchanged in appearance since medieval times, is **Dacre Castle** in Cumbria, built like a fortress with walls sixty-six feet high. All it contained was a large hall on the ground floor, a room above, and little chambers in the corner towers. Its adaptation began in the seventeenth century, when the Lord of Dacre had large windows put in to provide more light. Over the years the interior has

been altered and modernised to make it a comfortable private residence.

When the English were not fighting off invaders, they were often fighting each other. Most of the defences they needed were already there – castles, fortified mansions, town walls – but one unusual military building in Norfolk may have been purpose-built for the Civil War. Just outside the little village of **Sedgeford**, not far from the Royalist stronghold of the le Strange family at Hunstanton, stands the Magazine, an arms store which is now a Grade II listed private house.

Its appearance does not immediately suggest a military store. The elegant two-storey building has stone quoins, parapets and mullioned windows, with a rather odd first-floor window tucked discreetly between two chimneys. It looks more ecclesiastical than military – maybe it was already an Adaptable from some previous, more peaceful, existence.

When it came on the market recently, the estate agents seemed to be uncertain which side in the Civil War used it. One advertisement described it as 'a former Cromwellian arms store', but

Two early fortifications, now private residences: the Barbican at Sandwich in Kent, once a fortified gateway...

...and Dacre Castle in Cumbria, one of a chain of pele towers built to fend off marauding Scots

a subsequent report credited it to the Royalists, and that seems far more likely, with the le Stranges not far away. As for its appearance, perhaps they designed it like that quite intentionally, so Cromwell's men would not recognise it – which would be rather sensible, having built it in the middle of open countryside, instead of, much more conveniently, in Hunstanton itself. If they really did build it, that is...

Anyway, everybody seems to be agreed it was an arms store for somebody – and with an asking price of £129,950, a distinctly up-market arms store at that.

During the Napoleonic Wars, an extensive range of military establishments were built in England, from magnificent Georgian hospitals to gloomy little Martello towers. There were over a hundred Martellos, extending round the coast from Hampshire to Suffolk. They were started in 1796, when there seemed an imminent threat of invasion and, even after the French fleet was defeated at Trafalgar, the towers kept on multiplying – just in case.

The biggest and most northerly one, at **Aldeburgh** in Suffolk, was not finished until ten years after Trafalgar. Like all the others, it never saw active service – but it has seen a variety of action since.

The name makes it sound like some kind of ice-cream – 'Just one Martello...' – but the name actually comes from Point

The Magazine at Sedgeford in Norfolk may look like a chapel, but it was built as an arms store during the Civil War

Mortella in Corsica, where the French built the original. The British fleet attacked it in 1794 and found it impregnable, so the British commander, Lord Hood, borrowed the idea and had it copied over here. Presumably the name was changed slightly to avoid infringing copyright...

Nelson himself is said to have suggested the Aldeburgh site, though he died before building began. Three-quarters of a million bricks were brought by barge from London, and the total cost was some £10,000, equivalent to fifty times that amount today. There seemed to be no great urgency – it took six years to complete.

The tower had four cannon on the roof, five more on an emplacement in front of it, and a garrison of thirty to man them, but they were never fired in anger. In 1856 it was finally decided that the French weren't coming; the garrison moved out and the coastguards moved in. Then it was used as a signalling station, and in the First World War the army used it as a

No mistaking the Martello tower at Aldeburgh in Suffolk, even though it has now been adapted as an unlikely holiday cottage

Not many wartime pill-boxes have proved useful Adaptables, but the one on West Mersea beach in Essex has become a successful concrete café

billet. After the war nobody could think what to do with it next, until it was bought by Lord Redesdale, head of the famous and sometimes eccentric Mitford family, presumably for use as a rather bizarre summer retreat.

Subsequently, according to official records, 'it was owned by either Debenham or Freebody'; perhaps one of these well-known trading partners decided to decorate and restore the tower using goods from their own store. Certainly, it was furnished lavishly, gas heating was installed, and a sun-room built on the roof.

The luxury did not last for long. In the Second World War the Martello was again taken over by the military as a lookout tower and signalling station, and afterwards was allowed to fall derelict.

Finally, in 1971 the Landmark Trust bought it, 'sadly damaged', and restored it all over again. The by now disintegrating sun room was removed, the brickwork was repaired and the parapet made safe. Instead of cannon on the roof there are now holiday-makers admiring the view. But the Martello tower still looks as forbidding and impregnable as it did in Nelson's day. As one visitor noted in the logbook: 'Rule Britannia has an especial feeling sung here...'

There have been few successful attempts to adapt the twentieth-century successor to

the Martello tower, the coastal pill-box. Nobody seems too keen to convert these unsightly chunks of concrete into holiday homes. But, on Mersea Island in Essex, a pill-box on the beach at **West Mersea** has been used for years as a seasonal seaside café, and in the summer sunshine, with ice-cream posters decorating the concrete walls, tables and chairs outside, and a throng of suntanned holiday-makers in bathing trunks and bikinis, the 'Two Sugars Café' can look almost festive...

While the Martello was being built at Aldeburgh, further north round the East Anglian coast a much grander military building was taking shape. The Royal Naval Hospital at **Great Yarmouth** is also said to owe its existence there to Lord Nelson, who

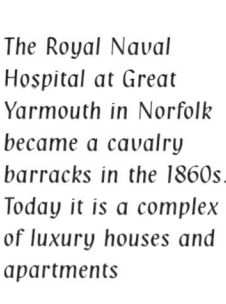

The Royal Naval Hospital at Great Yarmouth in Norfolk became a cavalry barracks in the 1860s. Today it is a complex of luxury houses and apartments

The Peninsula Barracks at Winchester look as martial as ever, but they are privately occupied now

was advisor to the naval committee which carried out the preliminary work. He is also said to have visited the first patients, 'casualties from the Battle of Copenhagen', but if he did, it could only have been in spirit. At the time of the first Battle of Copenhagen the hospital's foundations had only just been laid and, by the time the second one was fought, Nelson had been dead for two years. But no matter. In Norfolk everyone knows that their local hero had exceptional powers.

The hospital is a quite magnificent complex of Georgian terraces, four of which surround a grassed courtyard to form an elegant square. Instead of the humble London bricks used in the Martello, all the buildings are dressed with Portland stone. The approach is just as impressive; the main drive passes through an arch in the northern guardhouse, then across a yard into the main courtyard. It is, in fact, an oasis of luxurious calm which must have been relished by the wounded who were brought there direct from battle.

Subsequently, it became a cavalry barracks, then a civilian hospital. When it was vacated in the early 1990s it became an obvious candidate as an up-market Adaptable. Kit Martin, a developer specialising in the conversion of stately homes into smaller houses and

apartments, did the same thing with the Royal Naval Hospital. The terraces around the main square were divided into forty separate dwellings, the guardhouses became cottages, and the rest of the buildings on the ten-acre site were converted, too. But the hospital chapel has been preserved for the use of the residents, and there are plans to use one building as a museum of memorabilia to commemorate – who else? – Lord Nelson...

A similar transformation has taken place at another imposing military establishment from the same period, the Peninsula Barracks at **Winchester** in Hampshire, but in that case there is no local hero to be commemorated by a museum. Otherwise, the adaptation has been much the same, on an even grander scale. Behind the magnificent pillared frontage bearing the royal coat of arms, the soldiers' quarters have been converted into over a hundred houses and flats – and there is a restaurant instead of a canteen.

In total contrast to all this large-scale military grandeur, humbler even than the Martello towers, there were the little buildings which operated the then-primitive telegraph system between the Admiralty and the defence establishments around the coast. They were strung out across the countryside much as telegraph poles are today, but instead of messages being transmitted electronically, they were signalled by hand.

These telegraph stations looked rather like outsize cricket scoreboards, simple wooden huts with a huge frame on the roof, twenty feet high, containing slatted shutters. Levers were pulled in the hut below to convey signals to the lookout at the next telegraph station, ten miles away. Each combination of shutters could represent a different letter and, like signal flags at sea, there were some which conveyed complete phrases. But not all the phrases in the manual were very helpful on land; it would have been rather disconcerting, for instance, for a signaller on a hilltop in Hertfordshire to receive the order: 'Steer North'...

Working these shutters must have been exhausting work, even in phrases. By the end of a long message the operator must have been – well, shuttered. But life became simpler when someone invented the semaphore, with just two signal arms on a mast, then in 1847 the new electric telegraph made the whole system redundant anyway.

The signal huts had not been built to last for posterity, and most of them have long since disappeared. Just a name sometimes remains, like Telegraph Hill on the old Icknield Way near Lilley in Hertfordshire. And, just occasionally, you may find a Telegraph Cottage, like the one on Jardwick Hill, just outside **Plympton** in Devon. Once it was in a chain of thirty signal stations between Plymouth and London. Today, it is a private house. Sadly, the wooden frame on the roof has long since disappeared, but there are still beams remaining in the attic which formed part of the old signalling system. It would be nice to think that, for its final message, someone thought of sending the signal 'England expects...'

This innocuous cottage outside Plympton in Devon was one of a chain of telegraph stations, with a block of wooden signalling shutters above the roof, twenty feet high

There is another survival from the Napoleonic Wars which, perhaps, does not qualify as a full-scale Adaptable, since it has merely been adapted from military to civilian use, but because so many people immediately think of it in this context, it should not be omitted.

Dartmoor Prison was built to contain French prisoners of war, not by the nineteenth-century equivalent of the Ministry of Defence, but by a rich industrialist who used the prisoners as cheap labour. At one time there were nine thousand French prisoners enjoying the hospitality of Sir Thomas Tyrwhitt – he did after all provide the luxury of cast-iron pillars from which they could hang their hammocks – and they built much of Princetown for him. Then the wars ended, they all went home, and the building that served as their prisoner-of-war camp was left empty, along with much of Princetown itself. Thirty years later it was adapted – though not much adaptation was required to house long-term criminals. It has done so ever since.

The twentieth century brought a new form of warfare, and a new kind of military installation to go with it. Fighting could now take place in the air, and planes continue to battle in the skies to this day. But one form of flying machine was shorter-lived, and the establishments built to cater for it were the first to become redundant and qualify as Adaptables.

In 1917 the Admiralty purchased a site at **Cardington** in Bedfordshire to develop its answer to the German Zeppelin. The first airship it produced there, the R31, was built just in time to see the war end in 1918, but the Admiralty, and then the Air Ministry, kept the production line going in what became known as the Royal Airship Works. In 1921 the newest model, the R32, crashed soon after it was built with the

The giant hangars at Cardington in Bedfordshire once housed the ill-fated R101 and its sister airship the R100. One crashed, the other was scrapped

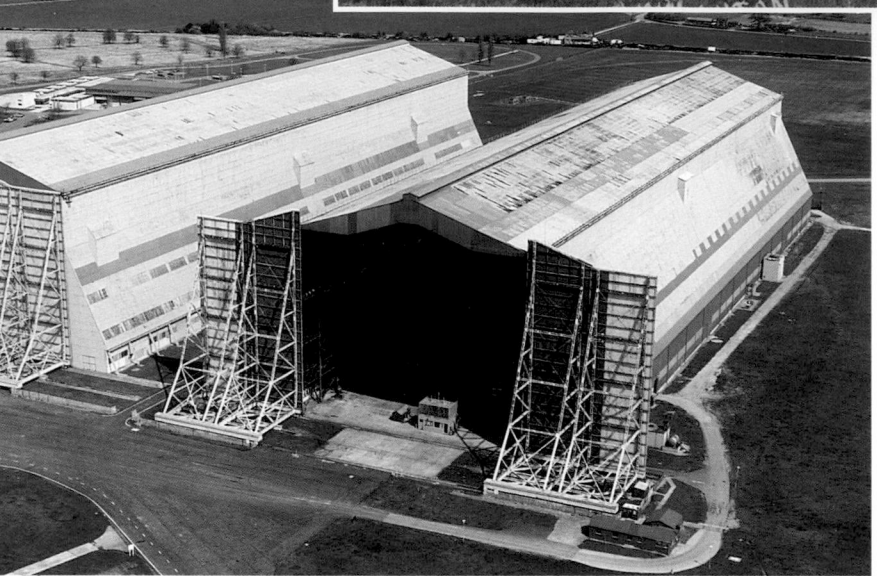

R100 was broken up and sold for scrap. The two hangars were used to store aircraft until the Second World War, when the balloon really did go up – several of them, in fact, but rather smaller than the R100 and R101. Cardington became an RAF training centre for balloon operators, and twenty-two thousand of them passed through the giant hangars.

There was a balloon unit there until 1967, and research work continued for a few years after that, but in 1972 Hangar 2 said a final goodbye to balloons and became a fire research station.

In 1993 it had its final adaptation, to accommodate the Building Research Establishment, and the former home of the R100 became the largest enclosed laboratory in the world, over one hundred and fifty feet high with a floor space of five acres. Ironically it is used, among other things, for creating experimental fires and explosions, the very hazards which the early balloonists tried to avoid.

Not many reminders of the airship age survived after the last war, but rural England is bespattered with reminders of the wartime aircraft age. Some RAF stations are still in use, but in many cases the buildings survive in other roles. Old hangars and Nissen huts have become barns or store-rooms, married quarters

loss of forty-four lives. Knowing what was to happen later, that might have been seen as an omen.

But the building programme went on. The existing balloon shed was enlarged, and another one was brought from a former airship base at Pulham Market in Norfolk to be erected beside it, to accommodate bigger and – supposedly – better airships. From Hangar 1 in 1930 the R101 emerged for its maiden flight; it crashed in France and burst into flames, with a death toll of nearly fifty.

This time the message got through. Its sister airship in Hangar 2 did make a trial flight to Montreal, but the airship programme was then abandoned, and the

The former control tower at RAF North Creake in Norfolk is now a private house, but it still has the observation balcony where operations officers watched for planes to return

have been privatised, groups of airfield buildings have been absorbed in industrial parks.

Perhaps the most distinctive Adaptables on these old airfields are the control towers, which evoke so many memories for wartime fliers. It takes some ingenuity to adapt a control tower as a residence, but one successful example is at **Egmere** in Norfolk, the home of RAF North Creake during the war. It was originally a decoy airfield, with dummy planes and hangars illuminated at night to distract German pilots from the real sites nearby. But later it was a base for Halifax and Stirling bombers, which often had the unenviable duty of dropping foil strips ahead of the main stream of bombers, to jam the enemy radar.

After the war the task of RAF North Creake was more depressing than hazardous: it consisted of receiving and then scrapping redundant Mosquito aircraft until, in 1947, the base itself was made redundant. These days it has been taken over by a major agricultural seed merchant, with the former living-quarters now occupied by some of its staff.

The control tower, standing beside what used to be the perimeter track, is still unmistakable, even though it now has a sloping roof instead of the original flat one, which had a wooden lookout on top. It still has a balcony on three sides at first-floor level, and it is not too difficult to picture uniformed figures standing on it, watching for the bombers to return. But inside, the radio room which kept in contact with the aircraft, the operations room and all the other duty rooms have been converted into a six-bedroomed house. When it came on the market recently – 'thought to be the only such building converted to residential use in Norfolk' – the asking price was nearly £130,000.

Some entire airfields have been adapted to a new civilian use. A former Royal Naval Air Station near **St. Merryn** in Cornwall, for instance, found a new use as a holiday centre. And perhaps the most comprehensive conversion was at **Martlesham Heath** in Suffolk, where Sir Douglas Bader flew with 242 Squadron in 1941. The old airfield is now a new village, with the Douglas Bader pub standing beside what used to be the runway.

The Royal Naval Air Station near St. Merryn in Cornwall has a rather more frivolous role now, as a holiday centre

Sir Douglas opened it himself in 1979, even though he was a teetotaller. Among the original buildings which survive, the wireless station is now a private residence and the control tower is used by the village playgroup. The children are probably oblivious to the significance of the windsock which still flies nearby.

Perhaps the most common military Adaptables are the old wooden or corrugated-iron huts, some dating from the First World War, which have been uprooted and replanted for use as village halls, Scout huts, 'temporary' classrooms and the like. These are gradually disappearing as they get beyond repair and new sources of grants, like the National Lottery and the Millennium Fund, have become available.

However, some Ministry of Defence buildings are still coming on the market, as costs continue to be cut and personnel are 'rationalised'. The most spectacular military Adaptable currently available must surely be Admiralty Arch, the massive edifice in **Trafalgar Square** which spans the entrance to St. James's Park.

It was built in 1910 as a memorial to Queen Victoria and housed Britain's naval chiefs until the axe fell on their Lordships, like everyone else. It has been empty since 1994. When it first qualified as an

Adaptable the Government proposed selling it to a developer for conversion into luxury flats or a hotel, but there was an understandable outcry and the idea was soon dropped.

The problem with this unique building is that it is very awkward to adapt. In spite of its grand exterior, it is mostly a jumble of small offices which are inadequate for modern purposes and a nightmare in terms of fire and safety regulations. As an added complication, the First Sea Lord has a flat inside the Arch.

The latest idea is to make it the headquarters for bodies like the London Tourist Board, with part of it, perhaps, converted into a naval museum, but there is probably still time to suggest something else. So, if you can think of an appropriate use for one of London's best-known but most impractical landmarks, complete with a resident Admiral, you could earn yourself a niche, if not in Admiralty Arch itself, at least in the history of military Adaptables.

The RAF station at Martlesham Heath in Suffolk, where Douglas Bader once flew, has been transformed into a new village; the control tower is now used by the village playgroup

England's best-known military Adaptable? Admiralty Arch in Trafalgar Square is awaiting a new role

Healthy Adaptables

● ● ● ● ● ● ● ● ● ●

Leper hospitals, bath-houses, hospitals, sanatoria – and morgues

	Location	Old use	New use(s)
1	Barsby, Leicestershire: Godson's Folly	Mortuary chapel	Private residence
2	Buxton, Derbyshire: Devonshire Royal Hospital	Stables	Hospital
3	Cromer, Norfolk: Bath House Hotel	Bath-house	Hotel
	Overstrand Road	School	Doctor's surgery; private residence
	Cottage hospital	Hospital	Conservative Club
	Ambulance station	Ambulance station	Jehovah's Witness HQ
4	Great Yarmouth, Norfolk	Bath-house	Hotel; amusement arcade
5	Hoar Cross, Staffordshire: Hoar Cross Hall	Stately home	Health spa
6	Launceston, Cornwall	Hospital	Food distribution centre; offices
7	Norwich, Norfolk	Mortuary	Restaurant
	Sprowston	Hospital	Dovecote; barn; cottages; parish hall; library
8	Seaham, Durham: Seaham Hall	Stately home	Sanatorium; hospital; hotel; nursing home; flats
9	Skipton, North Yorkshire	Hospital	Private residences and holiday accommodation
10	Sunderland Point, Lancashire	Bath-house	Holiday attraction; garage; equipment store
11	Threlkeld, Cumbria: Far End Row Farm	Sanatorium	Youth hostel; field studies centre

Adaptation can be good for your health

Ever since the Romans constructed their elaborate baths complex at the city they called *Aquae Sulis*, and which we know more simply as Bath, England has had establishments which were constructed specifically for the purpose of improving our health. And ever since the Saxons knocked most of it down, and adapted the rest as up-market accommodation for their families and animals, many other health-care buildings have become redundant and qualified as Adaptables.

Advances in medical science have meant new specialised medical treatment in new specialised buildings – even if, in the early days, it was just a purpose-built hut outside a village to isolate infectious diseases. In due course, as more advances were made, they joined the ranks of health-care Adaptables.

The original 'hospitals' were primarily charitable homes for the elderly and infirm, the earlier version of the almshouse, but medical hospitals as we know them only started to appear in any great numbers in the eighteenth century. 'The age of Philanthropy gave sober expression to its feelings, just as the age of Faith had sunk its soul in the stones of cloisters and cathedral aisles', as G.M. Trevelyan so weightily puts it in his *English Social History*.

In the course of that century about a hundred and fifty new hospitals and dispensaries were established, including many of the great teaching hospitals. Since then, some diseases have been wiped out completely, and new methods of treatment have developed for those that remain. Many of the specialist hospitals – asylums for the mentally ill, isolation hospitals for infectious diseases, sanatoria for tuberculosis patients – have had to change their roles.

That includes some of the original 'hospitals', even though the poor, of course, are always with us. Many of the medieval hospitals are still functioning as old people's homes, their facilities vastly improved, but often the original premises still in use. There are exceptions, though, like **Beamsley Hospital**, near Skipton in North Yorkshire.

This has the standard row of almshouses just off the road, but behind them stands a much more unusual building – a one-storey circular stone edifice with a stunted little tower in the centre, flanked by a couple of tall chimneys. It looks like a Templar's chapel gone wrong and, indeed, there is a little chapel in the centre under the tower, but seven rooms open off it, originally occupied by seven deserving women. Their only way in or out of the building was through the chapel – the next best thing, presumably, to a full monastic life.

The hospital was founded by the Countess of Cumberland in 1593 and continued to function for nearly four hundred years. In the 1970s, however, the supply of monastically minded deserving women must have run low and, while the almshouses were let to long-term tenants, the circular building at the back was adapted as a holiday cottage. It must be rather like living in a very squat lighthouse, but the former chapel gives quite a different meaning to 'seeing the light'.

The entrance to Beamsley Hospital in North Yorkshire. where a chapel surrounded by seven rooms is now a holiday cottage

The Roman health spa at **Bath** is not really adaptable for anything, and it has been carefully preserved in its original form. So have many other famous spas that came much later, treasured because of their historic significance, and some of them still function. On the other hand, their more humble relative, the bath-house, has had to join the ranks of the Adaptables, or perish.

They are mostly around the coast, built in the days when sea bathing was still something of an adventure. It did, in fact, take some time for doctors to recognise the health-giving qualities of sea air and salt water. Trevelyan wrote in his usual solemn style: 'The sea was the Englishman's common, his way to market, his fishpond, his heritage. But no one sought the seaside for the refreshment it could give to the spirit of man.'

When they did, many people still preferred to enjoy the benefits of the seaside from the comparative comfort of a bath-house. In Georgian times, for instance, **Cromer** in Norfolk already had a marine baths on the beach before 1824, when a local entrepreneur called Simeon Simons extended a reading room on the promenade to set up a genteel bath-house in competition. He aimed unerringly at the top end of the market, and he responded to any attempt at undercutting by his rival with the sort of publicity that Harrods or Claridges might be proud of: 'S. Simons begs to inform the Nobility and Gentry visiting Cromer that having received repeated testimonials to the Superiority of his Baths as regards both Respectability, Cleanliness and Comfort, he finds it unnecessary to reduce his charges.'

In 1836 the elements took a hand, and a storm wrecked both the Marine Baths and Mr Simons's bath-house. But while the Marine Baths were moved away from the

beach, Mr Simons rebuilt his bath-house on the same exposed site, and this time it stood firm. He continued in business for another thirty years, until his death. A few years later it was enlarged to become a licensed hotel, and the Bath House Hotel still stands on the promenade today, with an equally ingenious line in publicity material: 'Out of season, come and see a wild sea from the warmth and comfort of the Bath House!'

The bath itself has long since gone, but Simeon Simons would be gratified to see on the front wall the old-fashioned lift pump he used to operate, with the inscription: 'The original Bath House pump, installed 1834.'

Incidentally, there are three other health-care Adaptables in **Cromer** which have been converted rather more recently than the Bath House Hotel. One of them, a doctor's surgery in

The Bath House on the promenade at Cromer in Norfolk, which really was a bath-house before it became a hotel. The pump dates back to those days

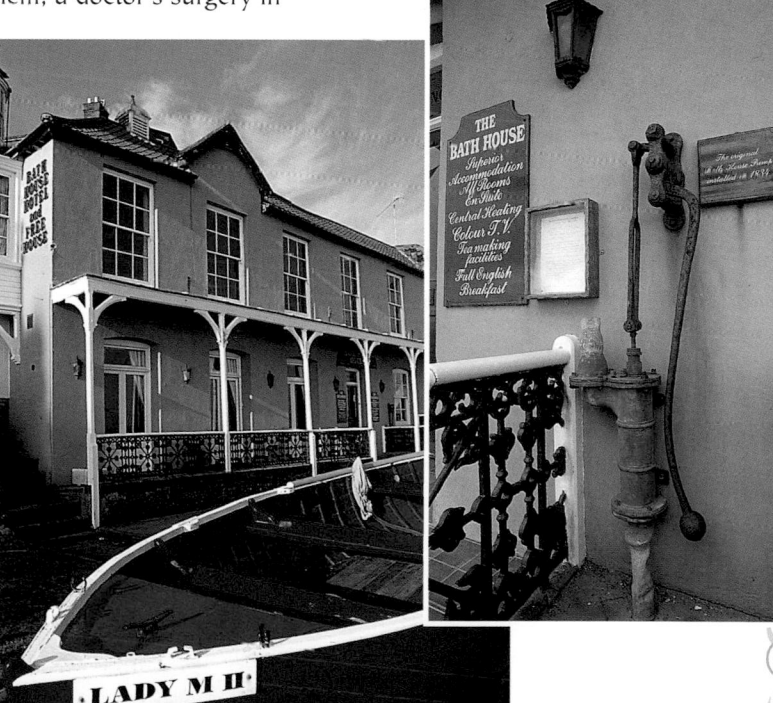

first consisted of two big plunge baths with dressing-rooms, where ladies and gentlemen changed and bathed separately, and a 'heat room' with big windows on each side. The sea water was raised every high tide by horse power – literally.

Sea-water bathing became sociable as well as medicinal and, during the next ten years, a new owner added an assembly room overlooking the sea, where the ladies and gentlemen were able to mingle over cups of coffee. In due course, it was a natural development to turn the place into the Bath Hotel, which thrived until the turn of this century.

Then came a more dramatic adaptation. A new owner, Michael Gilbert, knocked down the stables and replaced them with a circus building, the still-famous Hippodrome, and he demolished part of the hotel to provide a forecourt. Where the bath-house and assembly rooms used to stand, there is now an amusement arcade.

But not every bath-house was built for the benefit of health-seeking holiday-makers. They could be in a much less desirable location and fulfil a much more down-to-earth function. One example was at **Sunderland Point** in Lancashire, now a remote and lonely community connected to the mainland by a causeway, which is often covered at high tide, but in the eighteenth century it was the main seaport for Lancaster. It was also one of the principal English ports involved in the slave trade, and conditions on board the slave

Overstrand Road, was itself an Adaptable. It started life in 1821 as a Free School, and is now a private house, but memories of its earlier roles still survive. The doctor who used the surgery recalls how some of his older patients used to point out the exact spot in the surgery where the headmaster had caned them.

In addition, the former cottage hospital at Cromer is now the local Conservative Club, and the former ambulance station was adapted in 1996, in the space of a single weekend by a party of skilled volunteers, into the Kingdom Hall, headquarters of the Jehovah's Witnesses.

Like the one at Cromer, bath-houses usually occupied premier positions on the sea front at popular holiday resorts and, when they became redundant, there was no shortage of ideas for converting them into other seaside attractions. This happened to the handsome bath-house which was erected on waste ground near the jetty at **Great Yarmouth** in 1760. It

The bath-house at Great Yarmouth became the Bath Hotel at the turn of the century; today its appearance has rather changed

The bath-house at Sunderland Point in Lancashire was used by slaves and ships' crews to clean up and de-louse after weeks at sea. In 1900 it was part of a hotel, and today it is just a workmen's store

ships were almost as appalling for the crews as for the human cargo.

The bath-house, therefore, provided an essential health service for sailors as well as slaves. This is where they shed the grime – and often the lice – accumulated during many squalid weeks at sea. It was situated in a group of warehouses and other buildings on the Point, owned by a wealthy merchant trading with the West Indies.

After the slave trade was abolished, early in the nineteenth century, Sunderland Point felt the pinch, but it revived again when sea bathing became the vogue. One of the warehouses became the Maxwell Arms, and the bath-house followed the example of its more respectable counterparts in seaside resorts elsewhere, and became a holiday attraction. But, in more recent times, the holiday-makers disappeared too, and the bath-house was adapted to serve as a garage. These days it has an even humbler role as a store for workmen's equipment.

In medieval times there were other ways of being considered 'unclean', which no bath-house could put right. Leprosy was still prevalent in England, and the only form of treatment was to isolate lepers in a lazar house – named after the Lazarus in the parable, who was brought daily to the rich man's gate – and leave them there to die. Many big towns and cities had a lazar house outside the gates, but very few are still standing; they were not exactly built for posterity.

One exception is in **Sprowston**, now virtually a suburb of Norwich, but in those days well outside the city. The Hospital of St. Mary Magdalene by Norwich, as it was officially called, was founded early in the eleventh century by Bishop Herbert de Losinga, who also founded Norwich Cathedral. The building that survives, which served primarily as the chapel, but also accommodated the lepers in a gallery

127

Two stages in the adaptation of the Lazar House on the outskirts of Norwich, long after its days as a leper hospital. In the last century it was called the Magdalen Chapel; in 1923 it was opened as a branch library

over the nave, is now the Lazar House Library. But there were numerous other uses in between.

The hospital was closed during the Reformation. Any lepers or paupers who still lived there were shunted into other hospitals. It was sold in 1548 to a local lawyer, John Corbett, who was enlarging his estate at Sprowston, and he converted it into a dovecote, installing his doves where the lepers used to sleep. But, within a year, Robert Kett launched his rebellion against the local landowners, and one of his targets was John Corbett. His men were persuaded not to burn down Corbett's house but, instead, according to a contemporary writer, 'they spoiled his goods and defaced a dovehouse of his, which had been a chappell...'

Just how badly they defaced it is not recorded, but the damage could not have been too serious, because when the building was next mentioned, a hundred and fifty years later, it was functioning as a barn. A succession of farmers used it at harvest time, driving corn-wagons through the great doors in one wall. Then it was converted into cottages and, when the farm was split up and the farmhouse demolished, in about 1900, the old leper hospital was in danger of being demolished too.

It was saved by a local antiquary and restored by Eustace Gurney, the local

squire, for use as a parish hall, 'St. Magdalen Chapel Working Men's Club'. The restoration was not entirely sympathetic – the architect gave the old Norman building a mock Tudor entrance and windows – but at least it survived.

In 1921 Sir Eustace, as he was by then, presented the old place to Norwich Corporation, to be adapted as the city's first branch public library. It was opened two years late by a local dignitary, H.R. Copeman, who recalled that the Lazar House had been founded 'for the purpose of ministering to suffering humanity and the healing of the body', and it was appropriate it should finally be dedicated 'to the furnishing and nourishing of the mind'. It has been furnishing and nourishing local minds ever since.

Leprosy has now been wiped out in this country, but another disease which afflicted our forebears lingers on, though it can now be controlled. It used to be called consumption. These days we have a longer word for it, tuberculosis, but mostly we call it TB. In the big industrial cities in the last century it wiped out vast sections of the poorer population, until doctors grasped the idea that what their patients primarily needed was a dose of good fresh air.

That was little consolation to those who had no way of moving out of the dust-clogged, fume-filled atmosphere that surrounded them, but richer folk who contracted the disease made tracks for the hills, where sanatoria were built to accommodate them. Some of these were subsidised by charities and medical institutions to give poorer patients a bed, but mostly only the fresh air was free.

One of the pioneers involved in all this at the turn of the century was the National Association for the Prevention of Consumption and Other Forms of Tuberculosis. In 1902 the Cumberland branch bought Far End Row Farm, a thousand feet up on the south-facing slope of Saddleback, above **Threlkeld** in Cumbria. Saddleback is also called Blencathra, and even if you don't know Blencathra you will 'ken John Peel', founder and Master of the Blencathra Pack, which still hunts in that area.

John Peel had no need of a sanatorium, but a lot of city folk did, and the Association's venture was in immediate demand. It opened in 1904, only the second of its kind in the country, with twenty patients, no electricity, no running water – but lots and lots of fresh air. Even in the worst gale or snowstorm the windows were kept wide open. And there

were quite a lot of windows. During the Second World War it took workmen a fortnight to black them out – all eight hundred of them. By then there were eighty patients, so the ratio worked out at ten windows to a patient – all wide open.

By the end of the war, however, streptomycin and other forms of treatment had been introduced, and cures could be effected without the permanent chattering of teeth. For the first time in the sanatorium's history, heating was installed, and it became a long-stay hospital for the elderly and infirm.

Other sanatoria underwent similar adaptations, or were closed altogether. But the one on Blencathra, in the heart of superb walking and climbing country, fared rather better. In 1975 it was offered to the National Parks Authority and became a youth hostel. Then, in 1990, it welcomed its first students as one of eleven Field Studies Council Centres in England and Wales. Its cure was complete.

There has been no reprieve, though, for some of the smaller hospitals which have closed in recent years because of inadequate facilities, outdated premises, or that bane of modern commercial existence, 'rationalisation'. Cottage hospitals like the

The Field Studies Centre on Saddleback in Cumbria, as it is today, and when it was a tuberculosis sanatorium – with all the windows wide open, of course

The cottage hospital at Launceston in Cornwall, like many others, was declared redundant; it has been converted into offices

Seaham Hall in County Durham was a stately home in stately grounds when Byron stayed there. It became a sanatorium, then a chest hospital; now it has to find a new use

one at Cromer, now a Conservative Club, have been among the casualties, and even in larger towns like **Launceston** in Cornwall, for instance, the original hospital was closed down by the borough council during the last war and used as a food distribution centre. It is now the offices of a firm of accountants.

But it has not all been one-way for health-care Adaptables. Some stately homes have become hospitals, often providing specialist forms of treatment. **Seaham Hall** in County Durham is one such example. It played a pioneering role in the development of cardiac surgery in the 1960s but, alas, its future is now uncertain.

It was in an attractive setting when Sir Ralph and Lady Judith Milbanke built the hall in 1792 – but Lord Byron didn't seem to think so. He married Sir Ralph's daughter Anne Isabella in 1815, and it was fairly typical of him that at this ceremony it was the bridegroom, not the bride, who arrived late – by several days. It should have taken place before Christmas in the parish church, but he failed to turn up until January, and it was held, instead, in the drawing-room at Seaham Hall.

Byron spent three months there, and seemed to dislike every minute. 'Upon this dreary coast,' he wrote, 'we have nothing but county meetings and shipwrecks. I have this day dined upon fish, which probably dined upon the crews of several colliers lost in the gales.'

Even when his bride asked him to write an epitaph for her pet dog, Prim, he was still pretty sour. 'Alas poor Prim, I'm sorry for him,' he wrote, which hardly rated as immortal verse. He did not exactly improve matters by adding: 'I wish by half, it had been Sir Ralph.'

With an attitude like this to his father-in-law it was not entirely surprising that his marriage lasted for less than a year. Perhaps to get away from the scene of this unfortunate liaison, the Milbankes moved out of Seaham Hall a few years

later. They sold it to the third Marquess of Londonderry, who used it as his headquarters to mastermind the development of the East Durham Coalfield and Seaham Harbour.

This would not have improved the view from the hall, but the Londonderrys did not seem to mind too much. It was, after all, their personal empire. They lived there for a hundred years, until the seventh Marquess, perhaps not quite so thrilled by collieries and blast furnaces, tried to sell it in 1923. Prospective buyers were not thrilled by them either, so he gave Seaham Hall to Durham County Council as a hospital. In 1928 it opened as a sanatorium for tuberculosis sufferers; presumably there was sufficient fresh sea air to counteract any dust from the mines.

Like other sanatoria it became redundant in the 1940s, and it was transferred to the National Health Service, specialising in heart and chest complaints. It remained in the forefront of cardiac surgery for thirty years, and there was a public outcry when it was closed in 1978. But its days of glory were over, and it went through a difficult period when all kinds of roles were suggested for it, from luxury flats to a refuge for Vietnamese boat people. But they all failed to materialise.

It was six years before it re-opened as a thirty-five bedroomed hotel, with backing from a Middle Eastern sheikh, but that only lasted until 1988. Then it went back into the health-care business and became a nursing home. That, too, closed in 1995 and, as I write, it still stands empty. Only the stable block is serving a useful purpose, having been converted into flats.

Hoar Cross Hall in Staffordshire has a happier story to tell as a health-care Adaptable. It was built in 1860, complete with private chapel, by Hugo Meynell Ingram and, three years later, he brought

there his bride Emily, daughter of Viscount Halifax. Unfortunately, he died young, and his widow rebuilt the parish church in his memory. It contains alabaster monuments to both of them, alhough there is a private family chapel at the hall.

The chapel has been carefully preserved, along with the oak-panelled long gallery and the dining-room with its gilded ceiling and crystal chandeliers, and there are still four-posters in some of the bedrooms, but these days the four-posters are fitted with waterbeds, and there are also five hydrotherapy massage baths, a whirlpool spa, a sauna, solaria, and a cruciform swimming pool. It is, in fact, Hoar Cross Hall Health Spa Resort, which claims to be the first in England to offer a complete range of Continental thalassotherapy treatment. Thalassotherapy has no connection, I gather, with roping steers in the Wild West.

If all this healthy treatment had been at Hoar Cross Hall in the days of Hugo Meynell Ingram the poor chap might have lived a little longer. Or perhaps not.

As well as stately homes which have become health-care Adaptables, a set of stately stables has achieved the same distinction. Appropriately, it happened in **Buxton** in Derbyshire, which first became health-conscious when the Romans discovered the medicinal value of its waters, nearly twenty centuries ago. When the fifth Duke of Devonshire decided to establish Buxton as Derbyshire's answer to Bath, he commissioned the architect John

Stately stables at Buxton in Derbyshire which are now used as a hospital. They once housed a hundred horses; now they house patients

Finally, two examples of Adaptables which had the original purpose of being used when all health care had failed. In the little hamlet of **Barsby**, near Gaddesby in Leicestershire, there is an ordinary Victorian house in Church Lane which was actually built as a mortuary chapel in 1860 by a Mr Godson. Alas, it seems, he over-estimated the local mortality rate, and the chapel it was that died. It is known locally as Godson's Folly.

The other Adaptable in this category found a rather different role to play. A building by the River Wensum in **Norwich** which was used to store the bodies of suicides and other unfortunates who were found drowned in the river, has now been incorporated in a restaurant…

An ill-fated mortuary chapel at Barsby in Leicestershire. It was privately built, but its owner over-estimated the local mortality rate. It is now a private house

There used to be so many deaths in the River Wensum in Norwich that a mortuary was built on the riverbank. Happily the casualty rate has dropped, and it is now part of a restaurant

Carr 'to design a town where visitors could stay'. Carr duly built the famous Crescent, close to the original St. Ann's Well, incorporating the Natural Baths on the site of the old Roman ones.

Behind the Crescent he also built the Great Stables, large enough to accommodate over a hundred horses around an open exercise yard. The yard was later covered by a massive slate dome, nearly a hundred and sixty feet across. When the dome was built in 1881 it was said to be the largest in the world of its kind, and the Great Stables must have rated amongst the most luxurious.

The time came, of course, when nobody taking the waters at Buxton needed to stable a horse any more, let alone a hundred. These days the Great Stables house the Devonshire Royal Hospital – and, happily, it still treats its rheumatic patients with the water the Romans used, all those years ago.

Landmark
Adaptables

● ● ● ● ● ● ● ●

*Windmills,
drainage mills, and
old mills by the stream*

	Location	Old use	New use(s)
1	Alcester, Warwickshire: Arrow Mill	Flour mill	Hotel
2	Aldeburgh, Suffolk	Windmill	Laundry; private residence; flats
3	Bixley, Norfolk	Windmill	Water tower
4	Blockley, Gloucestershire	Watermill	Private residences
5	Bradford-on-Avon, Wiltshire	Windmill	Guest-house
6	Briningham, Norfolk	Smock mill	House
7	Diss, Norfolk	Windmill	House
8	Flatford Mill, Suffolk	Watermill	Field study centre
9	Fleggburgh, Norfolk	Drainage mill	Restaurant
10	Hartfield, East Sussex: Bolebroke Watermill	Watermill	Hotel
11	Horning, Norfolk	Drainage mill	Tourist attraction
12	Hoveton, Norfolk	Drainage mill	Private residence
13	Madingley, Cambridgeshire	Post-mill	Hay store; tyre store
14	Necton, Norfolk	Mill base	Grocer's shop
15	Reedham, Norfolk	Drainage mill	Private residence
16	Reigate, Surrey	Post-mill	Chapel
17	Roydon, Norfolk	Roundhouse	Cottage; private residence
18	Sandringham, Norfolk	Water tower	Holiday accommodation
19	Steyning, West Sussex	Water tower	Private residence
20	Sudbury, Suffolk	Watermill	Hotel
21	Tottenhill, Norfolk	Windmill	Garden store
22	Wendover, Buckinghamshire	Windmill	Private residence
23	Witton, Norfolk	Roundhouse	Summerhouse

They ground to a halt – but it didn't end there

'Did I not tell you they were windmills, and nobody could think otherwise, unless he also had windmills in his head?'

But that little lecture by his faithful squire did not discourage poor old Don Quixote from having a go at them with his lance, convinced that they were giants with flailing arms, and he has been an emblem of quixotic dottiness ever since.

Nonetheless, windmills are not always what they seem, and even the down-to-earth Sancho Panza could be deceived by some of the skilful adaptations that have taken place during recent years. They still look like windmills, but they may be restaurants, or holiday homes, or even permanent homes for agile folk who don't mind climbing six storeys to go to bed.

For hundreds of years, windmills dominated the English rural landscape. When the first ones appeared in the twelfth century, primitive wooden

structures revolving on a central post, they must have caused just as great a stir as the wind farms which annoy so many conservationists today.

Then they became more sophisticated, built on a brick 'roundhouse' to protect the revolving machinery – and some of these bases still survive as actual 'round houses' today. In the fifteenth century, someone had the bright idea of revolving just the cap and sails instead of the entire building, so the more solid wooden smock mill appeared and then the brick tower mill, the most common still seen today. Instead of being turned manually to face the wind, the sails were steered by a fantail on the back of the cap, the ultimate in eighteenth-century high technology.

But the fantail and the revolving caps were not enough to keep up with progress. Along came steam power and, ultimately, the internal combustion engine. Roller mills took over from the windmills and their close relations the water mills, and by the 1930s, they had virtually succumbed. In Norfolk, where the windmill was so common, it was almost regarded as the county emblem; the last one to operate commercially ground to a halt – literally – in 1956. The countryside was littered with redundant mills.

By then, however, the adaptors were already at work. As far back as 1880, some enterprising cleric at **Reigate** in Surrey realised the potential of the post-mill on Reigate Heath, which had not been working for more than a decade. Its roundhouse was converted into a chapel, which became a subsidiary of the parish church of St. Mary Magdalene.

The little circular chapel was equipped with an altar, an oak lectern, a small organ and seating for fifty. In the mill above it, most of the machinery was left in place, but the sails were blown off during the last

This postmill from Ellington in Cambridgeshire was moved to Madingley and finished up as a tyre store

TIMPSON'S *Adaptables*

A roundhouse could fare rather better if the less durable part of the post-mill was taken away altogether. At **Roydon**, on the Norfolk-Suffolk border, a two-storey brick roundhouse was given a jolly little conical roof with a chimney, some rather nice Georgian windows and a coat of black paint, and became a cosy little circular cottage. Since then it has been incorporated into a modern house.

Little circular brick buildings are not uncommon in former windmill country. They may either be a roundhouse which has lost its wooden superstructure, or the base of a tower mill which has been chopped off at one-storey or two-storey level. There is a cheerful-looking one at **Necton** in Norfolk, alongside a little wooden shop called 'Mum's Delight', which boldly claims to be 'Your Nursery Superstore in the Country'. The superstore has overflowed into the one-storey base of the old mill, which is painted an eye-catching, if slightly bilious, yellow. Cuddly toys peer out of the big front window, and around the edge of its circular flat roof stand the diminutive figures of

One of the mills of God? A postmill at Reigate in Surrey is now used as a church

A tower mill at Necton in Norfolk was chopped off above the ground floor. The base is now a toy store, surmounted by Popeye, the Flintstones and other 'guardian angels'

war, and it was later given a dummy fantail and dummy sails. Services are held in this unlikely place of worship once a month, in friendly competition with the adjoining golf club. It is said that the absence of a choir is not because of lack of space, but because the choirboys preferred supplementing their pocket money by hunting for lost golf balls on the course just outside the windows. The mill did, in fact, belong to the golf club, but the Borough Council took it over in 1962. It no longer grinds, even slowly, let alone exceeding small, but in its new role it must surely qualify as one of the Mills of God…

Other roundhouses have been put to much humbler uses. A post-mill, which was transferred from Ellington in what was Huntingdonshire to **Madingley** in Cambridgeshire, to replace a previous one which had collapsed, never actually worked on a commercial basis, and the roundhouse was used as a hay store for the nearby stables. These days, it serves a more modern form of transport; it is owned by a racing driver, who stores his tyres in it. The body of the mill rotated on the roof of the roundhouse, a familiar feature in the Midlands, though unusual in East Anglia. But to the stable lads who used to fork hay beneath it, and the mechanics who now stack tyres, it is no doubt just another roof.

Popeye, Fred Flintstone, the Pink Panther, and other improbable guardian angels.

The truncated mill was once used as a grocer's shop, and in the early 1970s it had a chimney sticking out of the middle of the roof, looking like the spindle of an upturned wheel. You can get an idea of what it originally looked like, at its full height and complete with sails, from the inn sign outside the village pub next door – The Windmill.

Another Norfolk mill base, at **North Tuddenham**, was given rather different treatment. Four stone pillars were erected around it, and a square ridge roof of asbestos sheeting was put on the pillars, so the round brick building underneath it looked like a classic example of a round peg in a square hole...

A roundhouse at **Witton**, near the Norfolk Broads, fared rather better. It was converted into quite an elegant summerhouse, with big French doors, a glass roof shaped like a pyramid, and a rather dashing weathercock.

The original millers would just about recognise all these partial windmill adaptations, but they might have difficulty

identifying a curious protuberance like a giant onion in a garden at **Tottenhill**, near King's Lynn. It is actually the ogee cap from a windmill which used to function at Sporle, some thirty miles away. It stands on the site of Tottenhill's former post-mill, perhaps for old times' sake, and it has found a modest new career as a garden store.

Even when a complete windmill is adapted for a new purpose, its origin is not always obvious. At **Briningham** in north Norfolk there is what many people believe to be either a lookout tower or just a folly, now converted into a house. One guidebook says categorically it was built by the Astleys, the local landowners, and was used as a lookout post at the time of the Armada, the Napoleonic wars and the two World Wars. And so it may have been, though it is difficult to understand why a lookout tower should be built ten miles inland.

The experts, however, say it was actually a smock mill, and it bears the date 1721, which was a little late for spotting

The roundhouse base of a windmill at Witton in Norfolk has become an elegant summerhouse...

...and the ogee cap from another Norfolk windmill at Sporle has finished up as a garden shed at Tottenhill, thirty miles away

There is no mistaking, however, the majority of windmill Adaptables which have been converted into living accommodation, even though few of them have retained their sails, so they don't qualify for calendars or the front covers of local guidebooks. It can also be a problem to keep up their appearance; not every painter and decorator fancies tackling the outside of a windmill. But I must mention the one at **Diss** in Norfolk, five storeys high with a splendid view over the town, because it occurred to me when I first saw it that it would be a wonderful setting for the opening line of a thriller: 'He climbed to the top of the windmill, went to look out of the window – and Diss appeared…'

There is a much grander windmill Adaptable at **Aldeburgh** in Suffolk. The Old Mill House on Fort Green, overlooking the sea, which also functioned as a laundry, was converted into a house in 1902 by a local parson. Unexpectedly, this very English building was given a Danish inscription over the door. It means: 'The Lord shall preserve thy going out and thy going in.' It is not a reminder of a Viking

A smock mill at Briningham in north Norfolk was first distinguished as a lookout tower, then became a private residence…

the Armada, even if it had sailed into the Channel the long way round. The three-storey octagonal base was originally surmounted by a wooden 'smock', but that has been replaced by a two-storey circular tower, with little battlements and a conical cupola on top. No wonder it causes confusion.

…but when a mill at Diss was adapted, the only outward alteration was the top storey

storm in 1904, but the mill went on grinding corn by steam-power for another twenty years. When it was converted into a residence, the cap was rebuilt and covered with aluminium, making it a distinctive local landmark.

The mill is, in fact, as much a publishing house as a home. Its owners, Mr and Mrs Kenneth Roberton, are music publishers, and its five storeys are packed with scores, books and manuscripts. Happily, there is still room for a grand piano in the ground-floor living-room, a reminder of Mr Roberton's musical antecedents, as well as his music publishing; his father founded the Glasgow Orpheus Choir.

The panoramic views which a windmill can provide have encouraged their

The Old Mill House at Aldeburgh in Suffolk (above) was converted by a local parson in 1902; the inscription was in honour of his Danish wife

invasion; the parson's wife happened to be Danish.

Nikolaus Pevsner, the architectural historian, paused during his tour of Aldeburgh's buildings to take a sideways glance at the former windmill. 'A fantasia', he noted – and moved on. These days the 'fantasia' and its adjoining buildings forms a complex of flats.

Wendover Mill in Buckinghamshire is another windmill-into-house Adaptable, but it has a special feature, a cap which is said to be the biggest of its kind in the country. The sails were damaged by a

The very up-market water tower on the Sandringham estate in west Norfolk – its foundation stone was laid by the Princess of Wales, later Queen Alexandra

Square, which in a round building indicates a certain ingenuity in design. It must have been a bit tricky squeezing in the *en suite* bathrooms – one visitor reported that he had difficulty fitting his face into the bathroom mirror – but the problem of furnishing the Round Room was solved very logically – with a round bed.

There is another ingenious use for which windmills are ideally suited, and Norfolk had an example of that, too. When **Bixley Mill** was built in 1838 it was one of the largest in the county, eleven storeys high. However, its size didn't save it when steam power arrived, and it became redundant like all the rest. But the village needed an improved water supply, and the mill was adapted to provide it. The upper storeys were lopped off, a conical tiled roof replaced the cap, a tank was installed, and the mill became a temporary water tower.

This was actually the reverse of the usual water tower adaptation; it is more common to find a water tower adapted for something else, generally a high-rise holiday home. The most elegant of these is on the **Sandringham Estate**, with all its royal connections. The foundation stone – and how many water towers can boast a foundation stone? – was laid in 1877 by the Princess of Wales, later Queen Alexandra, and there was living accommodation below the water tank for the man who looked after it.

An outside stairway goes up to a viewing room, and the dignified little turret which rises above the tank would delight any passing mullah. The Victorian designer had his own anti-freeze system for the water tank; all the chimney flues from the fireplaces below actually pass through the middle of it. The top of the tank, with its cast-iron railing, is now used as a lookout by the holiday-makers who rent the tower from the Landmark Trust.

conversion into holiday homes, restaurants and even small hotels, catering for fairly energetic guests who enjoy the novelty of near-perpendicular stairs and circular rooms for short periods, knowing they will return to their two-storey semis when the novelty wears off. One of the less taxing examples is the Old Windmill overlooking **Bradford-on-Avon** in Wiltshire.

As a mill it could hardly have been very successful – it was completed in 1808 and stopped functioning in 1817 – but its surviving four storeys have fared rather better in their current role of a four-bedroomed guest-house. The rooms are named Round, Oval, Rectangular and

Wendover Mill in Buckinghamshire when it was still functioning, and as the interior is today, complete with baby grand piano

The not-so-up-market water tower at Steyning in West Sussex – more like a concrete helter-skelter

At the other end of the aesthetic scale in live-in water towers is the ferro-concrete structure covered in pebble-dash which dominates the countryside near **Steyning** in West Sussex. It looks more like a giant helter-skelter than a water tower, but it is actually occupied – and the water still flows. The ten-thousand-gallon tank supplies the neighbouring farms, and the tenant, whose bedroom is immediately below it, gets woken before dawn each morning by great gushings when the water is drawn off for the cattle's early feed. The only access to this bedroom is by the outside stairway, which is not too convenient in an emergency – the bathroom is on the ground floor.

No ingenious heating from the chimneys here. There is just a wood-burning stove, which I gather is inclined to smoke when the wind is in the wrong direction. The concrete walls seem to attract the cold and damp, and in the winter the choice can sometimes lie between choking and freezing.

Even so, this is a Grade II listed building, and the tenant, who lives there permanently, has developed quite an affection for it, in spite of its unpicturesque appearance and assorted inconveniences. 'My home is like an old enemy,' he once said, 'but I think we sometimes love old enemies more than friends.'

Different fashions in adapted Norfolk windmills: a distinctly Dutch flavour at Horning on the River Bure...

Another kind of tower, which used to be a familiar sight in the English countryside, particularly in East Anglia, has now become as redundant as the windmill, which it strongly resembles. Drainage mills operated in the same way as corn mills; the wind turned the sails, the sails turned the machinery. But, instead of the machinery turning a grindstone, it turned a scoop-wheel, which lifted water from the marshland into higher channels, which took it away into rivers and the sea.

Like corn mills, they were superseded by steam at the turn of this century, and although some corn mills have been restored to grind corn again – if only to entertain the tourists – scooping water is rather less exciting, and most surviving drainage mills are now derelict. Norfolk has the highest concentration of them in the country, thanks to the Broads and the Fens, but, of the seventy-odd that survive, fifty are derelict. A handful have been restored by a preservation trust, the rest have been adapted as dwellings.

Living in a drainage mill can have advantages over living in a corn mill. They are usually beside a river, which is always an attraction, and often in an isolated position, where peace and quiet is

...an all-round viewing gallery at Reedham...

...a lighthouse effect at Hoveton Marshes...

...and the mill at Fleggburgh which has been adapted as a restaurant

guaranteed. Corn mills had to be built where the corn was, with easy access and often with other buildings nearby. And although the countryside around drainage mills is generally flatter, that does not detract from its charm, as any Norfolkman will forcefully confirm.

The popularity of the Broads has done away with some of the peace and quiet, and one of the most attractive drainage mills, at **Horning**, has a constant procession of pleasure boats passing by on the River Bure during the summer months. It is one of the few in this area which was built as a wooden smock mill instead of a brick tower, and it has been given flared wooden boarding around the base too, so it looks more like a Dutch mill than the homegrown variety, but with its dummy sails and smart white paint it is one of the showpieces of the Broads.

At **Reedham Ferry** and **Repps** the adaptors have added balcony-cum-sun-lounges to the second storeys, and at **Hoveton Marshes** there is a lookout on top which gives the impression more of a lighthouse than a mill. The mill at **Fleggburgh** was given a studio-style lookout too, but these days it is

St. Margaret's Restaurant. Surviving scoop-wheels are very thin on the ground – or the water – but one or two mills still retain the wheel casing, as a reminder of what these Adaptables were originally built for, a couple of centuries ago.

Water-mills were built for quite the opposite purpose, for the water to turn the wheels instead of the wheels scooping up the water. The majority were used like windmills, to grind corn, but in some areas they had a more specialised purpose. At **Blockley** in Gloucestershire, the brook turned twelve mill-wheels which powered factories making pianos, soap and collars; silk mills which made thread for weaving ribbons, and an iron foundry. A visitor wrote in 1836: 'The produce of the mills is sold at Coventry chiefly, some of it in London. Bengal and Turkey silk are here manufactured into silk thread. The process seems simple and the operation chiefly by young females and boys from 8 to 10 years of age.' The writer was a parson, the Reverend F.E. Witts, but he seemed undisturbed by this use of child labour.

Blockley was, in fact, quite an industrial village, thanks to the brook,

survive; it disintegrated after the mill went out of use fifty-odd years ago.

Arrow Mill, near **Alcester** in Warwickshire, was a working flour mill until 1962, and the paddle wheel and gear machinery are still turned by the force of the stream. As further reminders, there are cast-iron gearwheels and grooved grindstones around the open-plan ground floor, but these days the mill is another hotel, with the Miller's Bar where the real miller used to be.

The most famous mill of all, however, was not adapted as an hotel but as a field study centre. **Flatford Mill**, near the Suffolk–Essex border, was owned by John Constable's father, and the painter worked there for a year as a miller before going to London to study art. In 1816 he started his painting of the mill, and became so engrossed in it that he tried to postpone his wedding. His fiancée took a poor view of that, so he only postponed it for a month, leaving the painting unfinished. He must have enjoyed the honeymoon, because he only got around to completing the picture in the following year.

It was quite a picture. *Flatford Mill* became one of his best-known works and finished up in the Tate Gallery. The mill itself, after various vicissitudes, finished up as a study centre, still much photographed but not accessible to the public. Like all the other mills which became Adaptables, it has found a useful new role to play, after going, one might say, through the mill…

One of the water-powered mills which used to function at Blockley in Gloucestershire. Most of them are now attractive private residences

Bolebroke Watermill at Hartfield in East Sussex is now an hotel, but there are plenty of reminders of its past

which was fed by so many springs that it flowed strongly all the year round. But these days, the silk mills have been converted into up-market residences, and the homes of the youthful factory workers are probably holiday cottages.

Like the silk mills at Blockley, most of England's other water-mills are redundant but, happily, they are easier to adapt than their high-rise wind-driven cousins, and they are nearly always set in picturesque surroundings. They are rather big for holiday homes, but ideal for hotels and restaurants; diners always seem to relish having a drink while watching water – so long as it isn't water.

These Adaptables range from imposing hotels like the Mill at **Sudbury** in Suffolk, with the massive waterwheel separating the restaurant from the bar (wisely encased in glass to protect both the wheel and unsteady customers) to the less sophisticated Bolebroke Watermill at **Hartfield** in East Sussex, where parts of the machinery are liable to turn up in the bedrooms. In the Pond Room, for instance, the original pulleys are just above the bed. The waterwheel itself has failed to

Perhaps the most famous mill of them all: Flatford Mill on the Suffolk–Essex border, immortalised by John Constable

Custodial Adaptables

• • • • • • • • • •

Houses of Industry, Correction and Detention

	Location	Old use	New use(s)
1	Abingdon, Oxfordshire: Old Gaol	Prison	Leisure centre
2	Barley, Hertfordshire	Lock-up	Tool store
3	Bawdeswell, Norfolk: 'The Gables'	Workhouse	School; private residence
4	Berwick upon-Tweed, Northumberland	Prison	Town Hall
5	Brisley, Norfolk: 'The Clink'	Prison quarters	Holiday cottage
6	Deeping St. James, Lincolnshire	Market cross	Lock-up; lamp-post
7	Diss, Norfolk	Police station	Private residence
8	Farndon, Cheshire	Lock-up	En suite bedroom
9	Folkingham, Lincolnshire	House of correction	Holiday cottage
10	Gressenhall, Norfolk	Workhouse	Old people's home; museum
11	Hartfield, East Sussex	Workhouse	Pub and guest house
12	Helmsley, North Yorkshire	Police station	Café and shop
13	Launceston, Cornwall	Police station	Offices
14	Slaidburn, Lancashire	Courtroom	Inn
15	Wells, Somerset	Prison	Inn
16	Wirksworth, Derbyshire	Police station	Holiday accommodation
17	Wymondham, Norfolk: Bridewell	Prison	Court and police station; offices and accommodation; museum and tea-shop

When prisons reach their cell-by date...

Lock-ups, jails, workhouses, Houses of Correction – by definition, these are not the most attractive places to live or work. But, again by definition, they are generally so solidly made that it takes a great deal of time, effort and money to demolish them when they are no longer required. So, a considerable number of early examples still survive in the English countryside and, in spite of their generally forbidding appearance, a number of them have become successful Adaptables.

For the extremely big ones or the extremely small ones, there are not too many alternatives open. A vast, gaunt place like **Gressenhall** workhouse in Norfolk, for example, originally known as a House of Industry, did become an old people's home for several years, but that was not exactly an Adaptable. Beech House, as it was officially christened, still looked exactly the same outside, and not very different inside. In spite of curtains and carpets and fairly comfortable furniture, the general atmosphere seemed to be much the same, too.

It has finished up, like so many of these enormous white elephants, as a museum, with no attempt to disguise its original use. On the contrary, the old punishment cell, for instance, where inmates were put for such heinous offences as talking at mealtimes, is still carefully

The former village lock-up at Deeping St. James in Lincolnshire started life as the market cross; now it is an elaborate lamp-post

preserved. With a building like that, if you can't beat it, flaunt it...

Similarly, there are few uses to be found for the little lock-ups that were put on village greens to accommodate the local drunks and minor felons. A number of them were circular with conical roofs designed, presumably, for offenders with pointed heads, and they had very small doors and no windows to speak of. There are good examples at **Harrold** in Bedfordshire, and **Kingsbury Episcopi** in Somerset. The design is taken a stage further at **Wheatley** in Oxfordshire, where the entire lock-up is cone-shaped, with a jolly little stone ball on the point. At the last count they had still defied the adaptors and were simply preserved as museum pieces, too.

The lock-up at **Barley** in Hertfordshire offered a little more scope because, unlike the others, it was built of wood with a slate roof, rather like an up-market garden shed. It is older than most, dating back to the seventeenth century, and it remained in use until 1890. Then, like the others, nobody knew quite what to do with it, except for one period when the local roadman stored his tools in it. These days, it has joined the ranks of the OAPs – Officially Adopted and Preserved.

In one or two rare cases, village lock-ups were themselves adapted from an earlier use. The stone-built lock-up at **Deeping St. James** in Lincolnshire, for instance, started life as the market cross. When it became redundant in 1819, an ingenious fellow called Tailby Johnson turned it into an Adaptable by hollowing out the centre to make a thoroughly gloomy little cell.

In due course, that too was made redundant, and it qualified as an Adaptable again. This time it was considered as impractical to convert as all

'The Clink' at Brisley in Norfolk, where warders stayed overnight while escorting prisoners from King's Lynn to Norwich Prison. The prisoners were locked in the church crypt

The courtroom at the Hark to Bounty Inn at Slaidburn in Lancashire is now a party room; the witness box is the bar

Although it is called the Clink, it is thought that it was actually where the warders stayed, after they had locked up their prisoners in rather less attractive accommodation, the crypt of the parish church just up the road. These days the crypt is unoccupied, but the Clink has been modernised as an unusual holiday cottage, a sort of vertical flat.

The courtrooms where these and other prisoners were sentenced have often become Adaptables, too. One which achieved a much more congenial role was at **Slaidburn** in Lancashire, where, for centuries, the only courtroom between Lancaster and York was on the upper floor of the quaintly named Hark to Bounty Inn – Bounty was the squire's over-noisy dog. These days the inn uses it as a party room, where the revellers can relax on the jury benches which still line one wall, and the witness box is used as bar.

Early in the last century, some of the standard lock-ups were being built on a rather larger, and comparatively more luxurious, scale than the primitive little structures on the village greens. They were given windows, albeit heavily barred, and there was room for the occupant to sleep full-length. When they eventually fell out of use they offered rather more scope as Adaptables, and they have turned out to be quite an attraction for holiday-makers looking for novel accommodation.

the others – until a latter-day Tailby Johnson realised what an excellent site it occupied to provide street lighting. Today, it is possibly the only village lock-up to be converted into a lamp-post.

At **Brisley** in Norfolk there is another unusual little building, known locally as 'The Clink'. It was built in the days when prisoners, who had been tried and convicted in King's Lynn, were walked the fifty-odd miles across the county to Norwich Jail. The journey took two days, and as Brisley was about halfway, this was where the walkers stayed the night.

A little two-storey tower stands beside the road, in what is now the front garden of the adjoining cottage. It is just large enough for one room on each floor.

The rather attractive little lock-up at **Farndon** in Cheshire, which adjoins a house in the High Street, is a good example. It was built in 1837 and qualified, in due course, as a listed building, but for some time after it became redundant and it was just used for storage. Five years ago the couple who lived next to it linked it to their house with a sun room, installed a

shower room in the lock-up itself, and adapted it as an *en suite* bedroom for two. The windows are still barred, but occupants are now provided with their own key to the cell door. As one write-up rather coyly explains: 'The Village Lock-Up is completely self-contained, making it ideal for those wanting to lock themselves away – the sentence is entirely up to you...'

The Old Lock-Up at **Wirksworth** in Derbyshire was even more suitable for holiday accommodation as it was the local police station as well. There was much more room – and more cells – to play with. It was actually built in 1842 as a house for the magistrate, and his room is now the master bedroom. His handsome commode is no longer required (the room is *en suite*) so it has been moved into the lounge – but only for decorative purposes.

In the 1850s the magistrate moved out and a police inspector moved in. He had to

provide his own horse, but he was allowed a coach and coachman. Both were accommodated in the adjacent coach-house, which now has two bedrooms, one the former coachman's and the other the old hayloft.

The lock-up had four cells, all with vaulted roofs. Those on the first floor still have large boulders perched on the roofs, inside the loft, to prevent prisoners breaking out that way. Two of the cells are now bathrooms, a third has been preserved in its original state with steel-lined door and stone-flagged floor, and the fourth, where the local drunks sobered up after a heavy night, is now, perhaps appropriately, the bar.

Other former police stations with cells have found different uses. Some of them are difficult to spot, they have been adapted so thoroughly. The former police station at **Helmsley** in North Yorkshire, for instance, is now a small café and shop. The only visible evidence of its original use is just inside the entrance; there are two old cell doors set into the wall. And at **Launceston** in Cornwall the old police station is now fulfilling a new role in the legal system, as the office of a firm of solicitors. I gather the cell still exists, perhaps as a warning to clients.

A much larger police station complex at **Diss** in Norfolk, consisting of three police cells, an exercise yard and a police house, as well as the station itself, was only built ninety years ago, and remained in use until 1996. It has been fairly easily adapted by a housing association to provide accommodation for people with

Two guest houses equipped with cells: at Farndon in Cheshire the cell is an en suite bedroom...

...and at Wirksworth in Derbyshire the cells have become bedrooms and bathrooms; this bedroom has kept its steel-lined door. The drunks' cell is now the bar

New roles for old police stations: at Launceston in Cornwall it is a solicitors' office...

New roles for old police stations: at Launceston in Cornwall it is a solicitors' office...

urgent housing needs. The cells still have their original heavy doors and tiled walls, but the windows have been enlarged to provide more light. One cell has become a kitchen and bathroom, the others are bedrooms, and the exercise yard has been become a garden. The police station is now a three-bedroomed house, with the general office converted into a lounge, and the police house has become two flats.

...at Diss in Norfolk it is part of a complex run by a housing association...

A good many custom-built prisons seem to continue functioning long after their sell-by date, but some have been finally pensioned off. At **Berwick-upon-Tweed** in Northumberland it has happened twice. Prisoners were originally held on the second floor of the Town Hall and, judging by the elaborate appearance of the exterior, it looked as though they led a fairly luxurious life. But the Town Hall was specifically designed in the 1740s as a 'Tolbooth, Steeple and Proper Gaol', and the second floor is very different from the others.

The first floor has the Guild Hall, the Council Chamber, and the Mayor's Parlour, all rather sumptuous, but above them were the felons' cells – quite a bizarre assortment. The security cell was built like a cage, while the women's cell had one wooden bed big enough for four. The other women either took turns, or slept on the floor, or more likely kept everyone awake all night arguing whose turn was next.

There was a different problem in the drunkard's cell. It had one large bed which

...and at Helmsley in North Yorkshire it is a café and shop

sloped so, presumably, the drunks had hardly climbed on to it before they slid off the end – no doubt thinking it was all the fault of the drink. Finally, the condemned cell was the grimmest of the lot, pitch dark with no windows. The last person to be hanged in Berwick, a woman called Grace Griffiths, spent her final days in it in 1823.

A corridor leads directly from the cells to the bell chamber on the same floor. If any of the prisoners had got out of their cells they could have celebrated by ringing the bells in the steeple – though it might have been rather ill-advised. There was also a flight of steps leading up to the flat roof, so prisoners could go outside for exercise. It might also have occurred to them to use it for escaping, if they were athletic enough to abseil down the wall, but there are no reports that anyone did.

The gaol was in use for nearly a hundred years,

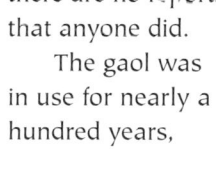

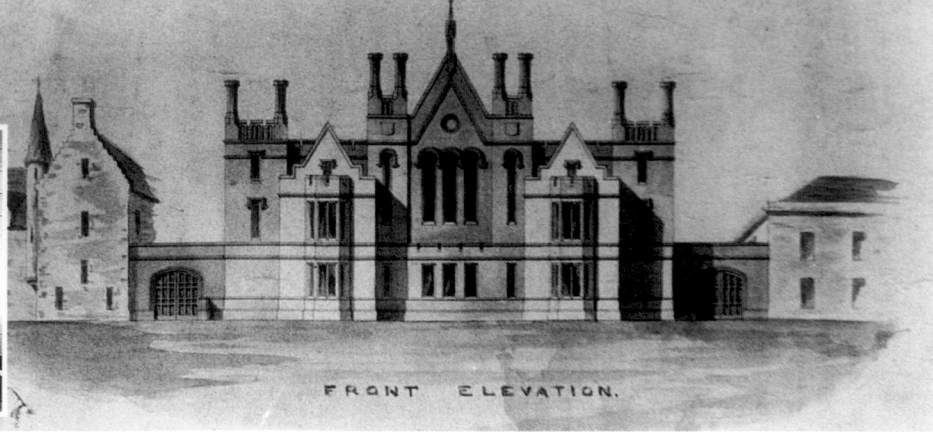

FRONT ELEVATION.

One of two former prisons at Berwick-upon-Tweed. The first occupied one floor at the Town Hall; the second was in Wallace Green, and is now the Borough Council offices

until a new prison was built in **Wallace Green** at the end of the 1840s. It did not become a true Adaptable, because the cells have been preserved in their original form as the Cell Block Museum – but its successor did. The Wallace Green prison became redundant in its turn, and is now the Council offices.

Wells in Somerset has also had more than one prison. The main one was in the old tithe barn, and in 1591 the town Shambles was converted into another, more up-market, where it is said prisoners were sent if they could

The City Arms pub at Wells in Somerset used to be the town jail in the eighteenth century; only a barred window and some leg irons survive

Abingdon Gaol had a pleasant setting, and it now has a more pleasant use, as a leisure and entertainment centre

afford to pay. There was an extra charge for one of the upstairs rooms, which would normally be occupied by the prison officers.

In 1801 it became an Adaptable and was converted into an inn; it has been the City Arms ever since. After nearly two centuries there is little evidence left of its previous role, though some say you can tell that the ladies' toilet was once a cell – I am not sure how. There is, however, a window display of leg irons, which may just possibly have been worn by the inmates.

The Old Gaol at **Abingdon** in Oxfordshire was built by French prisoners

during the Napoleonic Wars in the early nineteenth century. In those days Abingdon was the county town of Berkshire, and the jail served the whole county for sixty years, until the town lost its title to Reading. The building was renovated in the 1970s and became – in contrast – a leisure and entertainments centre.

Houses of Correction were not quite as unpleasant as the prisons built for hardened criminals, but certainly a stage more uncomfortable than Houses of Industry. They accommodated the drunks and disorderlies, vagrants and other minor offenders. Some were just in there for being 'idle', which could cover almost anything. At **Folkingham** in Lincolnshire only the

gatehouse of the House of Correction survives – but it is quite a gatehouse. It was added to the main building in 1825, 'a bold and monumental work,' as one reference book describes it, 'borrowing from the styles of Vanbrugh, Sammichele and Leoux'. The offenders who passed through it had probably never heard of any of them, but they must have felt their influence; it was like entering some kind of fortress, as imposing as the medieval castle that originally stood on the site.

The House of Correction was closed in 1878 and most of the buildings converted into dwellings, then demolished in 1955. The gatehouse, once occupied by the turnkey and the governor's horses, was rather amazingly turned into a holiday cottage by the Landmark Trust. From the front it looks as forbidding as ever, with its parapet still inscribed: 'House of Correction, AD 1825', but at the rear there is no sign of the house itself, just an expanse of grass. 'Anyone who doesn't love their stay here deserves to be locked up,' wrote one holiday-maker. 'What a pleasure to be an inmate,' wrote another. A third added without going into detail: 'The children were particularly taken with the handcuffs…'

While workhouses could be as large and forbidding as Houses of Correction, like the imposing one at Gressenhall in Norfolk, there were smaller establishments, sometimes supported by local charities, which looked comparatively cosy, and which were eventually much more suitable as Adaptables. A dozen miles from Gressenhall, for instance, 'The Gables' next to the parish church at **Bawdeswell** looks like a large private house, and that, indeed, is what it has been in recent years, but it was actually built as a workhouse before the one at Gressenhall. It incorporated an earlier wing which probably dates back to the sixteenth century.

However, it fulfilled that function for less than sixty years before undergoing its first adaptation, as a school for seventy pupils. It is currently facing yet another, after being empty for a number of years. There is a plan to divide its twenty rooms into three dwellings.

The former women's workhouse at **Hartfield** in East Sussex has had a rather more drastic change of roles. In the last century it was owned by the Reverend Dr Rand's Charity, and was controlled by the Hartfield Board of Guardians. The control must have been quite firm, because ankle chains were discovered during recent restoration work. By the turn of the century, however, the need for ankle chains, and indeed the need for the workhouse, had faded, and it became a public house. Instead of ankle chains, the only reason for tripping over was the strength of the ale. It was first the Dorset Arms and is now the Anchor. In 1915 it was advertising accommodation for small parties, 'with carriages to meet trains by order'.

Since then it has prospered in the tourist trade, helped by its proximity to Pooh Bridge, immortalised by A.A. Milne. Indeed, it makes the most of the connection, rather than its earlier history. The Victorian-style

The gatehouse at Folkingham House of Correction in Lincolnshire was nearly as forbidding as the House itself – but it makes a novel holiday home

The attractive Anchor Inn at Hartfield in East Sussex was originally a women's workhouse, though it is difficult to recognise as such

bedrooms, which still accommodate small parties, are not decorated with ankle chains but Pooh paraphernalia, and instead of workhouse gruel, there is, no doubt, honey on the menu.

Back among the full-scale prisons, quite a revolutionary change has taken place at the **Wymondham Bridewell** in Norfolk, which itself was quite a revolutionary establishment in its time. It was built in 1785 to replace an earlier prison which had been condemned, in a House of Commons report, as the most insanitary and barbaric in the country – and the way prisons were in 1785, that was quite a damning condemnation. The new bridewell served as a model for prisons in Manchester and Liverpool, and for the first penitentiary to be built in the United States.

It was built in the form of four separate wings around a central courtyard, each with its own access, and this made it easier to convert when, eventually, it became an Adaptable. The first conversion was as early as 1879, when one wing was adapted as a magistrates' court, while the rest became the police station. Other sections were hived off over the years, with the Red Cross occupying part of one wing, and another used as accommodation for mentally handicapped patients returning to society. The original dungeons, dating back

The Bridewell at Wymondham remains unchanged from the front, but it now contains various local services, from a Citizens' Advice Bureau to a teashop

to the earlier prison condemned by the Commons, were occasionally put on show to the public.

In 1992 the whole building was put on the market, and the local Heritage Society managed to raise enough grants and local funds to take it over. Various other organisations occupied parts of it, from the Citizens' Advice Bureau to a local housing association, while the Heritage Society moved the Wymondham Museum into one wing and opened a teashop to go with it. It all took four years, a lot of determination, and £450,000, but it worked.

There was a final hiccup on the day of the official opening by the Duke of Gloucester in 1996. One of the organisers wrote afterwards: 'There had been much rehearsing of the walk and visits to all parts of the Bridewell, and much consultation with the police and palace officials over the split-second timing of the programme. Then I had a phone call that morning to say that His Royal Highness had missed the train in London. I thought this was the big leg-pull of the year...'

The Lord Lieutenant carried out the ceremony instead, and a slightly breathless Duke arrived an hour later and made the planned tour. It included a visit to the dungeons, just 216 years, almost to the day, after one Elizabeth Pulley had occupied one of them. She served three weeks for theft, but it failed to make much impact on her, and after further offences she was transported to Australia. Two of her descendants visited the bridewell, about the same time as the Duke, to see where their ancestor had started her life of crime, and they left behind a rather delightful memento of their visit. Elizabeth Pulley's descendants married into a family called Rope, and the Bridewell Museum now has a copy of the family newsletter as one of its exhibits. They are called the Rope-Pulleys...

Ecclesiastical Adaptables

Priories, convents, abbots' houses, an archbishop's palace – and a holy well

	Location	Old use	New use(s)
1	Abingdon, Oxfordshire	Abbey	Prison; theatre
2	Beverley, East Yorkshire: Beverley Minster	Friary	Youth hostel
3	Bisham Abbey, Berkshire	Priory	Abbey; private residence; football training ground
4	Cawood Castle, North Yorkshire	Manor house	Archbishops' residence; military prison; courthouse; holiday cottage
5	Conishead, Cumbria	Priory	Stately home; hotel; convalescent home; hospital; Buddhist centre
6	Exeter, Devon: Annuellars Refectory	Priory	Shops
7	Lamorna Cove, Cornwall	Hostel and chapel	Boarding house; private residence; hotel
8	Lingfield, Surrey	Priory	Library
9	Marrick, North Yorkshire	Priory	Church; residential centre
10	Osney Abbey, Oxfordshire: Weston Manor	Abbey house	BBC station; hotel; tyre company store; hotel
11	Pulham St. Mary, Norfolk	Guild chapel	School
12	South Elmham, Suffolk: St. Peter's Hall	Priory	Brewery
13	Taplow, Buckinghamshire	Country house	Abbey; apartments
14	Truro, Cornwall	Convent	Hotel
15	Woolston, Shropshire: St. Winifred's Well	Well	Chapel; courthouse; holiday cottage
16	Wymondham, Norfolk: St. Thomas à Becket Chapel	Guild chapel	Library

Henry did his worst – but abbey days are here again

Marrick Priory in Swaledale, North Yorkshire, is now a residential centre for young people...

When Henry VIII dissolved the monasteries, he could hardly have foreseen that many of them would be restored or rebuilt in centuries to come and qualify, in due course, as Adaptables – while often retaining their original titles. Any number of 'Abbeys' and 'Priories' these days are, in fact, private residences or, more likely, up-market hotels. Sometimes, they are easily recognisable as former ecclesiastical buildings: stone towers, lofty roofs, high arched windows. More often, they incorporate just a few of the original features – an arched doorway here, a stained-glass window there.

The ecclesiastical origins of Marrick Priory at **Swaledale** in North Yorkshire, are unmistakable, even though it became a young people's residential centre for outdoor education in the 1960s. In the Middle Ages it was the priory of Benedictine nuns, and on the other side of the River Swale there was a Cistercian priory. They were accessible to each other

...and Bisham Abbey in Berkshire is frequently a residential centre for the England football team. The painting by Francis Walker shows it as it was in 1907

by stepping-stones, and it might have been a temptingly romantic situation if the Cistercians had been monks – but, in fact, that priory was an all-female establishment too.

Marrick Priory was founded in the twelfth century by Roger de Aske, and it was a descendant of his, Robert Aske, who led the Pilgrimage of Grace in 1536, protesting against the suppression of the monasteries. It did little good for Roger de Aske's priory, and even less good for Robert; he was hung in chains at York Castle as a punishment.

The priory fell into ruins but in 1811 the monastic church was rebuilt for use as a parish church. However, it is in a remote spot, and the parishioners were very scattered. By the middle of this century the church was disused and abandoned. It was finally closed in 1960 and, in its isolated position, it hardly seemed an ideal

Adaptable. Then the Diocesan Board of Finance had the bright idea of adapting it as a residential centre for young people. A new building was erected beside it, containing a kitchen and other services, with accommodation for the warden. The church itself was converted into a dining area and sitting-room, with the chancel being used as a chapel. The upper floor and gallery became dormitories.

Roger de Aske's Benedictine nuns would, no doubt, be startled to find young men sleeping in their church, but the Augustinians of **Bisham Abbey** in Berkshire might be rather gratified to meet the England football team limbering up in the grounds and relaxing in their great hall. The name of the abbey has become familiar to all sporting fans as the national training ground. Before big matches no television news bulletin is complete without distant shots of international football stars strolling through its portals.

Bisham Abbey was first an Augustinian priory, where four successive Earls of Salisbury were buried. It is also the burial place of Richard Neville, Earl of Warwick, known to generations of schoolboys as 'Warwick the Kingmaker'.

After Henry VIII destroyed it, the Hoby family took over. Sir Philip Hoby started building a house from the ruins, incorporating the decorated porch and doorway, part of the chapel wall and the great hall. He died before finishing it and his half-brother, Sir Thomas, completed the job. They both loll nonchalantly, side by side, in the

A former Augustinian priory at Conishead in Cumbria is now the Manjushri Mahayana Buddhist Centre

Hoby Chapel at the parish church, no doubt marvelling at the energy of the young men who rush round the grounds of their old home, kicking footballs.

Another Augustinian priory, at **Conishead** in Cumbria, has had a much more complicated history since Henry VIII evicted the monks, dismantled the building and sold off the bells, the lead roof and the timbers. In the early days, the priory estate passed through a number of hands, including a William Sandys, who suffered from the backlash against the Crown in 1558 and was 'very riotously and wilfully murdered at Conishead'.

When Colonel Thomas Braddyll of the Coldstream Guards, High Sheriff of Lancashire, took over the estate in 1818 he decided the building was too dilapidated to be repaired, and completely rebuilt it in Victorian Gothic.

But its origins were not forgotten. Between the twin octagonal towers, a hundred feet high, a traceried window depicts St. Augustine and the main benefactors of the priory, including Edward II, who bestowed a royal charter on it – not that it cut much ice with his descendant King Henry. There are also eighteen stained-glass windows depicting scenes from the life of Christ, and a vaulted

New uses for ecclesiastical Adaptables: a Dominican friary at Beverley in East Yorkshire is now a youth hostel...

...while a Carthusian guest-house at Lingfield in Surrey has found a new role as a county library

priory, but the Manjushri Mahayana Buddhist Centre. The objectives and activities are much the same as they were five or six centuries ago – to teach and study their religion, to meditate, and to spread their beliefs.

The homes of other religious communities which have become Adaptables mostly switched to more secular activities. A medieval Dominican friary next to **Beverley Minster**, in the East Riding of Yorkshire, which was mentioned in Chaucer's *Canterbury Tales* and still has fifteenth-century wall paintings, is now a youth hostel. The sixteenth-century Annuellars Refectory at Cathedral Close in **Exeter**, home of the chantry priests who said masses for their benefactors' souls on the anniversaries of their death, has been absorbed behind a row of shops. The Convent of the Sisters of the Epiphany at **Truro** in Cornwall is now the Alverton Manor Hotel, which has adapted its Gothic-style chapel for use as an exhibition hall. And the guest house of a Carthusian college established in the 1430s at **Lingfield** in Surrey later became a county library.

Perhaps the most recently built abbey to become an Adaptable is at **Taplow** in Buckinghamshire. It was actually designed by Sir Edwin Lutyens as a private residence called Nashdom, one of the last great country houses built in England, but it has been occupied by Benedictine monks for most of its existence.

Lutyens was commissioned by a wealthy lady from Lancashire, who had acquired the unlikely title of Princess Dolgorouki by marrying a Russian prince she met in Cannes. Nashdom was completed in 1909, but she and her husband only occupied it briefly before the Great War broke out and they moved abroad. Neither of them ever returned. The

corridor which is vaguely reminiscent of a cloister – but that's about it.

The new priory took fifteen years to build, and £140,000 of Colonel Braddyll's money. As it turned out, he could ill afford it. He lost the remainder of his fortune in unwise investments, and was declared bankrupt in 1848.

Conishead came on the market again, and its story took some unlikely turns. A Scottish syndicate converted it into a hydropathic hotel, then the Durham Miners Welfare Committee bought it as a convalescent home for sick miners. During the last war it was used as a hospital, then it was returned to the miners. When they vacated it in 1972 there was an unsuccessful bid to turn the site into a holiday camp. Then it remained empty for nearly five years until, finally, it reverted to its original use as the home of a spiritual community – not an Augustinian

prince died in Paris in 1915, the princess retired to the Pyrenees.

The Benedictines took over the house in the 1920s and lived there for the next sixty years. It was an improbable-looking abbey. Lutyens had to build it to the princess's instructions, and became thoroughly exasperated: 'She wants a mad house looking like three houses of different heights, sizes and kinds in a row,' he fumed to his wife.

He managed to tone it down a bit, and finished up with two large blocks of equal size, which do, indeed, look like separate buildings linked by a Palladian portico. It might seem more suited to house Whitehall office workers than Benedictine monks, but they must have settled in very happily and became well established in the community. So much so, in fact, that after the Profumo affair it is said that Lady Astor asked one of them to exorcise Cliveden, her great house nearby, which played such a prominent role in the scandal.

When the monks moved out in 1988 there was no shortage of developers hoping to make it an Adaptable, but it took nearly ten years to achieve. In that time Nashdom deteriorated to such an extent that it was placed on the 'Buildings at Risk' register, but it has now been successfully converted into fourteen apartments.

In contrast to this comparatively new building, **Abingdon Abbey** in Oxfordshire was founded in the seventh century, wrecked by the Danes, re-founded by the Saxons and wrecked again by Henry VIII. Miraculously, some elements of it still stand, though the abbey church has long since gone. The room above the gateway was used as a prison until the nineteenth century, and still survives as the Abbey Room, but the most distinctive building, dating back to the thirteenth century, houses the Checker Room, with its

remarkable gabled chimney – the smoke comes out of vertical slits below the gable.

'Checker' did not mean this was the monks' games room. It is a shortened version of 'Exchequer', where the abbey's finances were handled. The building has now achieved a new role as the home of the Unicorn Theatre.

The link between St. Peter's Hall, **South Elmham** in Suffolk, and another of Henry VIII's suppressed priories is a little obscure. The hall dates back before his time, to the thirteenth century, but a lot of the stonework is said to come from the priory ruins. Alternatively, they may come from Elmham Minster, which some Suffolk folk say was the seat of the Saxon bishops after they left Dunwich, but the claim is hotly disputed in North Elmham, which definitely had a Saxon cathedral – and happens to be in Norfolk...

Whatever religious establishment the stonework came from, the monks who lived in it would appreciate the new role

It may look like a Whitehall office block, but it was an Augustinian priory at Taplow in Buckinghamshire for sixty years. It is now split into apartments

Part of Abingdon Abbey in Oxfordshire is now the Unicorn Theatre

St. Peter's Hall at South Elmham in Suffolk is now a commercial brewery. The monks would have enjoyed that

The Thomas à Becket Chapel at Wymondham in Norfolk is now a branch library

which St. Peter's Hall is playing. In 1996 it became St. Peter's Brewery – and monks were renowned for enjoying, as well as brewing, their own beer.

At the lower end of the ecclesiastical scale in medieval times were the tiny guild chapels, built by parish guilds or fraternities in rural areas as independent chantries for their own use and benefit. Two survive in Norfolk, the St. Thomas à Becket Chapel in **Wymondham**, which is now a branch of the county library, and a chapel at **Pulham St. Mary** dedicated to St. James the Greater, patron saint of the Guild of Hatters, Cappers and Hurers, which was built in his honour by the local hat-making community.

The St. Thomas à Becket chapel, erected soon after his murder and rebuilt in the fourteenth century, was permanently staffed by two monks, but when the hat makers of Pulham St. Mary rebuilt their chapel in 1401 they made do with a hermit called Walter. In 1670 one of the Lords of the Manor, William Pennoyer, left an endowment to provide Pulham St. Mary with a free school, to be housed in the chapel, and it thus became an early Adaptable. The Victorians added extra classrooms, and Pennoyer's School survived until 1988, when falling pupil numbers caused it to close. It has been empty ever since then, but recently a village committee has been trying to find yet another role for the former home of Walter, the hat-maker's hermit.

While medieval monks and nuns lived rather frugally on the whole – except for the beer, of course – abbots and priors were inclined to indulge themselves when it came to building or acquiring their own residences. They could often do useful deals with the local landowners, and take over the odd manor house in return for some religious favour.

The Abbots of Osney in Oxfordshire, for instance, had quite a record for this sort of profitable arrangement. Indeed, the abbey itself was founded in 1327 as part of just such a deal. A local lady of the manor, Edith d'Oilley, wanted to atone for her part in Henry I's extra-marital activities, and she persuaded her husband Robert, egged on by her religious advisers, to build Osney Abbey as a penance on her behalf. He not only built it – on the site of the Oxford Railway Station – but also endowed it with a grant of land in **Weston Manor**, plus the parish church.

Eight years later Edith atoned still further – her relationship with King Henry must have given her quite a guilt complex. She gave some more land to another new abbey in nearby Otmoor. Unfortunately, that gesture was not quite so effective, because the land was very marshy, the monks got rheumatism, and they packed up and moved to Thame.

The Abbey of Osney, however, continued to prosper. A hundred years after its foundation, a descendant of its original benefactor fell deeply into debt and sold nearly all his land to the Abbot at a knock-down price. As part of the deal, he also gave him Weston Manor, in return for a promise that, when he died, he would be buried before the abbey's high altar.

The house remained the property of the Abbey for three hundred years. The Abbot's bailiff occupied it for most of the time, and held his courts in the Baron's Hall. But then along came Henry VIII and put an end to it all. The abbey was dissolved, and Weston Manor became involved in a new kind of deal, along with many other properties that Henry had acquired from the monasteries. He distributed them as pay-offs to those who had lent a hand in his, sometimes questionable, activities.

In the case of Weston Manor, he gave it to Sir John Williams of Thame, who had surveyed the monastic lands in Oxfordshire for him, and managed to finish up with quite a good share of them for himself. In due course, the house passed to his son-in-law, Lord Henry Norreys, and it stayed with the Norreys family and their relations by marriage, the Berties, until the last Bertie heir died in the Great War.

Between the wars Weston Manor passed through several hands until finishing up as one of the wartime retreats of the BBC. When these unlikely tenants moved out, a consortium of local farmers and shopkeepers bought it to run as a country club. It seems they were not too successful, because it was soon acquired by an enterprising gentleman called Mogford, who persuaded the Ministry of Labour to let him have fifty prisoners-of-war to help restore the place and turn it into a three-star hotel.

This was not the final adaptation. During the Cold War the Dunlop Tyre Company wanted to acquire it as a safe retreat to be used if the Russians turned

At Weston Manor in Oxfordshire, the abbot's bailiff used to hold court in what is now the dining-room of Weston Manor Hotel

nasty, and with the backing of the Home Office – perhaps anxious to ensure a steady supply of tyres for the Minister's limousine – they made an offer which Mr Mogford couldn't refuse.

However, the Russians decided not to invade, and Dunlop sold the house to a family who recreated Weston Manor Hotel. It has remained an hotel, in various private hands, ever since. The Baron's Hall, where the Abbot's bailiff held court, is now the dining-room, and the little chapel next door is used as an ante-room. The original moat has been restored and restocked with fish which, in the Abbot's time, would have been caught and eaten, but today they are just for decoration. While the abbots might recognise the moat, they could be baffled by the swimming-pool and squash court.

The tithe barn attached to the manor, where the tithes extracted by the bailiff were stored, became an Adaptable in its own right. According to local legend, Prince Rupert hid in the barn's chimney during the Civil War, while his famous opponent General Fairfax billeted himself in the manor house for the night. Rupert escaped early next morning disguised – as refugee Royals were inclined to be – as a maidservant. When the manor house became an hotel, the barn was converted to provide extra bedrooms and a lounge; it is now called 'Rupert's Cottage'.

Weston Manor must have looked as grand in medieval times as it does today, but the comforts enjoyed by the Abbots of Osney and their like were quite Spartan compared with the luxurious accommodation provided for archbishops. For over seven hundred years the Archbishops of York lived in what is still called **Cawood Castle**, though in their time it was more of a palace.

The original manor house was given to the See of York in AD 937 by King

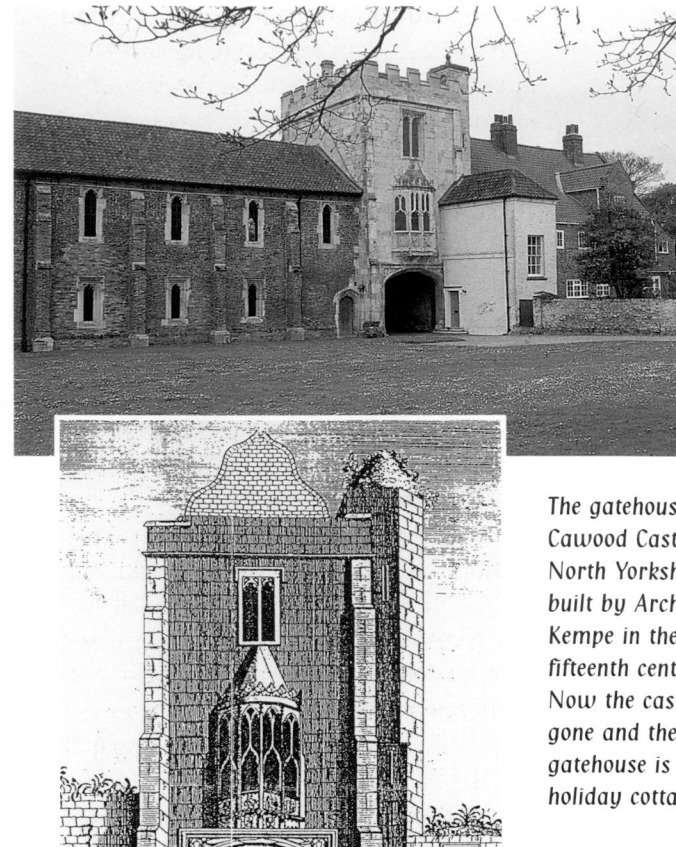

The gatehouse of Cawood Castle in North Yorkshire was built by Archbishop Kempe in the fifteenth century. Now the castle has gone and the gatehouse is a holiday cottage

Athelstan, as a thank-offering for his victory over the Danes, and subsequent archbishops made it literally fit for a king. The courts of several medieval monarchs made it their base camp while they went off to fight the Scots, and King Edward I even left his wife in residence there while he conducted his campaigns.

The archbishops were lavish in their hospitality – which, perhaps, is why Cawood was so popular among the Royals. Archbishop George Neville, for example, celebrated his enthronement in 1466 with a banquet for two thousand guests which lasted for four days. The subsequent hangovers probably lasted even longer.

Cardinal Wolsey is said to have had grandiose plans for extending and refurbishing the castle on the lines of Hampton Court, when he was sent there by Henry VIII but, before he could even book an architect, his volatile master had one of his frequent changes of mind. He was arrested for high treason, and died on his way back to London.

Archbishop Kempe fared rather better, and added the imposing gatehouse which is virtually all that remains of the castle. It was he who embellished it with the Cardinal's hats which feature on the carved stone shields over the archway. Archbishop George Mountain might have added even more, if he had not died a fortnight after his enthronement in 1628. 'He was scarcely warm in his seat than he was cold in his coffin,' as one contemporary writer succinctly observed.

Actually, George Mountain was quite a dab at the crisp *bon mot* himself. He was still Bishop of London when King Charles consulted him on whom to appoint to the vacancy at York. 'Hadst thou faith as a grain of mustard seed,' he rather brazenly responded, 'thou wouldst say to this Mountain, be removed to that See.' The King took the hint...

After Mountain's death Cawood Castle went downhill. During the Civil War it was held alternately by Royalists and Parliamentarians, and suffered considerable damage each time it changed hands. When Cromwell took over, the main building was dismantled and only the gatehouse remained serviceable. For a time

it was used as a courthouse, and a new staircase was installed to supplement the medieval spiral one leading up to the handsome old room on the first floor.

This proved a great help when the gatehouse came on the market as an Adaptable. It has been acquired in recent years by the Landmark Trust, and part of the adjoining house, which had been added later, was acquired with it to convert into a holiday cottage. The steep spiral staircase is still the only route up to the top floor, but it may be consoling to think you are following in the footsteps of Archbishop Kempe who, no doubt, climbed it when he was inspecting his new gatehouse, four hundred-odd years ago.

Perhaps the most improbable ecclesiastical Adaptable is St. Winifred's Well, at **Woolston** in Shropshire. It was dedicated to a seventh-century Welsh saint who was decapitated by a frustrated suitor on learning that she was dedicated to a life of chastity. Fortunately, her uncle happened to be a saint as well, and miraculously brought her back to life.

A little medieval chapel was built above the well, which was used as a courthouse after the Reformation. The well itself was

The medieval chapel at St. Winifred's Well at Woolston in Shropshire is now a holiday cottage, but some of the arrangements are still slightly medieval – the toilet facilities are on the far side of a public footpath

A Victorian quarry owner at Lamorna Cove in Cornwall built a workers' hostel incorporating a chapel they all had to attend. Now the hostel is an hotel and the chapel is the dining-room

Lamorna has an explosive Adaptable as well as an ecclesiastical one. The magazine house where gunpowder was stored for the quarry is now a holiday cottage, overlooking the cove

enlarged by a local squire who fancied having his own swimming-pool. Later, it was made available to the public, but it turned out to be an unwise move. There were all sorts of goings-on, entirely unsuited to a holy well, and it was closed altogether. That was during the reign of George II, and for the next two hundred years it was left undisturbed, but the little building is now used as a tiny holiday cottage, another adaptation by the Landmark Trust. One slightly medieval element still survives: the washing and toilet facilities are external – on the far side of a public footpath...

Finally, an Adaptable which was not entirely ecclesiastical, since it was built by a layman for laymen, but it did combine the ecclesiastical facilities of a residence and a place of worship for an all-male community, just like a monastery.

In 1856, on a wooded hillside above **Lamorna Cove** in Cornwall, a local quarry owner called John Freeman built accommodation for his manager and his quarrymen. Mr Freeman was a strict Baptist, and built the hostel in

the shape of a cross, incorporating a chapel large enough to take his entire workforce – who were all expected to attend.

In due course, the quarrymen moved out and the building became a kind of up-market boarding-house. In the early years of this century Lamorna Cove became very popular with London's artistic colony and in 1912 Sir Alfred Munnings forsook his native East Anglia to take a whole floor as his permanent residence. Many of his artist friends joined him at various times during the three years he lived there, including Augustus John and other notable figures. They could be quite Bohemian in their behaviour, and John Freeman would hardly have approved of some of the high jinks in what used to be his chapel.

Since then, the house has had its final adaptation as a peaceful country house hotel – with a no-smoking rule which Sir Alfred and his friends might have disapproved of in their turn. The vast chapel has been reduced to two-thirds its original size, and is now the Chapel dining-room.

Incidentally, the hotel is not the only Adaptable at Lamorna connected with the old quarry. The Magazine House, where the gunpowder for blasting the rock used to be stored, is now a small cottage. The occupier may still think twice before striking a match to light the fire...

View from Harbour, Lamorna Cove.

Eccentric Adaptables

• • • • • • • •

Caves and kiosks, clubhouses and outhouses, grandstands – and a grand finale

	Location	Old use	New use(s)
1	Alderley Edge, Cheshire	Telephone kiosk	Shower
2	Audlem, Cheshire	Market hall	Bus shelter
3	Eastbourne, East Sussex	Clubhouse	Youth hostel
4	Eyton-on-Severn, Shropshire	Summerhouse	Holiday accommodation
5	Fyfield, Essex: Fyfield Hall	Telephone kiosk	Aquarium
6	Hawkshead, Cumbria	Oak beam	Parish chest
7	Hexton, Hertfordshire	Village pump	Signpost
8	Huddersfield, Kirklees: Huddersfield Hotel	Telephone kiosk	Bar
9	Kirkby Lonsdale, Cumbria	Garden pavilion	Holiday accommodation
10	Long Compton, Warwickshire	Coach-house	Garage
11	Lund, East Yorkshire	Smithy	Bus shelter
12	Lympstone, Devon	Clock tower	Holiday accommodation
13	Marsden Bay, South Tyneside: Grotto	Cave dwelling	Mansion; restaurant and inn
14	Norwich, Norfolk: Unthank Road	Royal retirement room	Health promotion unit
15	Shenley, Hertfordshire	Buttery	Cottage
16	Sherborne, Gloucestershire	Grandstand	Cottages; dower house; stately home
17	Snape, Suffolk	Bridge	Bus shelter
18	West Burton, North Yorkshire	Smithy	Bus shelter and builder's store
19	Woodborough, Nottinghamshire	Stables	Farm outhouses; cottages
20	Woodford, Stockport: Davenport Arms	Telephone kiosk	Garden shed
21	Wothorpe, Cambridgeshire	Grandstand	Private residence

Ever sheltered in a shambles, or showered in a phone-box?

A cave at Marsden Bay in Tyne & Wear was hollowed out into a subterranean mansion; it is now a unique restaurant and inn, seen here from an adjacent cave

There are some Adaptables which are almost impossible to fit into any general category. How do you classify, for instance, the Grotto at **Marsden Bay** in Tyne and Wear? It was hollowed out of the cliff in 1782 by a local character known as Jack the Blaster. He made it into a home for himself and his family, and subsequent owners carried on where he left off, until his comparatively simple cave dwelling had expanded into a fifteen-roomed subterranean mansion. It was the manmade answer to one of Nature's marvels just offshore, Marsden Rock, which was pierced by a natural archway large enough for boats to pass through. It was only in 1997 that the archway was deemed unsafe, and a latter-day Jack the Blaster blew it to bits.

By then the Grotto had become an Adaptable – not everybody wants to live in a cave on a beach, no matter how many rooms it may have. It was converted into a unique restaurant and inn, reached by a lift down Marsden Cliff. From it the diners can watch the kittiwakes and cormorants on what is left of Marsden Rock.

Unfortunately, there were not enough Jack the Blasters to create an entire chapter of hollowed-out cave Adaptables. One of his contemporaries, a Yorkshire weaver called Thomas Hill, did carve out a dwelling for himself in the cliffside at **Knaresborough**, not far from the cave occupied by the renowned soothsayer

Mother Shipton, and there are some cliff dwellings at **Mansfield** in Nottinghamshire, one or two even graced by chimneys and pantiled roofs – but are they real Adaptables? After all, there is nothing new about living in caves, as all fans of the Flintstones well know. But the Grotto, converted from a cave home into a cave pub, gives Jack the Blaster a cave-shaped niche in the Adaptable Hall of Fame.

There is a rather better chance of finding Adaptables on the roadside than the cliffside. The old red telephone kiosks, for example, brain children of Sir Giles Gilbert Scott in the 1920s, and still regarded with great affection and nostalgia, have fallen victim to progress and new technology. Two or three thousand still survive on their original roadside sites, fulfilling their original roles, but thirty thousand more have disappeared into the scrap-yards. Only a few hundred, in varying stages of dilapidation, live on in the gardens of Friends of the Phone Box, generally just as bizarre ornaments, occasionally, as in the case of the Davenport Arms at **Woodford** in Stockport, as potential garden sheds. And just one or two, reglazed and freshly

This phone box has no phone – it serves as an unusual garden shed in a pub garden at Woodford, near Manchester

This phone box has left the roadside to become an unlikely aquarium at Fyfield Hall in Essex...

birdcages and bookcases – all adapted from redundant phone boxes. And those are just the indoor versions. If your house, unlike Fyfield Hall, would have difficulty in accommodating a chunk of cast iron, teak and glass, eight feet high and weighing three-quarters of a ton – which builds up to about three-and-a-half tons for a phone box aquarium like Mr White's, once it has been fitted with reinforced armoured glass and filled with water – then it could always find a place in the garden as a tool-shed or a greenhouse.

In some cases customers have gone full circle and asked for the phone box to be converted back into a phone box again, complete with bakelite telephone and 'Press Button A or B' mechanism. In that case, however, the royal crown above the door has to be covered up, and the box painted any colour but red.

'I love everything about old telephone kiosks,' says Mr White. 'I think they are a design classic and a national treasure.' And, of course, a nice little earner too, but Mr White takes a great pride in his Adaptables: 'Perhaps you imagine Sir Giles Gilbert Scott would have been bemused at what we are doing here – but I dare say he would have accepted a drink from his beloved K6 Kiosk!'

But he might draw the line at taking a shower in one. Mr David Hughes of **Alderley Edge** in Cheshire has no such qualms – though the wealth of windows on his telephone-box shower cabinet, which still had clear glass in when I last saw it, could make taking a shower something of a spectator sport...

Other roadside Adaptables have remained beside the road. The village pump at **Hexton** in Hertfordshire, for instance, which was presented to the village by a local benefactor in 1846, became redundant when a bore was sunk

painted, have been given a new life and purpose in new and unlikely surroundings.

One of the earliest telephone box Adaptables is in the **Huddersfield Hotel** in Yorkshire, where they claim it is the smallest bar in the world. There is just room in it for a couple of shelves of bottles, and the barman. But there is a rather more elaborate domestic version at **Fyfield Hall** in Essex. Mr Willy White's 'Kocktail Cabinet' is fitted with a cold cabinet, a wine rack, decanters, a shelf for bottles and a rack for glasses.

Mr White has, in fact, made quite a business out of kiosk Adaptables. In an elegantly illustrated glossy brochure he offers washing-machines, tumble-driers, self-contained cooking hobs, fridge-freezers, ice machines, saunas, aquaria,

...while the village pump at Hexton in Hertfordshire has been adapted as a signpost

The little market hall called the Shambles at Audlem in Cheshire is now used as a bus shelter...

The former smithy at Lund in East Yorkshire makes a convenient bus shelter, with seats and strip-lighting

nearby. It had a brief reprieve in 1935 when the borehole ran dry, but once the water supply had been permanently restored, a new use had to be found for it. Today, it serves as a rather ornate signpost.

On a slightly larger scale, a variety of roadside Adaptables have finished up as bus shelters. One of the most historic is the former Shambles at **Audlem** in Cheshire, built in the 1730s as part of the market. A century later the market more or less ceased to operate, and the little market hall closed down. It did have a brief revival after the First World War, but again became redundant in the 1920s. It never officially changed use, but these days it comes in very handy during bad weather for passengers waiting for the local bus. It is perhaps the only village bus shelter which has a roof supported by eight Tuscan columns.

There are a couple of humbler examples at **Lund** in the East Riding of Yorkshire and **West Burton** in North Yorkshire, where former smithies have been adapted for the same

purpose. The open-fronted smithy at **Lund** is still recognisable as such, with the brickwork of the forge left in place, but it now has a long bench seat at the back, modern lighting in the roof, a smart notice-board on the wall, and a substantial chunk of tree trunk in the middle of the floor to provide additional seating. In spite of all these comforts though, I suspect that passengers faced with a long wait may prefer to pass the time in the Wellington Inn next door.

At **West Burton** the smithy stands on the picturesque village green, a rather unattractive hut-like building which has one end adapted as the bus shelter, while the interior has been used for years as a builder's store. In 1997 the owner applied to make the old smithy a full-scale Adaptable and turn it into a tea-shop, which would be very handy for the bus passengers languishing in the shelter, but when I visited West Burton there was a strong anti-tea-shop lobby among the villagers, and it looked as though the shelterers would remain unrefreshed.

But perhaps the oddest origin for a bus shelter is at **Snape** in Suffolk. In 1959 a one-hundred-and-fifty-year-old humpbacked bridge across the river was replaced by a modern one. The bricks from

The roof of the bus shelter at Snape in Suffolk looks like a hump-back bridge – and that is exactly what it was

The rather splendid 'summerhouse' at Eyton-on-Severn in Shropshire – it was actually a guest annexe to the Big House, and is now a holiday cottage

The squire's personal carriage shelter outside the church at Long Compton in Warwickshire now copes with cars instead

the original bridge were used to build the bus shelter which stands on the common, and its 'hump' is now the curved roof of the shelter.

Another form of roadside shelter has itself been adapted to a different use. It is a building erected in the last century at **Long Compton** in Warwickshire, opposite the lych-gate to the churchyard – which itself is a kind of Adaptable, because it was a cottage with part of the lower storey removed to make an archway. One regular attender at the church in the 1830s was Sir George Philips, who rebuilt Weston House just outside the village. Sir George drove to Sunday morning services in an elegant carriage escorted by footmen, so as part of his building programme he erected a kind of waiting-room cum coach-house opposite the church 'to accommodate the equipage'. In more recent times its use has adjusted to the changing modes of travel, and it is now a garage.

This is one rather odd example of how an ancillary building connected with a great house can become an Adaptable, while the house itself remained unchanged, or was adapted to some quite different use, or disappeared altogether – as in the case of Sir George's Weston House, where only

the lodges survive. Sometimes the modest little buildings are picturesque enough to be adapted as holiday cottages, as in the case of the 'Summerhouse' at **Eyton-on-Severn** in Shropshire.

It is not quite the sort of summerhouse you see in suburban gardens, nor was it used for the same purpose. It was built in 1607 as extra accommodation for the guests of Sir Francis Newport. They could retire there after a banquet to gossip about their host and fellow guests over a couple of nightcaps, with no fear of being overheard by someone in the next bedroom. The mansion has long since disappeared, but the octagonal brick summerhouse still stands, commanding splendid views of the Shropshire countryside. Its staircase turret, with an ogee cap that looks rather like an elegant windmill, is a landmark for miles around. The Vivat Trust won prizes for restoring and adapting it, and it is now let for self-catering holidays.

This stone pavilion at Kirkby Lonsdale in Cumbria has become a holiday cottage, with a view that Ruskin admired and Turner painted

The clock tower at Lympstone in Devon, an unusual adaptation into a residence

The Trust carried out a similar adaptation with a garden pavilion at **Kirkby Lonsdale** in Cumbria. Here again, 'pavilion' is a misleading term. This is no wooden hut where cricketers' wives serve teas, but a solid stone building. Again the views are impressive, in this case across the valley of the Lune – 'one of the loveliest scenes in England,' as John Ruskin described it.

The other major operator in this type of Adaptable, the Landmark Trust, has dealt with a number of ancillary buildings in this way. One of the most unusual is the Peters Clock Tower at **Lympstone** in Devon, beside the Exe estuary. It was built in 1885 by William Peters, who lived in the nearby great house, as a memorial to his wife Mary. As the Trust observes rather wryly: 'It is no great work of architecture – a very distant and poor relation of St. Mark's in Venice.' But it stands on the water's edge, and again the views are spectacular. For a couple who enjoy very small rooms and very steep spiral staircases, the accommodation is ideal. They also won't need a watch; the clock still works.

Some ancillary Adaptables were built to provide a particular service for the mansion from which they originated. The Old Buttery at **Shenley** in Hertfordshire, for instance, was built to provide a steady supply of home-made butter for Porter's Park, once the home of Christopher Wren's fellow architect, Nicholas Hawksmoor, who is buried in the churchyard. The mansion became Shenley Hospital, which now stands empty surrounded by new estates. The buttery has been converted into a two-bedroomed cottage with an octagonal domed dining-room and, to keep it company from the old days, the chapel still functions too, but as a school for music, dance and drama.

There is an unlikely little group of Adaptables connected with horse-racing, apart from the more obvious stable conversions – though there is a very imposing example worth mentioning at **Woodborough** in Nottinghamshire. A range of Victorian racing stables, two storeys high with a gabled entrance, first became part of a market garden, then served as outhouses for Manor Farm, and has now become a row of terraced cottages, all of which have equestrian-related names like 'Hickstead' as a reminder of past glories.

But, in this field, it is the grandstand Adaptable which is understandably rare. Modern grandstands are rather Spartan on the whole, the public areas open to the elements, just the hospitality suites and directors' boxes allowed the luxury of windows, comfortable chairs and cocktail bars. In earlier times, however, grandstands were only built for the gentry anyway –

Sporting Adaptables: a former horse-racing grandstand at Wothorpe in Cambridgeshire...

...and a grandstand where guests at Sherborne House in Gloucestershire watched deer-coursing

The Old Buttery at what used to be Shenley Hospital in Hertfordshire, another unusual residential Adaptable

the public had to make do as best they could – so every comfort was provided, in buildings as lavish as the local landowner could afford.

In 1766 the Marquis of Exeter had a very elegant brick grandstand erected on what used to be the Burghley estate racecourse at **Wothorpe** in Cambridgeshire. It is claimed to be the oldest of its kind in the country, and the Marquis made sure it set a high standard to follow, with handsome archways on the ground floor, a good view through the windows on the first floor, and a better view still from the flat roof. It was from here in later years that privileged racegoers were able to watch the legendary jockey Fred Archer ride his first winner, and he also made his final appearance at the last meeting there in 1873. The grandstand was restored in 1996, ready to be adapted as a four-bedroomed house.

Although the Wothorpe grandstand was the first in the horse-racing field, an equally opulent version had already been built at

The racing stables at Woodborough in Nottinghamshire are now 'horsey' cottages

Sherborne in Gloucestershire in the previous century, for spectators at a very different kind of race. The runners were dogs, not horses, and they were not greyhounds chasing an imitation rabbit, but hunting dogs chasing a very real stag.

Deer-coursing was a popular spectator sport among landed gentry in the 1600s, before people thought of climbing on to horses and joining in too. And it was primarily of interest to the gambling fraternity, betting on which dog caught the stag first. This is what appealed to John Dutton of Sherborne House, who built the grandstand for himself and his guests.

'Crump' Dutton, as he was called because of his hunched back, was an inveterate gambler. At his splendid grandstand he and his guests could enjoy the chase and lose their money in comfort.

When deer-coursing fell out of favour and the gentry went fox-hunting instead,

Eccentric Adaptables

A final batch of odd Adaptables: a retiring room for King Edward VII during the Royal Norfolk Show in Norwich is now part of a health promotion unit...

Crump's grandstand became an early Adaptable. First it served as two gamekeepers' cottages, until a much later Dutton, Emma Lady Sherborne, had it converted into a dower house. In more recent years Lord and Lady Sherborne moved permanently into the former grandstand, now Lodge Park, and lived there until the 1980s. It is now owned by the National Trust, who are restoring it to its original condition – though without the deer-coursing. Sherborne House has itself become an Adaptable; it has been converted into luxury apartments.

...a tiebeam from the roof of Hawkshead Church in Cumbria was adapted as a parish chest...

Another spectator Adaptable of much more modest proportions, but for a much more distinguished spectator, is now part of a health promotion unit in Unthank Road, **Norwich** in Norfolk. It was built specifically for King Edward VII when he was Prince of Wales, to use as a retirement room during his visits to the annual Royal Norfolk Show, which used to be held in that area of Norwich.

A building at **Eastbourne** in East Sussex, which offered shelter and refreshment to spectators and players alike, is an unusual Adaptable because the adaptation generally goes the other way. A number of country mansions have been converted into golf clubhouses, but it is rare to find, in a game which is constantly growing in popularity, a clubhouse which

...and the nineteenth hole at Eastbourne Downs Golf Club in East Sussex, which opened in 1909 looking slightly different, is now a youth hostel. The club has moved into bigger premises

has been converted to something else. The one at Eastbourne Downs is now a thirty-two-bed self-catering youth hostel – though it still advertises 'a plethora of recreational opportunities', which presumably includes golf, because Eastbourne Downs Golf Club is still prospering. Indeed, it only vacated its original clubhouse, which dates back to the founding of the club nearly ninety years ago, in order to move into more spacious premises in 1973.

Finally, an Adaptable which fits into no obvious category, though it used to fit very neatly into a church roof. **Hawkshead Church** in the Lake District was once well known to William Wordsworth when he went to school in the village, and tourists are often shown the seat along the church wall where he used it sit. Or they may be told about the 'Buried in Wool' certificates which are held in the church archives, introduced to enforce the use of woollen instead of linen shrouds, to boost the wool trade. But they may not know about the curious little Adaptable which is kept in a side chapel.

It is an oak tie-beam which was removed from the roof during restoration work and might have been discarded altogether, until an ingenious carpenter hollowed out part of it, fitted a lid with three separate locks – one key for the vicar, two for the churchwardens – and presented them with what must surely be the Church of England's oddest parish chest. In this case it has the last word in Adaptables...

Regional Maps

• • • • • • • • • •

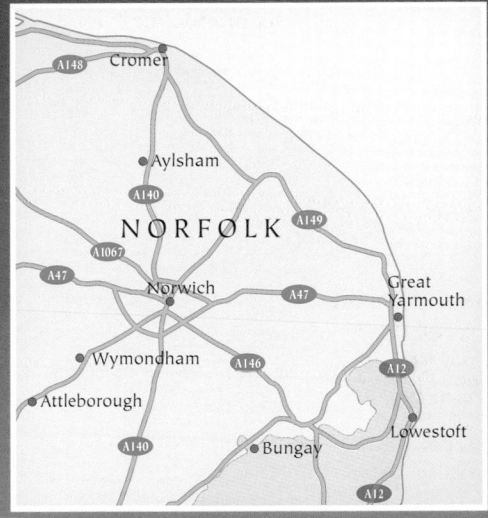

These maps show the positions of the Adaptables region by region. The map numbers, from 1 to 11, correspond to the cross-references given in the index. The locations shown on each map are listed in a key alongside which also includes page numbers.

These maps are intended only as a general guide to the location of the buildings featured in this book. They should not be used as route maps – a more detailed route-planner or road atlas is recommended for this purpose.

Brown areas on the maps indicate urban regions comprising several local authority areas which are too small to be shown clearly. However, the map key entries for Adaptables in these regions do include the name of the appropriate local authority area.

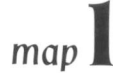

map 1

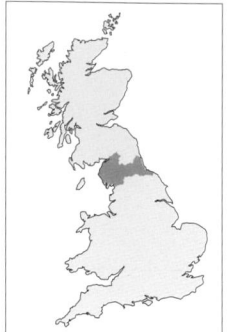

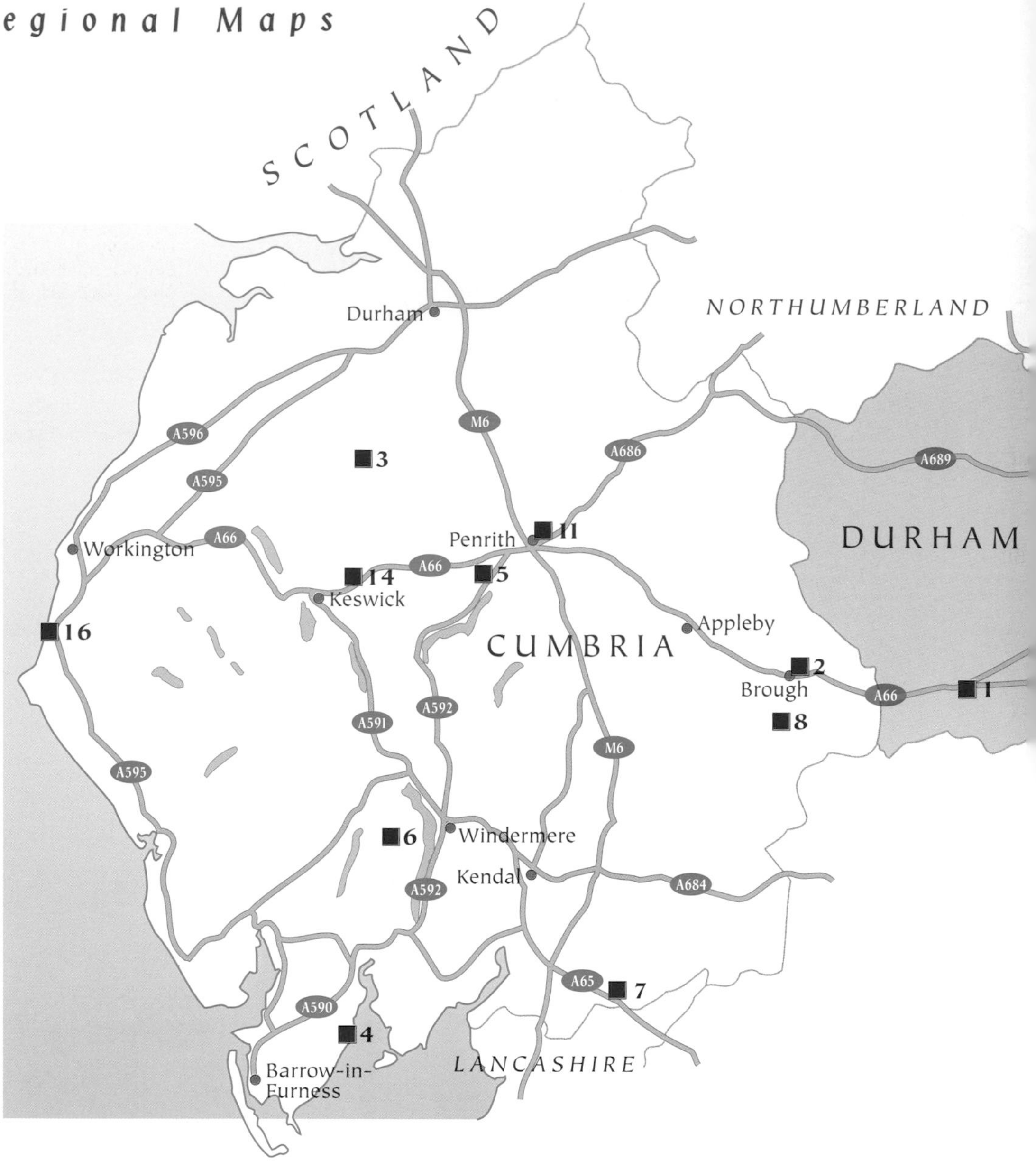

SCOTLAND
NORTHUMBERLAND
DURHAM
CUMBRIA
LANCASHIRE
Durham
Workington
Penrith
Keswick
Appleby
Brough
Windermere
Kendal
Barrow-in-Furness
M6
A596
A595
A66
A686
A689
A591
A592
A684
A65
A590
1
2
3
4
5
6
7
8
11
14
16

	Location	Page
1	Bowes, County Durham	103-4
2	Brough, Cumbria: Post office	87-8
3	Caldbeck, Cumbria	97
4	Conishead, Cumbria	153-4
5	Dacre, Cumbria: Dacre Castle	115
6	Hawkshead, Cumbria	168
7	Kirkby Lonsdale, Cumbria	166
8	Kirkby Stephen, Cumbria	57
9	Marsden Bay, South Tyneside: Grotto	162
10	Newcastle-upon-Tyne	64
	Balmbra's	86

	Location	Page
11	Penrith, Cumbria: Dame Birkett's School	104-5
12	Seaham, County Durham: Seaham Hall	130-1
13	Thorpe Thewles, Stockton-on-Tees: Castle Eden Walkway	69
14	Threlkeld, Cumbria: Far End Row Farm	129
15	Washington, Sunderland: Washington Arts Centre	23
16	Whitehaven, Cumbria: Coastguard station	14
17	Wilton Castle, Redcar and Cleveland	45-6

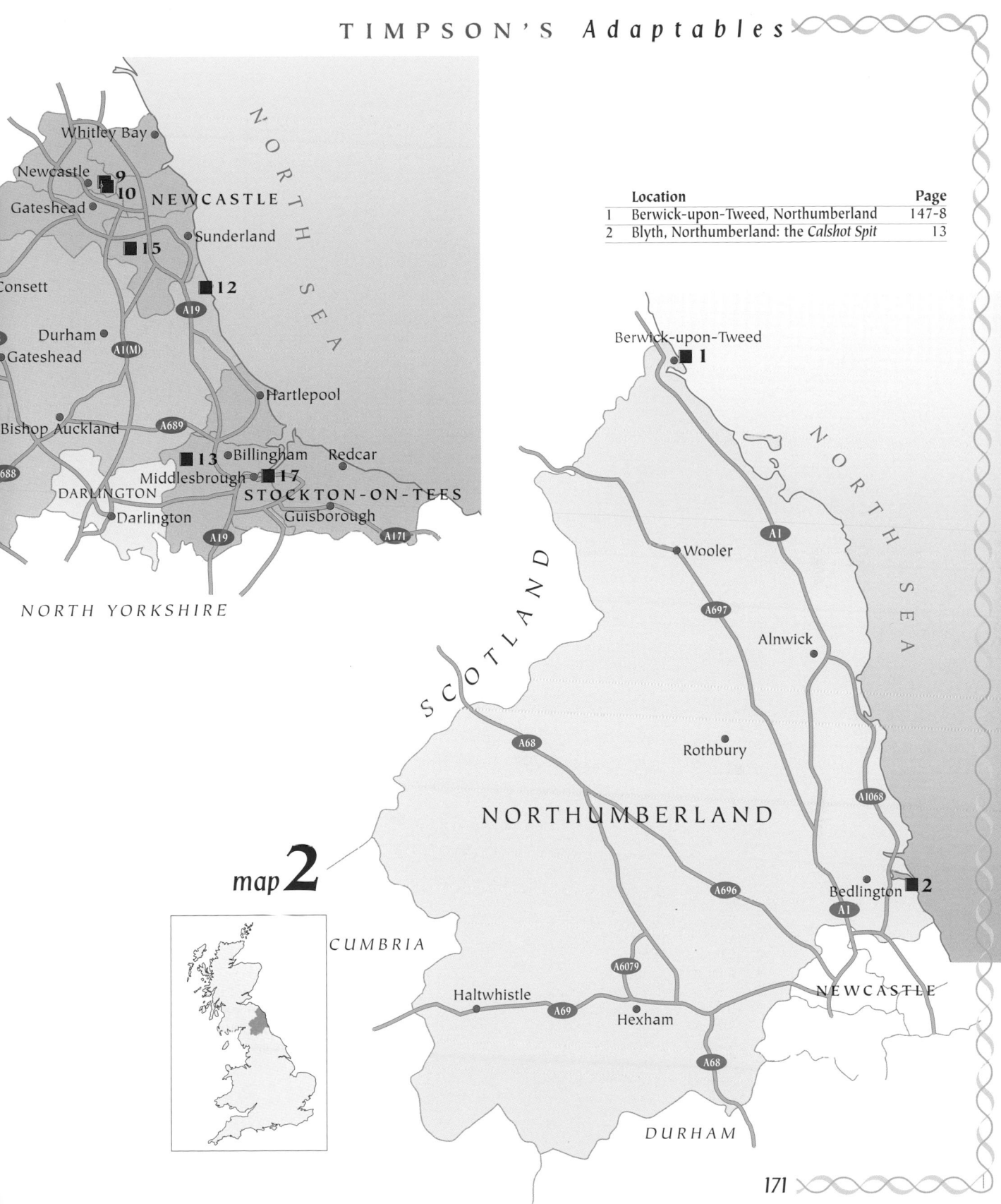

Location	Page
1 Berwick-upon-Tweed, Northumberland	147-8
2 Blyth, Northumberland: the *Calshot Spit*	13

Whitley Bay

Newcastle 9
10 NEWCASTLE

Gateshead

Sunderland

Consett 15

12

Durham
Gateshead A1(M) A19

Hartlepool

Bishop Auckland A689

688 13 Billingham Redcar
Middlesbrough 17
DARLINGTON STOCKTON-ON-TEES
Darlington Guisborough A19 A171

NORTH YORKSHIRE

NORTH SEA

Berwick-upon-Tweed 1

SCOTLAND

Wooler

A1

A697

Alnwick

A68

Rothbury

NORTHUMBERLAND

A1068

map 2

CUMBRIA

A696

Bedlington 2
A1

A6079

Haltwhistle

A69

Hexham

NEWCASTLE

A68

DURHAM

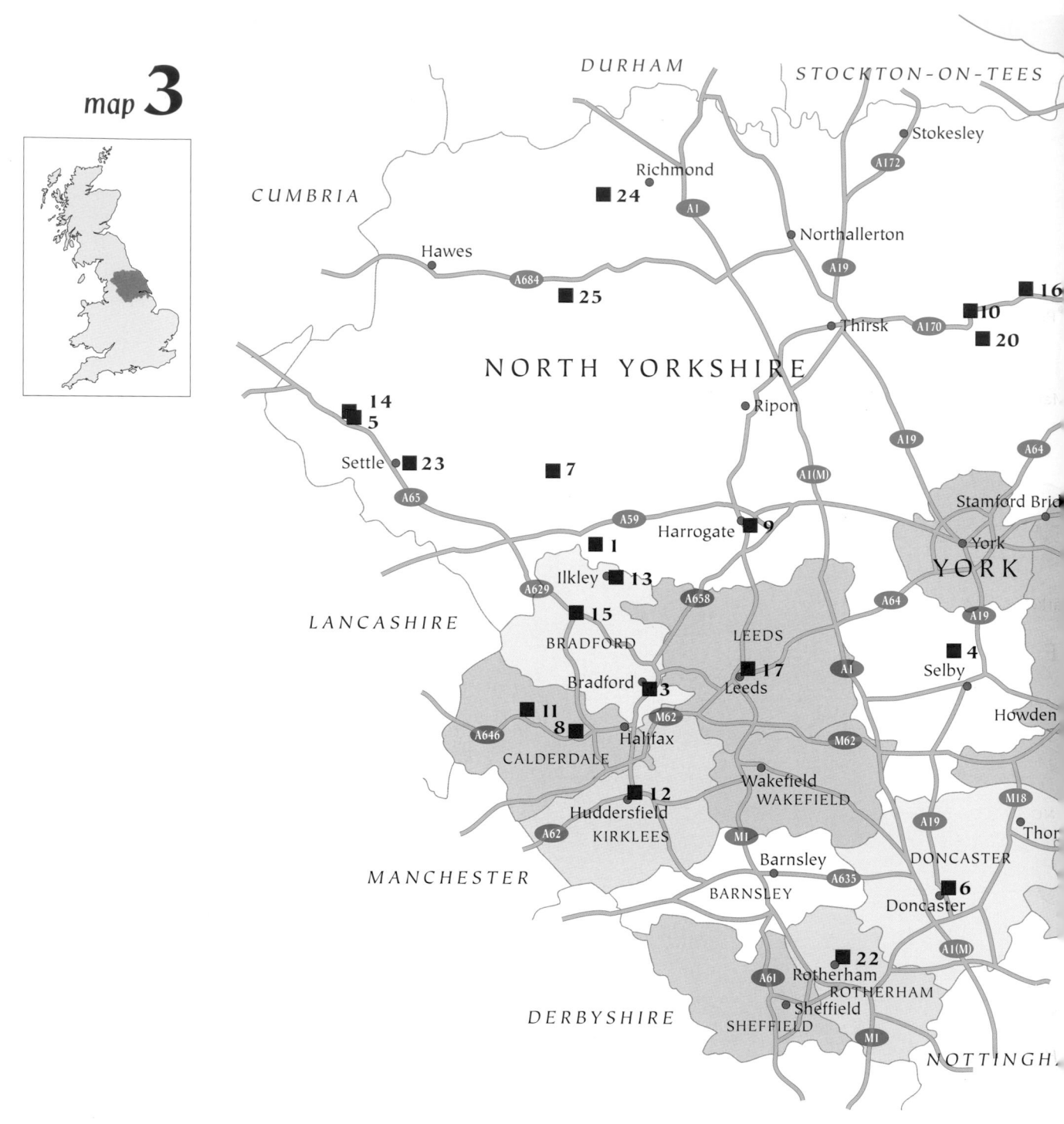

map **3**

DURHAM

STOCKTON-ON-TEES

Stokesley

A172

CUMBRIA

Richmond

■ **24**

A1

Northallerton

Hawes

A19

A684

■ **25**

NORTH YORKSHIRE

Thirsk

■ **16**

A170 ■**10**

■ **20**

Ripon

A19

A64

14

■

5

A1(M)

Stamford Brid

Settle ■ **23**

York

A65

YORK

A59

■ **7**

Harrogate ■**9**

■ **1**

A64

A19

Ilkley ■■ **13**

A658

LANCASHIRE

A629

15

■

LEEDS

A1

4

■

BRADFORD

Selby

A646

Bradford ■**3**

17

■

Leeds

Howden

11

■

M62

8■

Halifax

M62

M18

CALDERDALE

Wakefield

Thor

A19

WAKEFIELD

DONCASTER

■ **12**

Huddersfield

M1

Barnsley

A62

KIRKLEES

A635

6

■

MANCHESTER

BARNSLEY

Doncaster

A1(M)

22

■

A61

Rotherham

ROTHERHAM

DERBYSHIRE

SHEFFIELD

Sheffield

M1

NOTTINGH.

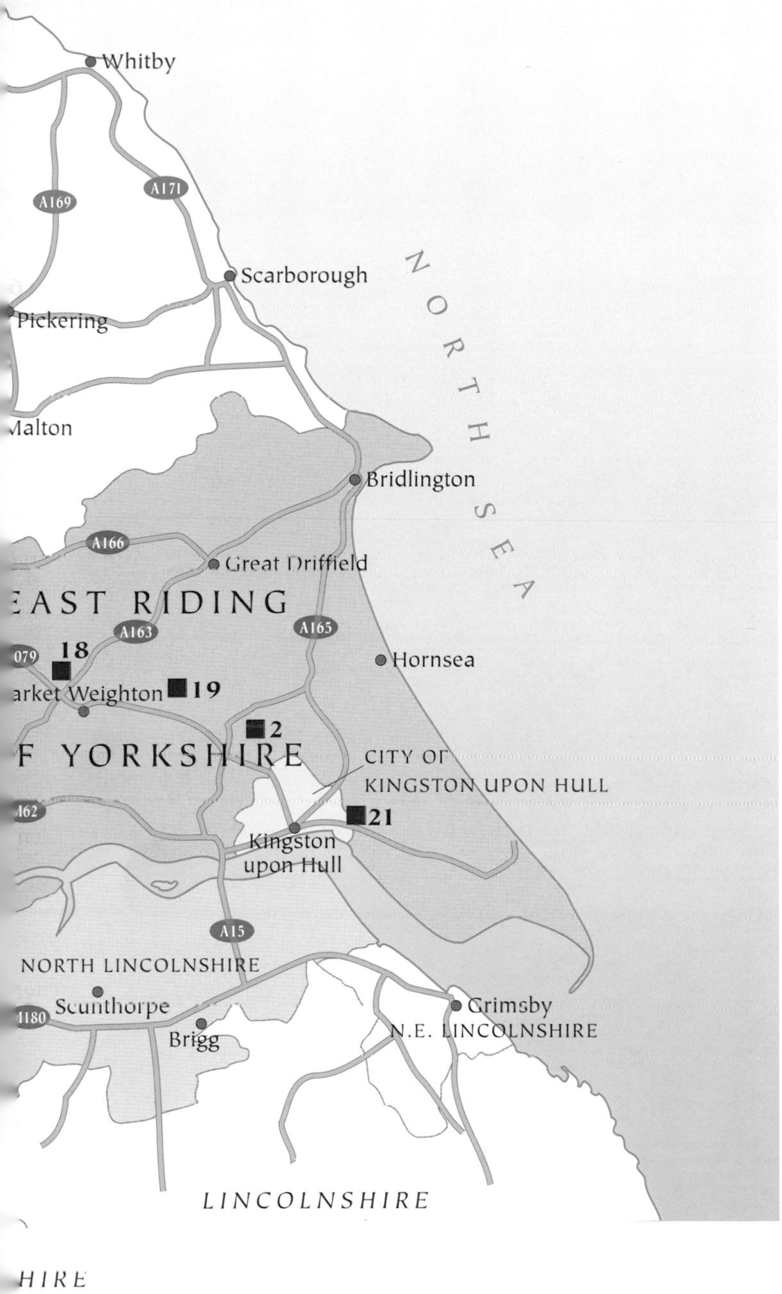

	Location	Page
1	Beamsley Hospital, North Yorkshire	124
2	Beverley, East Yorkshire: Youth Hostel	154
3	Bradford	79
	Sheik's restaurant	55
4	Cawood Castle, North Yorkshire	158
5	Clapham, North Yorkshire: Station House	66
6	Doncaster	55
7	Grassington, North Yorkshire: Pletts Barn	24
	Tom Lee's Smiddy	28
	Town Hall	105-6
8	Halifax, Calderdale: Piece Hall	79
	The Playhouse	54
9	Harrogate, North Yorkshire: St. Luke's Church	51
10	Helmsley, North Yorkshire	146
	Duncombe Park	109
11	Heptonstall, Calderdale	79
12	Huddersfield, Kirklees: Huddersfield Hotel	163
	Lawrence Batley Theatre	56-7
13	Ilkley, Bradford: Denton Hall	44
14	Ingleborough, North Yorkshire: Ingleborough Hall	109-10
15	Keighley, Bradford	55
16	Kirkbymoorside, North Yorkshire: Mr Towler's	89
17	Leeds	95
18	Londesborough, East Yorkshire: Village hall	97-8
19	Lund, East Yorkshire	27,164
20	Nunnington, North Yorkshire: Ryedale Lodge Hotel	66
21	Paull, East Yorkshire	11
22	Rotherham: Congregational Church	54
23	Settle, North Yorkshire: National Westminster Bank	72-3
24	Swaledale, North Yorkshire: Marrick Priory	152
25	West Burton, North Yorkshire	27, 164

Ryedale Lodge Hotel – once Nunnington Station

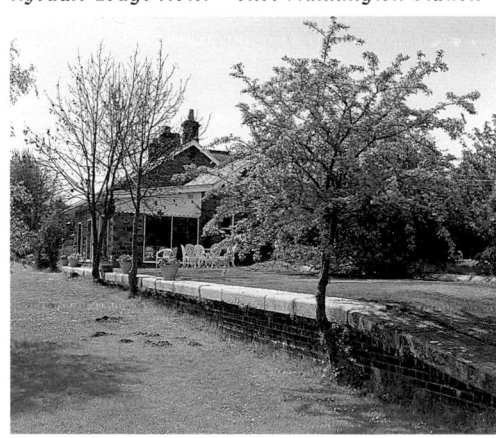

map **4**

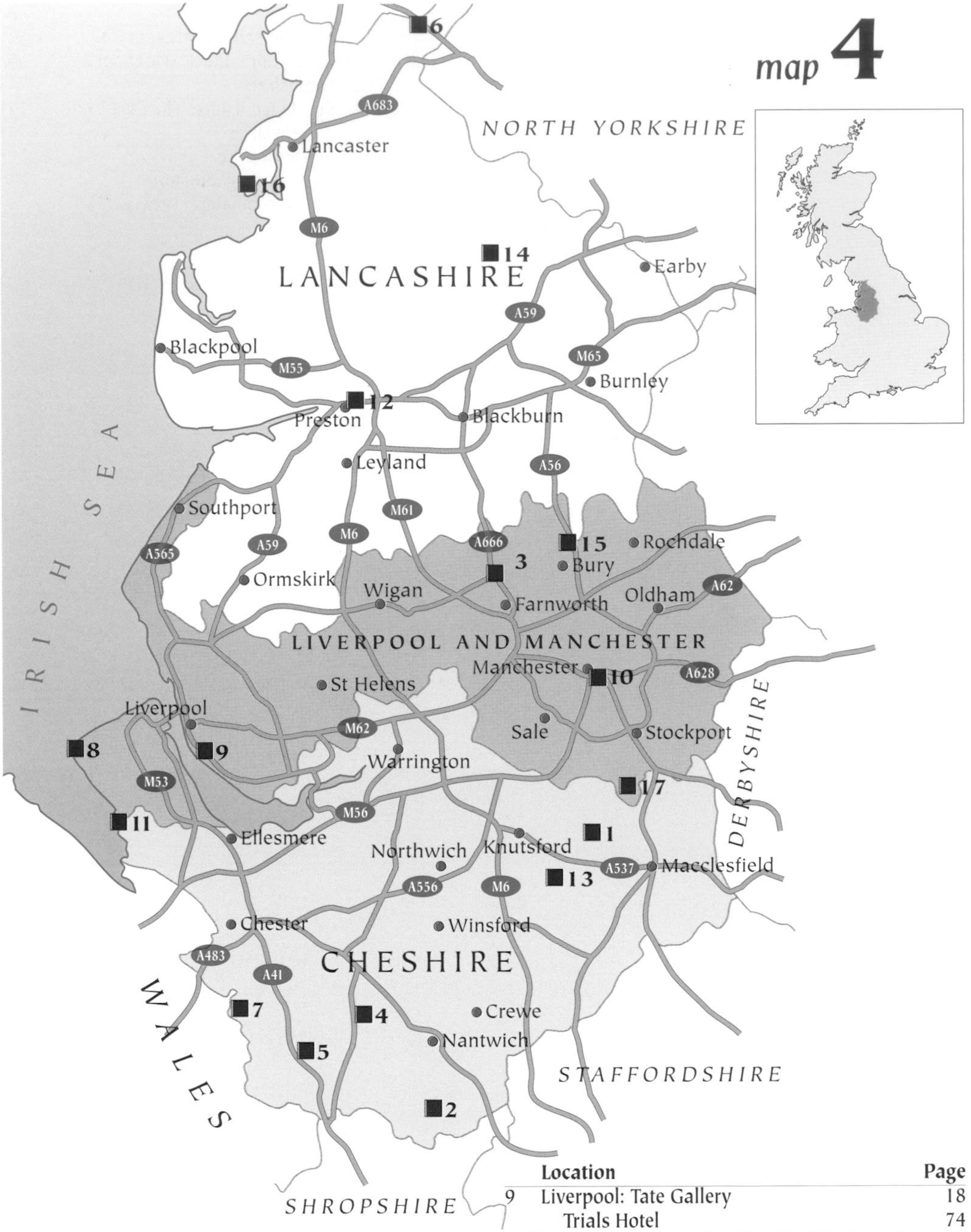

NORTH YORKSHIRE

Lancaster

■16

LANCASHIRE

■14

Earby

A59

M6

M65

Blackpool

Burnley

M55

■12

Preston

Blackburn

Leyland

A56

Southport

M61

■15

Rochdale

A59

M6

A666

3

Bury

A565

A62

Ormskirk

Wigan

Farnworth

Oldham

LIVERPOOL AND MANCHESTER

Manchester

■10

A628

St Helens

Liverpool

Sale

Stockport

M62

■9

■17

■8

DERBYSHIRE

Warrington

■1

M53

M56

Ellesmere

■11

Knutsford

Northwich

A537

Macclesfield

■13

A556

M6

Chester

Winsford

A483

CHESHIRE

A41

■7

■4

Crewe

■5

Nantwich

STAFFORDSHIRE

■2

IRISH SEA

WALES

SHROPSHIRE

Glossop

A628

Buxton

■3

A6

■1

DER

A515

■11

Ashborne

A52

STAFFORDSHIRE

A3

TIMPSON'S *Adaptables*

map 5

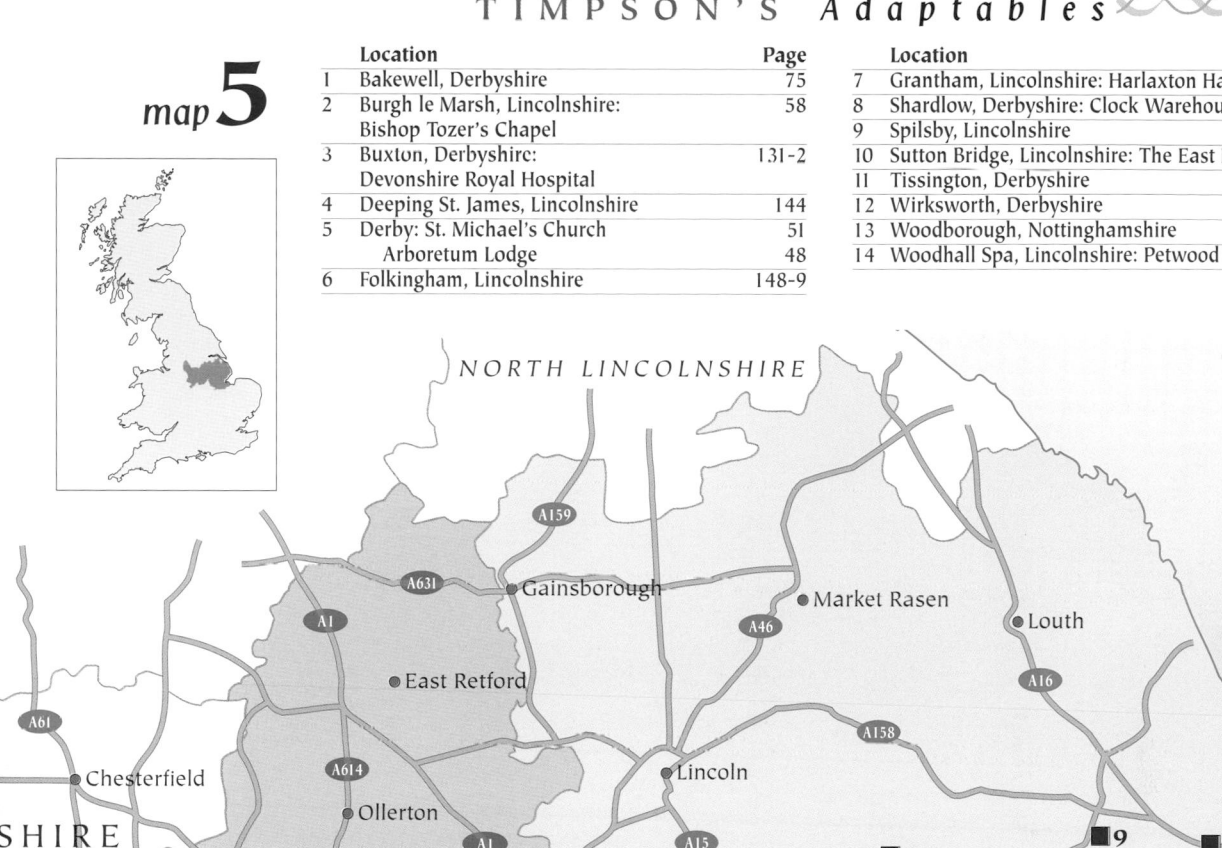

map **6**

The Old Lion, Dunchurch, where the Gunpowder Plot was hatched – now a private house

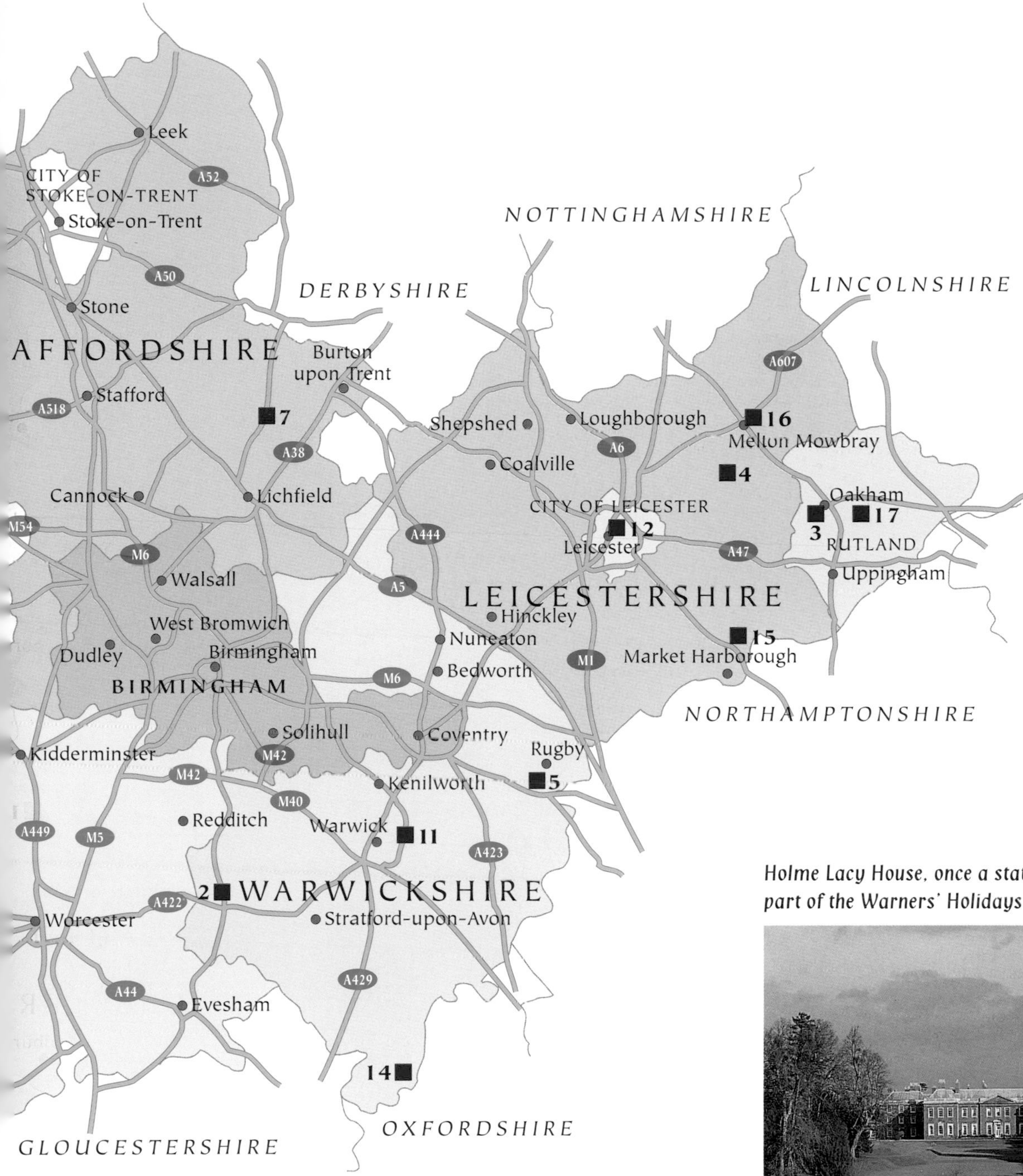

Leek

CITY OF
STOKE-ON-TRENT
Stoke-on-Trent

A52

NOTTINGHAMSHIRE

DERBYSHIRE

LINCOLNSHIRE

A50

Stone

AFFORDSHIRE

Burton
upon Trent

A607

■ 7

Shepshed

Loughborough

■ 16
Melton Mowbray

A518

Stafford

A38

Coalville

A6

■ 4

Oakham

A54

Cannock

Lichfield

CITY OF LEICESTER

■ 17
RUTLAND

M54

A444

Leicester

■ 12

3 ■

A47

Uppingham

M6

A5

LEICESTERSHIRE

Walsall

West Bromwich

Hinckley

Birmingham

Nuneaton

■ 15

Dudley

BIRMINGHAM

M6

Bedworth

Market Harborough

M1

NORTHAMPTONSHIRE

Solihull

Coventry

Kidderminster

M42

Rugby

Kenilworth

■ 5

M42

M40

Redditch

Warwick

■ 11

A449

M5

A423

2 ■ WARWICKSHIRE

A422

Worcester

Stratford-upon-Avon

A429

A44

Evesham

■ 14

GLOUCESTERSHIRE

OXFORDSHIRE

Holme Lacy House, once a stately home, is now
part of the Warners' Holidays empire

map 7

HEREFORD AND WORCESTER

Tewkesbury **25**

M50

M5

A40 **22**

Cheltenham

Gloucester

GLOUCESTERSHIRE

A48

A417 A429 **3**

Stroud

M5

Lydney

Nailsworth

Cirencester

A419

A433

A429

26 M5

M4

SOUTH GLOUCESTERSHIRE

Chipping Sodbury

M4

CITY OF BRISTOL

Avonmouth

8

Bristol

A46

Chippenham

Clevedon

N.W. SOMERSET

Weston-super-Mare

M5

BATH & N.E SOMERSET

Bath **2**

6

A4

Devizes

12

A37

Midsomer Norton

Trowbridge

WILTSHIRE

SOMERSET

Warminster

A360

A36

A303

A30

DORSET

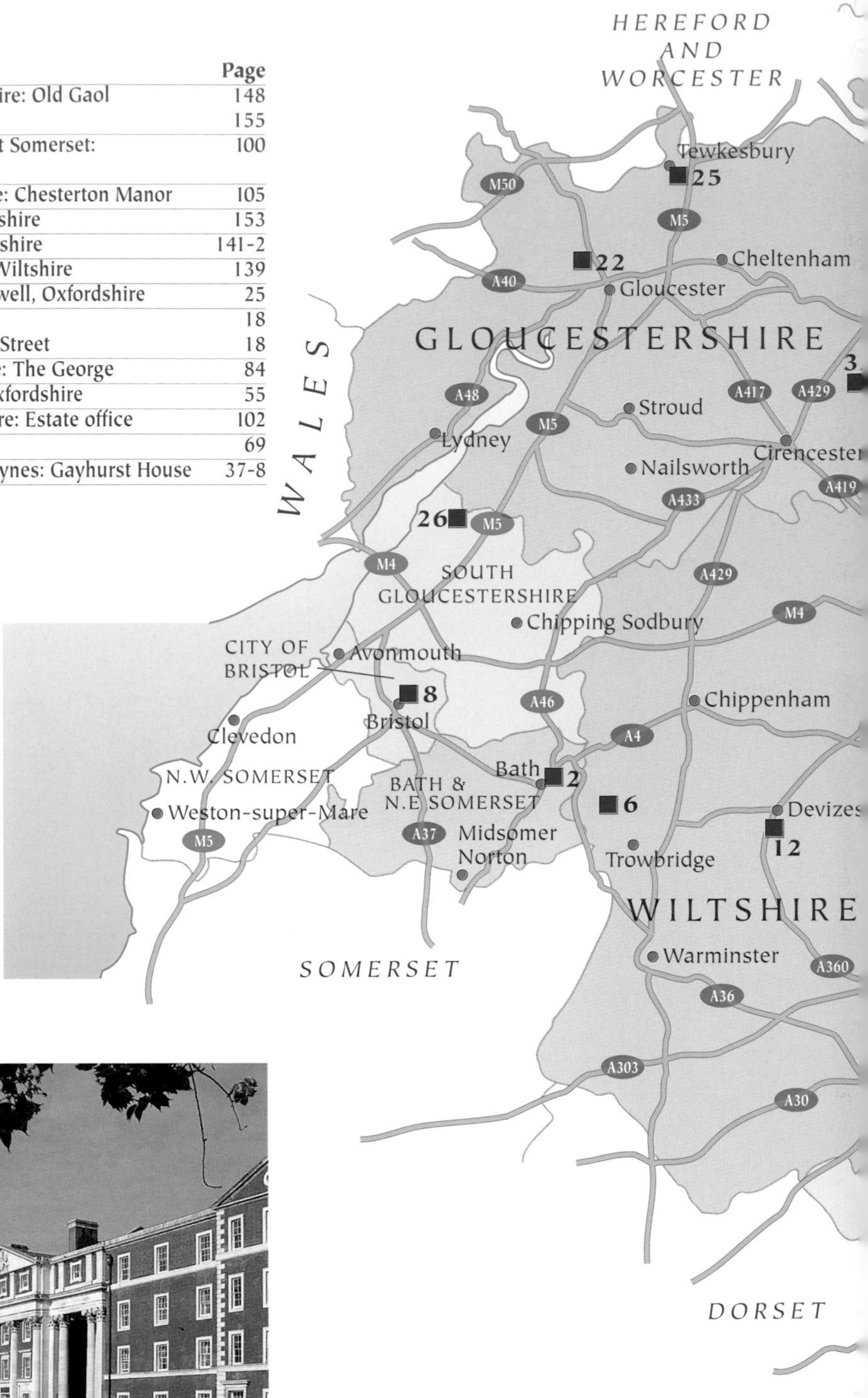

The Peninsula Barracks at Winchester, now privately occupied

WARWICKSHIRE

NORTHAMPTONSHIRE

17

13

M1

MILTON KEYNES

Banbury

Milton
Keynes

23

44

5

Buckingham

10

11

Stow on
the Wold

Chipping Norton

Bicester

3

BUCKINGHAMSHIRE

A4146

A413

21

Woodstock

29

Aylesbury

A41

40

20

9

A44

A41

Oxford

18

30

28

OXFORDSHIRE

Chesham

A420

A413

1

Abingdon

Wallingford

7

27

Wantate

15

High
Wycombe

THAMESDOWN

M40

Swindon

4

Lambourne

24

Slough

Maidenhead

BERKSHIRE

Windsor

M4

Reading

Marlborough

Bracknell

A4

Newbury

Wokingham

A322

A338

A33

A34

M3

SURREY

Basingstoke

Aldershot

A303

Andover

A338

M3

Alton

HAMPSHIRE

A31

A36

19

**WEST
SUSSEX**

Salisbury

Winchester

31

**CITY OF
SOUTHAMPTON**

Eastleigh

A3

338

16

Southampton

M27

A337

Fareham

CITY OF PORTSMOUTH

14

Portsmouth

Lymington

Ryde

Freshwater

Newport

ISLE OF WIGHT

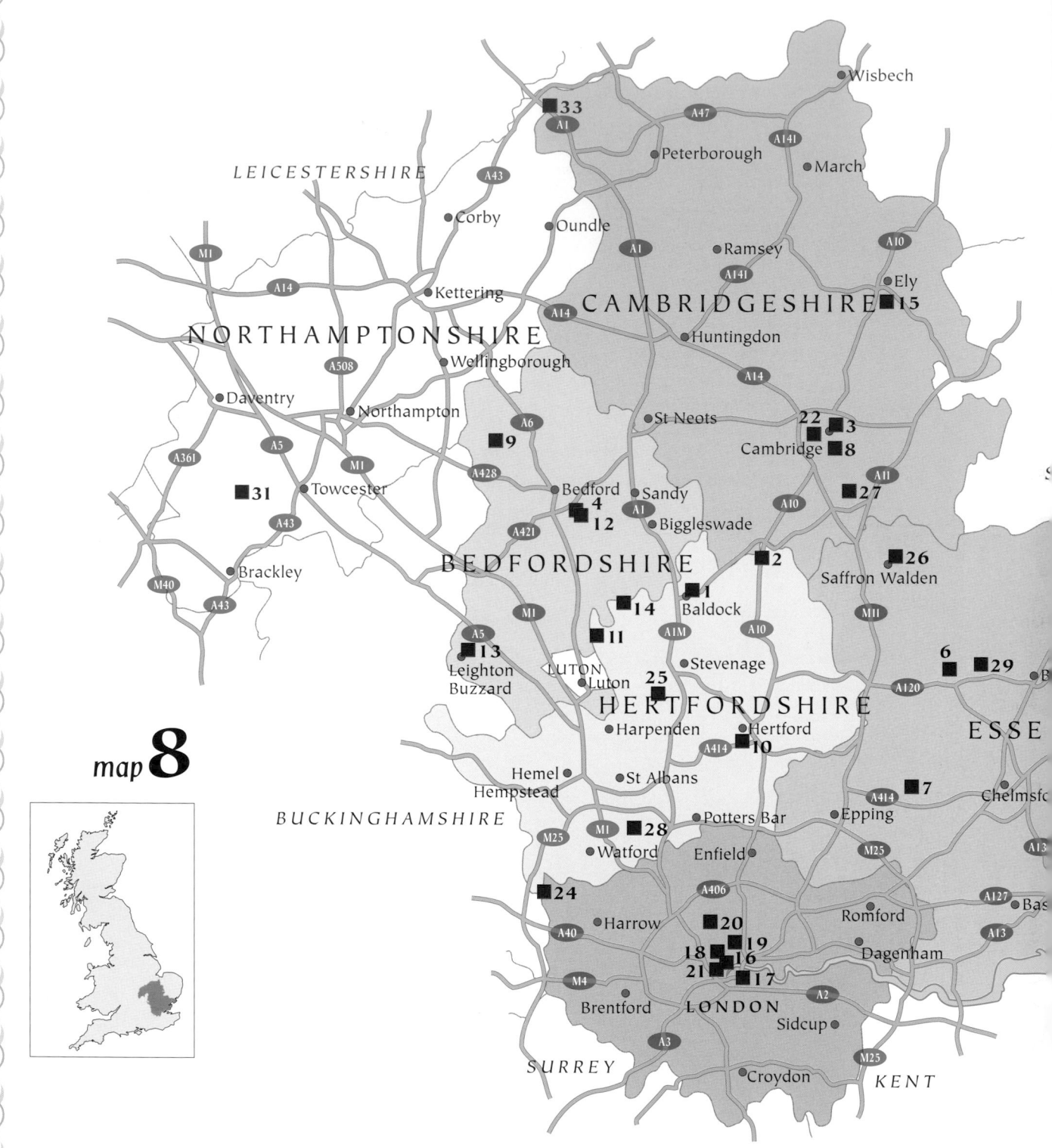

LEICESTERSHIRE

33

A1

Wisbech

A47

Peterborough

A141

March

Corby

A43

Oundle

A1

Ramsey

A10

A141

Ely

15

CAMBRIDGESHIRE

M1

A14

Kettering

A14

Huntingdon

NORTHAMPTONSHIRE

Wellingborough

A508

A14

St Neots

A6

9

22 **3**

A428

Cambridge

8

Daventry

Northampton

A11

A5

M1

A421

Bedford

Sandy

A1

A10

27

31

Towcester

4

12

Biggleswade

A361

BEDFORDSHIRE

A2

26

A43

A43

Saffron Walden

Brackley

M40

14

1

Baldock

A43

M1

11

A1M

A10

M11

A5

13

6

29

Leighton
Buzzard

LUTON

Stevenage

A120

B

Luton

25

HERTFORDSHIRE

ESSE

map **8**

Harpenden

Hertford

A414

10

Hemel
Hempstead

St Albans

7

A414

Chelmsf

BUCKINGHAMSHIRE

Potters Bar

Epping

M25

28

M1

Watford

Enfield

A13

M25

A406

Romford

A127

Bas

24

A406

A13

A40

Harrow

20

19

Dagenham

M4

18 **16**

21 **17**

Brentford

LONDON

A2

Sidcup

A3

SURREY

Croydon

M25

KENT

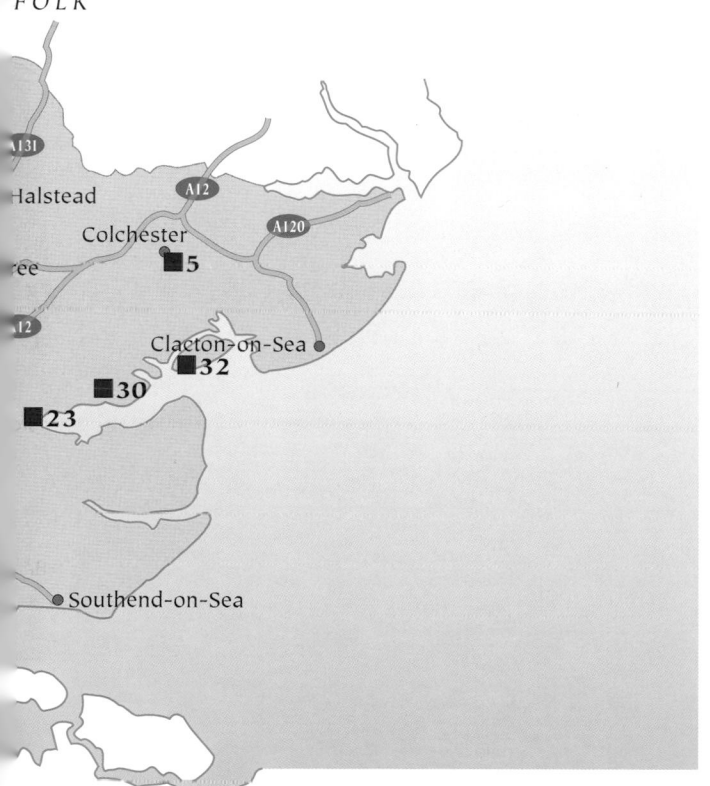

A new use for a Cambridge public convenience that no longer functions – it hires out bicycles so you can make a dash for one that does

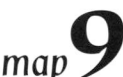

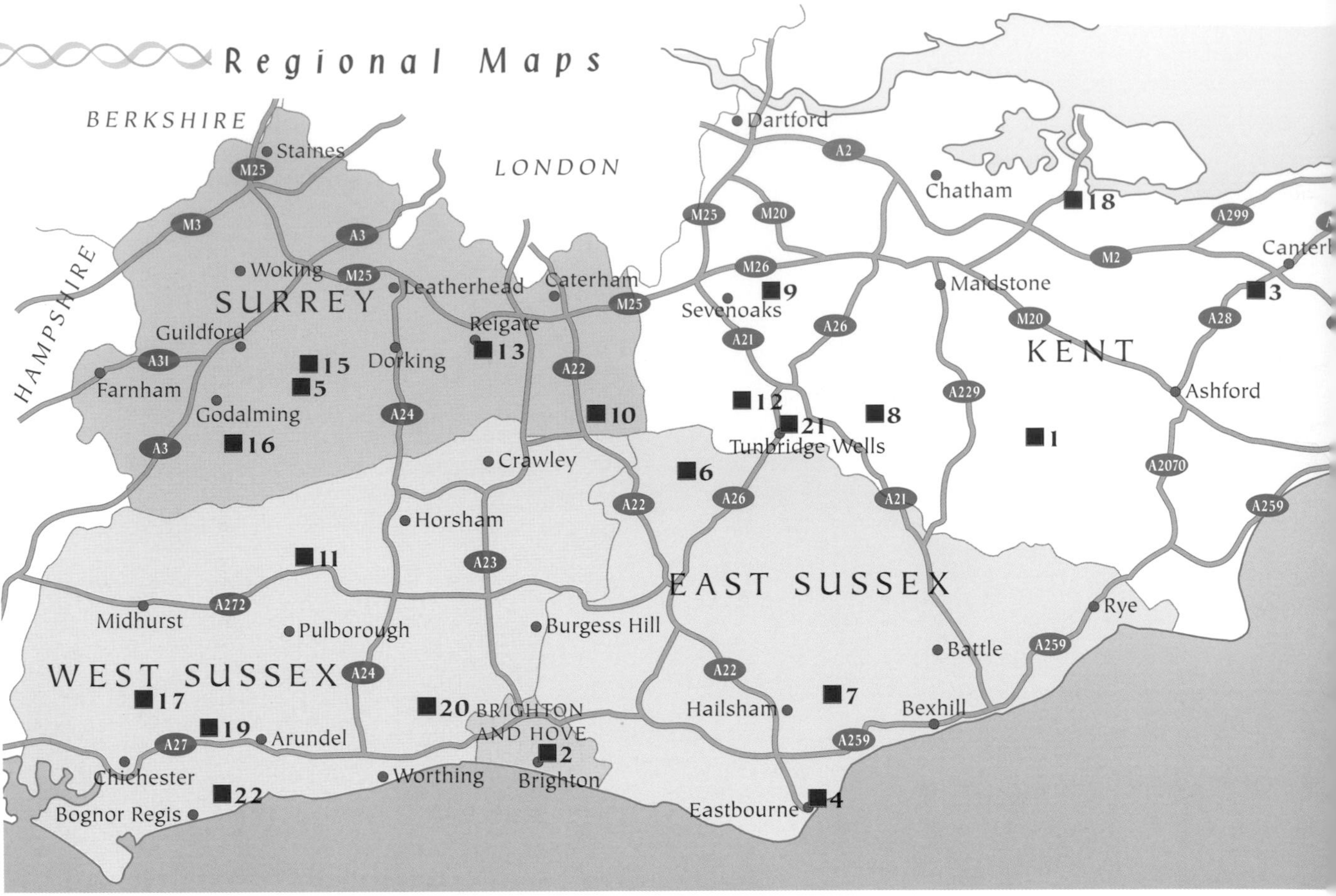
BERKSHIRE
LONDON
HAMPSHIRE
SURREY
KENT
EAST SUSSEX
WEST SUSSEX
Staines
Dartford
Chatham
Woking
Leatherhead
Caterham
Sevenoaks
Maidstone
Guildford
Reigate
Dorking
Farnham
Godalming
Ashford
Crawley
Tunbridge Wells
Horsham
Midhurst
Pulborough
Burgess Hill
Rye
Battle
Hailsham
Bexhill
BRIGHTON AND HOVE
Arundel
Chichester
Worthing
Brighton
Bognor Regis
Eastbourne
M25
M3
A3
M26
M20
M2
A2
A299
A28
A26
A21
A22
A229
A31
A24
A23
A272
A27
A259
A2070
1
2
3
4
5
6
7
8
9
10
11
12
13
15
16
17
18
19
20
21
22

map 9

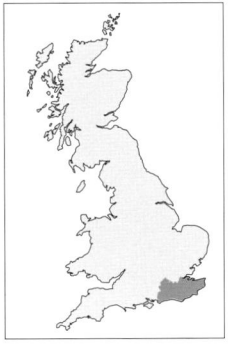

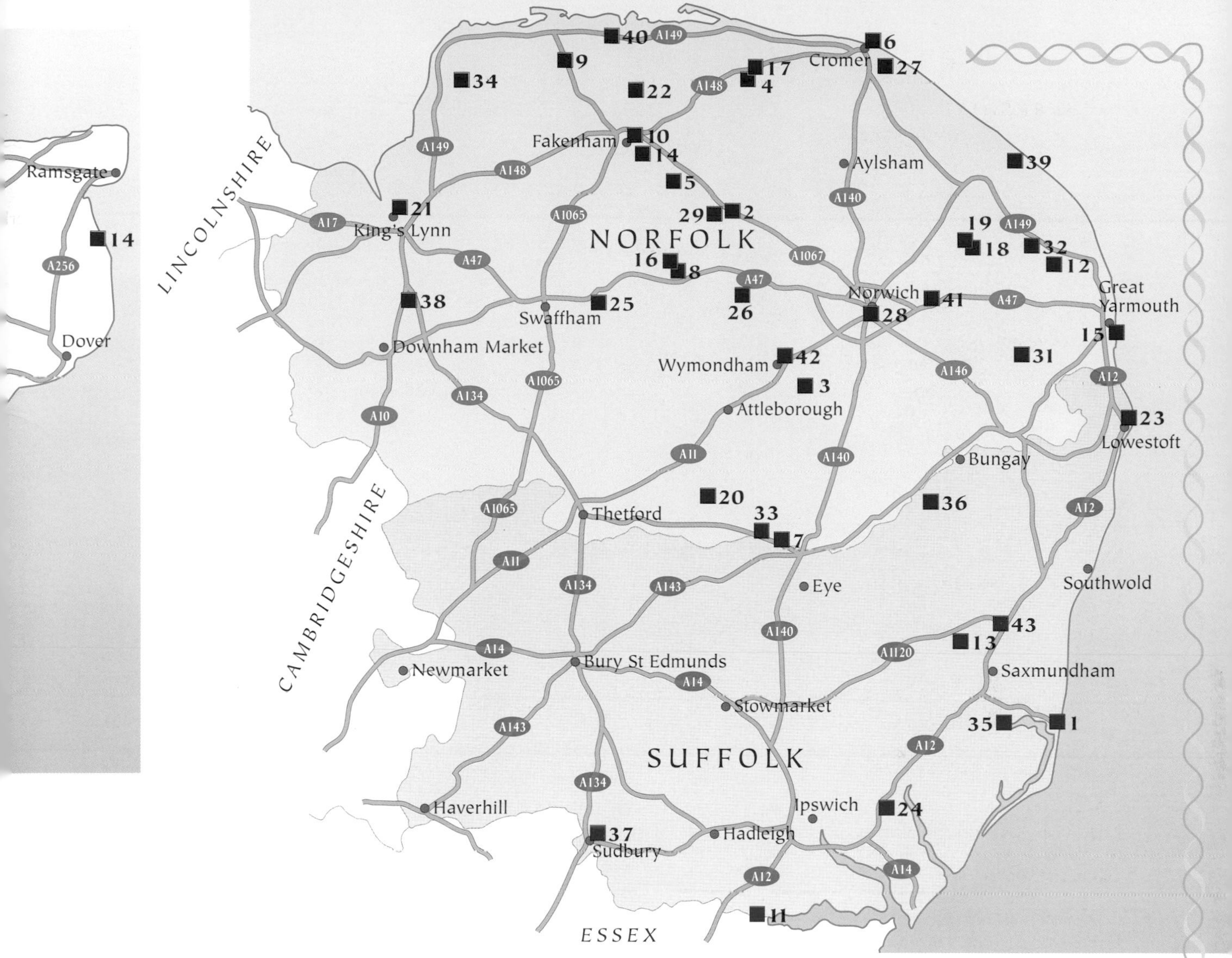

map **10**

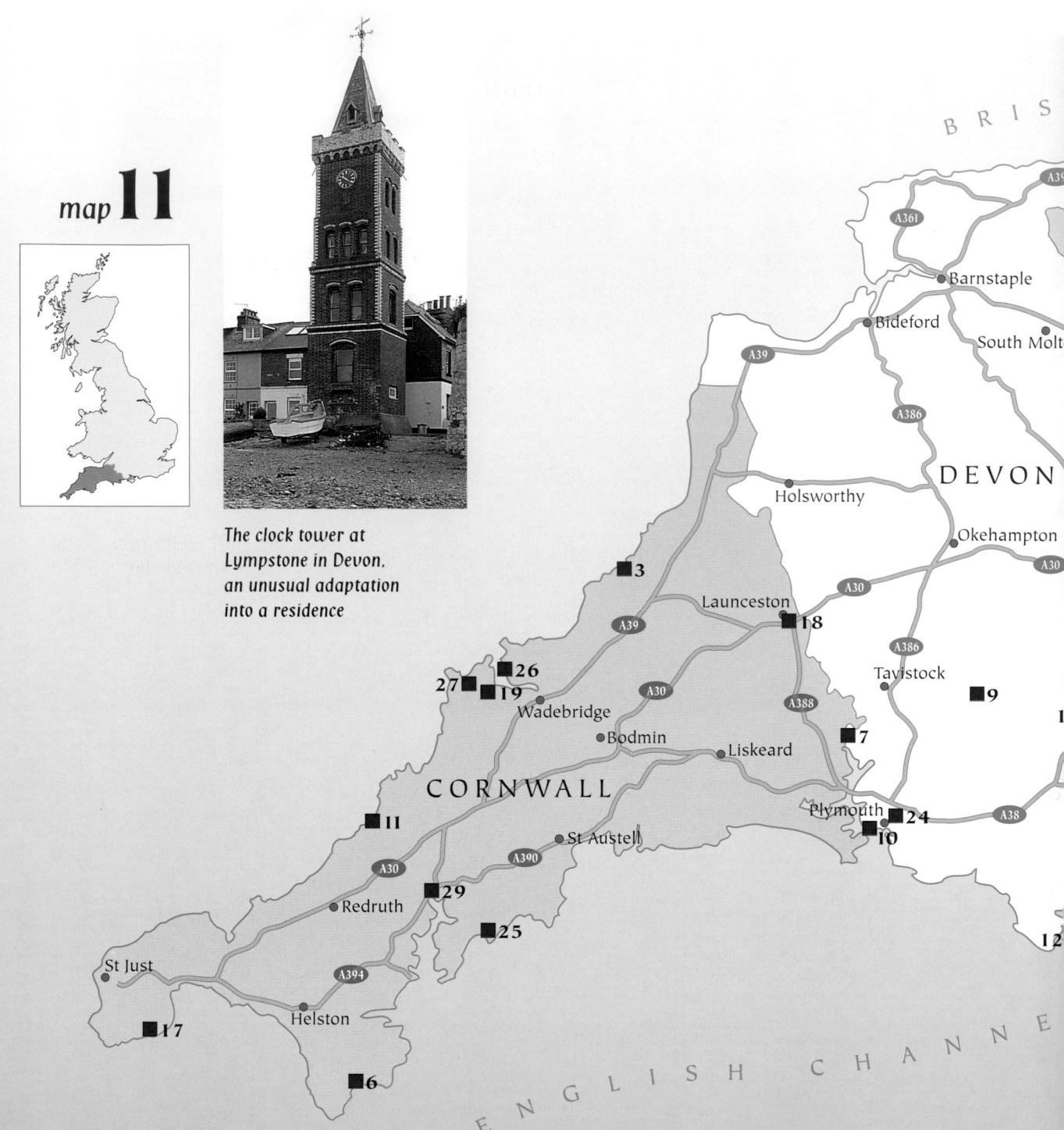

map **11**

The clock tower at
Lympstone in Devon,
an unusual adaptation
into a residence

BRIS

A39

A361

● Barnstaple

● Bideford

South Molto

A39

DEVON

A386

Holsworthy ●

Okehampton ●

A30

A386

Tavistock ●

■ 9

■ 3

Launceston

■ 18

A39

A30

A388

■ 26

27 ■ ■ 19

Wadebridge ●

Bodmin ●

Liskeard ●

■ 7

CORNWALL

Plymouth ●

■ 24

■ 10

1

■ 11

St Austell ●

A390

A30

■ 29

Redruth ●

■ 25

12

St Just ●

A394

■ 17

Helston ●

■ 6

ENGLISH CHANNE

A38

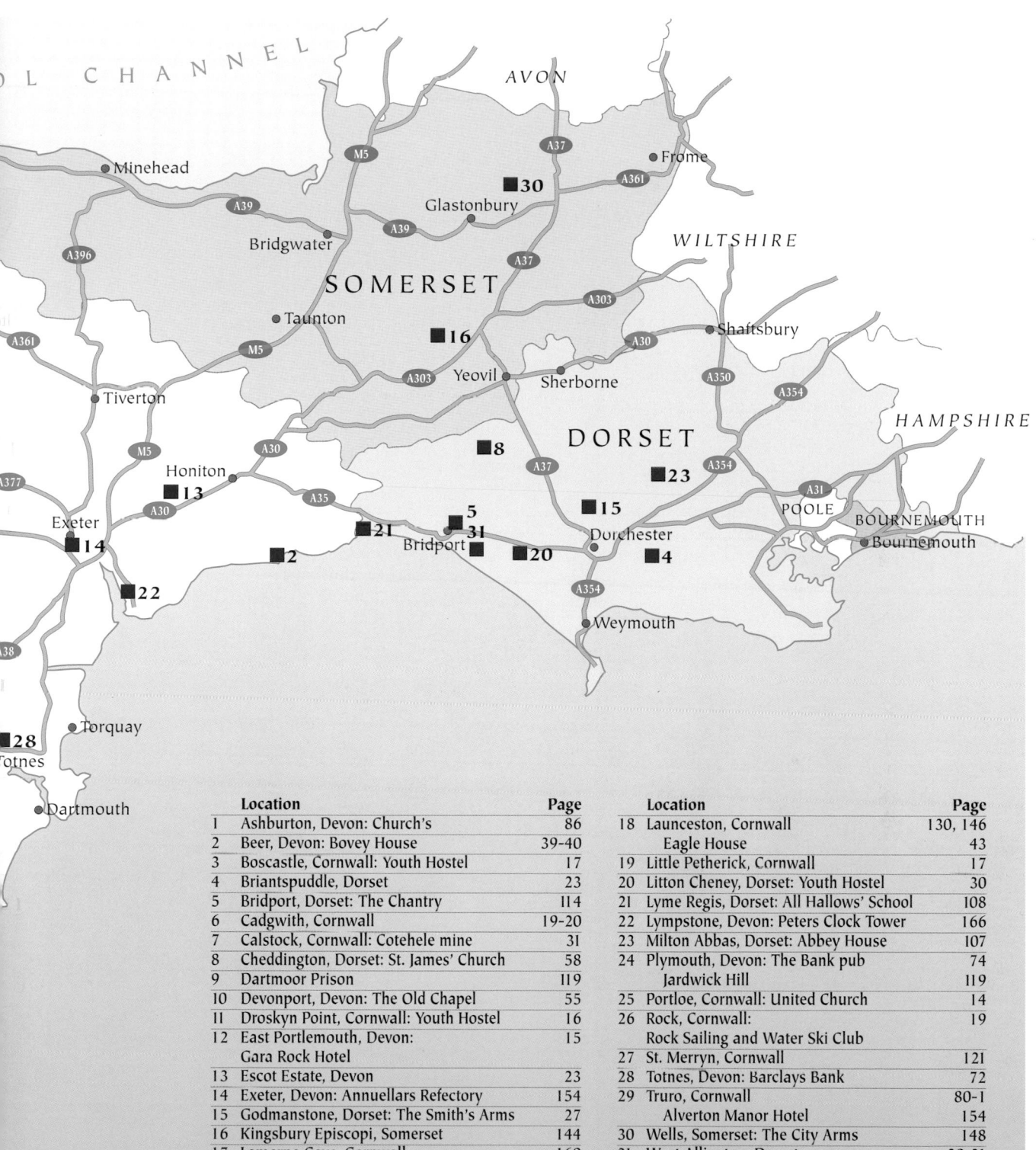

Index

Bibliography

AA Illustrated Guide to Country Towns and Villages of Britain, Drive Publications Ltd, 1985

AA Secret Britain, Automobile Association, 1986

AA Touring Guide to Britain, Automobile Association, 1981

AA Where to go in Britain, Automobile Association, 1992

Beautiful Britain, Drive Publications Ltd, 1988

The Book of the British Countryside, Drive Publications Ltd, 1973

Britain's Haunted Heritage, Jarrold Publishing, 1990

Distinctly Different Hotel Brochure, P. and P. Roberts, 1996

The English River by Alan Titchmarsh, Jarrold Publishing, 1993

ETB Somewhere Special, Jarrold Publishing, 1996

Gardens of England and Wales, National Gardens Scheme, 1993

Healthy Breaks, Jarrold Publishing, 1996

Jarrold Tour Guides, Jarrold Publishing

The Past All Around Us, Reader's Digest Association Ltd, 1979

New Shell Guide: North East England, Michael Joseph, 1988

The Shell Book of English Villages, Peerage Books/Rainbird, 1986

The Shell Guide to England, Michael Joseph/ Rainbird, 1970

The Signpost Hotel Guide to Great Britain, Signpost Ltd, 1990

Treasures of Britain, Drive Publications Ltd, 1968

Village England by P. Crookston, Promotional Reprint Co Ltd, 1992

The Visitor's Guide to North York Moors, York and the Yorkshire Coast, Moorland Publishing Co Ltd, 1984

Which? Hotel Guide, Consumers' Association, 1991

Acknowledgements

page

5 (top left) See details for page 38; (bottom right) See details for page 28

6 See details for page 42

10 (left) Mary Evans Picture Library

12 (bottom) Photo by C.J. Nicholas

13 (bottom) Photo by C.J. Nicholas

15 (top) Courtesy of The Gara Rock Hotel

16 (bottom right) Photo reproduced by courtesy of Eric Reading

22 (top, three photographs) Courtesy of Washington Arts Centre; (bottom left and bottom right) Courtesy of The Last Drop Hotel

25 (bottom) Reproduced by kind permission of Mrs Mary Dunn

28 (top and bottom left) Both pictures courtesy of Bishopsdale Oast Guest House, Biddenden, Kent

30 (top left) Essex County Council Libraries, Trustees of the Town Library, Saffron Walden

34 (bottom left and top right) Mary Evans Picture Library; (bottom right) Courtesy of Kit Martin

35 (top right) Courtesy of Kit Martin

36 Reproduced from *V.C.H.* Buckinghamshire, volume iv, plate facing p. 344, by permission of the General Editor

38 Courtesy of Thornbury Castle Hotel

39 Courtesy of The Bovey House Hotel

40 Courtesy of Petwood Hotel

41 Courtesy of Stapleford Park

42 (top) Mary Evans Picture Library; (bottom) Courtesy of Warners' Holidays

43 Courtesy of Satis House Hotel

45 (top) Mary Evans Picture Library

46 (top) Mary Evans Picture Library; (bottom) Courtesy of the secretary of the Moor Park Golf Club

48 (top left) Hertfordshire Record Office

50 Courtesy of Derek Latham

52 (bottom) Courtesy of Red Rose Radio;

54 (top) Photo by Paul Murphy

54 (centre and bottom) Photos by Paul Murphy

58 (top) Courtesy of Newton Vewton Flags & Banners

61 (top) Gloucestershire County Library Service, Gloucestershire Collection

64 (top) Courtesy of The East Coast Sail Trust

66 (centre left) Courtesy of the Ryedale Lodge Hotel; (bottom right) Lens of Sutton

67 (top right) Ipswich Record Office, Ref. No. SPS 51

69 (top) Photo by Paul Murphy

74 (bottom right) Laurence Shaw Antiques

77 (bottom left) Courtesy of The Borough Council of King's Lynn and West Norfolk

78 (bottom right) Courtesy of Norfolk Library and Information Service

81 (bottom right) Royal Institution of Cornwall, Truro

84 (bottom left) Oxfordshire Photographic Archive, DLA, OCC

87 (bottom) Newcastle Libraries and Information Services

88 (centre) Essex County Council Libraries, Trustees of the Town Library, Saffron Walden

90 Courtesy of the Severn Trow

92 (top and bottom) Photos by Andrew Perkins

93 (top) Photo by Andrew Perkins

94 (bottom two) Courtesy of the Britannia Hotel, Manchester

97 (bottom) Courtesy of J Strong & Son, Caldbeck

98 (bottom left) Lowestoft Record Office, Ref. PH–S/TRA/2

104 (bottom) Reproduced by courtesy of Penrith Museum (Eden District Council)

108 (top left) Courtesy of Abberley Hall School

109 (bottom three) Courtesy of All Hallows'

School, near Lyme Regis

112 (top) Mary Evans Picture Library

114 (left) Courtesy of Bridport Museum

117 (bottom right) Great Yarmouth Library, Norfolk County Council

117 (top) Photo by Charles Nicholas

120 (top) Bedfordshire Record Office; (bottom) Courtesy of the Building Research Establishment

122 (top right) Courtesy of Paul Firman

127 (top left) Norfolk County Council Library and Information Service, the Norfolk Studies Department; (bottom) Courtesy of Lancaster City Museums

128 (top left) Norfolk County Council Library and Information Service, the Norfolk Studies Department; (top right) Eastern Counties Newspapers

130 (bottom left) Courtesy of David Angus

134 (left) Cambridgeshire Heritage, County Record Office, Ref. No. PH 25/11

135 (top) Photo by Paul Murphy

138 (bottom right) Buckinghamshire County Museum

140 (top) Photo by Paul Murphy

142 (middle) Photo by Paul Murphy

146 (bottom) Courtesy of The Old Lock-Up, Wirksworth

148 (top right) Reproduced by kind permission of Berwick-upon-Tweed Borough Council; (bottom right) Photo by Paul Murphy

152 (bottom left) Mary Evans Picture Library

154 (bottom) Photo by Paul Murphy

155 (top) Courtesy of Nashdom Ltd

156 (centre) Courtesy of St. Peter's Brewery

157 (both) Courtesy of the Weston Manor Hotel

158 (bottom) Courtesy of The Landmark Trust

160 (top, bottom right) Courtesy of the Lamorna Cove Hotel

173 See details for page 66

177 See details for page 42